Electrical Machines-II

AF668673

Dr. P. S. Bimbhra

Ph.D., M.E.(Hons.), F.I.E. (India), M.I.S.T.E.

Ex-Dean. Ex-Professor and Head,
Electrical and Electronics Engineering Department
Thapar Institute of Engineering and Technology
Patiala-147004

KHANNA BOOK PUBLISHING CO. (P) LTD.

Publisher of Engineering and Computer Books

4C/4344, Ansari Road, Darya Ganj, New Delhi-110002
Phone : 011-23244447-48 **Mobile:** +91-9910909320
E-mail : contact@khannabooks.com
Website : www.khannabooks.com

Dear Readers,

To prevent the piracy, this book is secured with HIGH SECURITY HOLOGRAM on the front title cover. In case you don't find the hologram on the front cover title, please write us to at contact@khannabooks.com or whatsapp us at +91-99109 09320 and avail special gift voucher for yourself.

Specimen of Hologram on front Cover title:

Moreover, there is a SPECIAL DISCOUNT COUPON for you with EVERY HOLOGRAM.

How to avail this SPECIAL DISCOUNT:

Step 1: Scratch the hologram
Step 2: Under the scratch area, your "coupon code" is available
Step 3: Logon to www.khannabooks.com
Step 4: Use your "coupon code" in the shopping cart and get your copy at a special discount
Step 5: Enjoy your reading!

Price: ₹ 332.00

ISBN: 978-93-86173-60-7

Electric Machines II
by Dr. P.S. Bimbhra

First Edition: 2018
Reprint: 2025

To view complete list of books, Please scan the QR Code:

KPH

Published by:
Khanna Book Publishing Co. (P) Ltd.
CIN: U22110DL1998PTC095547

Visit us at: **www.khannabooks.com**
Write us at: **contact@khannabooks.com**

Printed in India.

Preface

This book on "Electrical Machine-II" is intended to serve as a text book for the students of Electrical Engineering in general and for those studying in institutions where AICTE model curriculum has been adopted. This book serves as a supplement to the already published book on "Electrical Machines-I".

The topics covered in this book pertain to the syllabus contents as prescribed by AICTE for the course on "Electrical Machines-II".

Chapter 1 describes the fundamental of AC machine windings. Here, general terms associated with armature windings are defined first. Then, air-gap mmf waves produced by concentrated and distributed windings are explained. Concept of winding factor is also given in this chapter. Chapter 2 describes the concepts of constant magnetic field, pulsating magnetic field and rotating magnetic field.

In chapter 3, three-phase induction motor is described in detail so far as its constructional features, principle of operation, rotor and stator equivalent circuits and torque-slip characteristics are concerned. This chapter also includes methods of starting, speed control techniques, electric braking, three-phase induction generator working and doubly-fed induction machines. In chapter 4, constructional features, principle of operation, double-revolving field theory and starting methods of single-phase induction motor are described.

Chapter 5 pertains to the analysis of three-phase synchronous machines. In this chapter both cylindrical-rotor type and salient-pole type machines are discussed in detail. Steady-state phasor diagram of each type is developed for analysis purposes. Steady-state power-angle characteristics and operating characteristics are also presented in this chapter.

The book contains a large number of worked examples to highlight the principles and concepts of the topics covered in this book. Unsolved problems at the end of each chapter are included for practice. Objective type questions included at the end of each chapter will help the readers to evaluate their comprehension of the chapter topics. For the text material presented in this book, the author has taken the help of several text books available in the market.

Some errors might have crept in despite utmost care to avoid these. The author will grateful if such errors are pointed out.

Any suggestions or constructive criticism leading to improvement of this book are welcome.

Dr. P.S. Bimbhra

Contents

Chapter

1

Fundamentals of AC Machine Windings

The functions of ac machine windings are to *(i)* develop emfs in a number of phases when designed with hetropolar structure and to *(ii)* develop pulsating or rotating mmfs when phase windings are suitably excited. Here, first terms pertaining to machine windings, like turn, coil, pole-pitch etc. are explained. Then, fundamental of ac machine windings are presented.

1.1. GENERAL TERMS FOR MACHINE WINDINGS

Various terms associated with armature windings of ac machines are presented here.

Conductor : Active length of wire in the slot along the axial length of machine is called a conductor. In Fig. 1.1. *(a)*, *AB* is one conductor and *DE* is another conductor.

Turn : One turn is made up of two active conductors. In Fig. 1.1 *(a)*, two active conductors *AB* and *DE*, suitably connected, form one turn.

Coil : Two conductors separated by nearly a pole-pitch and connected in series form a **single-turn coil**, Fig. 1.1 *(a)*. Two conductors placed in almost at the same position as in Fig. 1.1 *(b)* form a two-turn **Coil**. More conductors placed in the same position constitute a **multiturn** coil. A multiturn coil is illustrated as shown in Fig. 1.1 *(c)*.

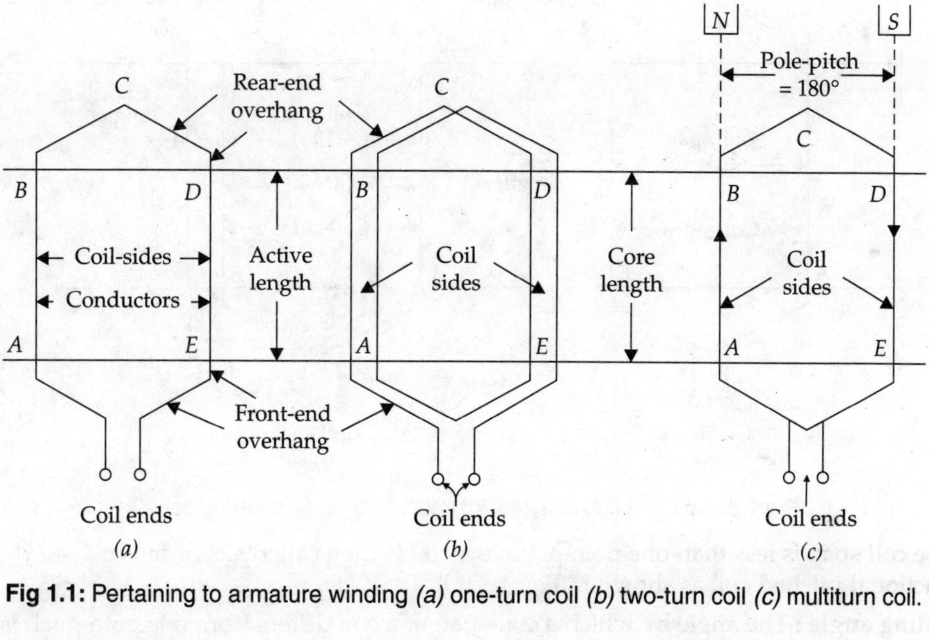

Fig 1.1: Pertaining to armature winding *(a)* one-turn coil *(b)* two-turn coil *(c)* multiturn coil.

Coil-side : One coil with any number of turns has two coil-sides. In Fig. 1.1 *(a)*, *(b)* and *(c)*, *AB* and *DE* are the two coil-sides of a coil.

Single and double-layer windings : If one coil-side occupies the total slot area, it is called **single-layer winding** as shown in Fig. 1.2 *(a)*. In case one slot contains even number (2, 4, 6 etc.) of coil-sides in two layers, the winding is called **double-layer winding**, Fig. 1.2 *(b)*.

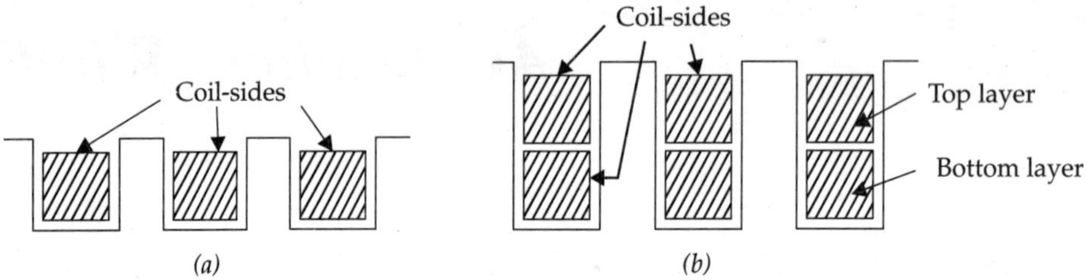

Fig 1.2: Coil-sides *(a)* single-layer winding and *(b)* double-layer winding.

Most of the polyphase ac armature windings are double-layer windings with multiturn coils. In general, a double-layer winding *(i)* has lower value of leakage reactance and *(ii)* produces better emf waveform, as compared to single-layer winding.

Pole-pitch : The peripheral distance between identical points on two adjacent poles is called pole-pitch. A pole pitch is always equal to 180° electrical as shown in Fig. 1.3.

Coil-span or coil-pitch : The distance between the two coil-sides of a coil is called coil-span or coil-pitch, see Fig. 1.3.

Chorded coil : When the coil span is equal to one pole-pitch, the coil is a full-pitched coil as shown in Fig. 1.3 *(a)*.

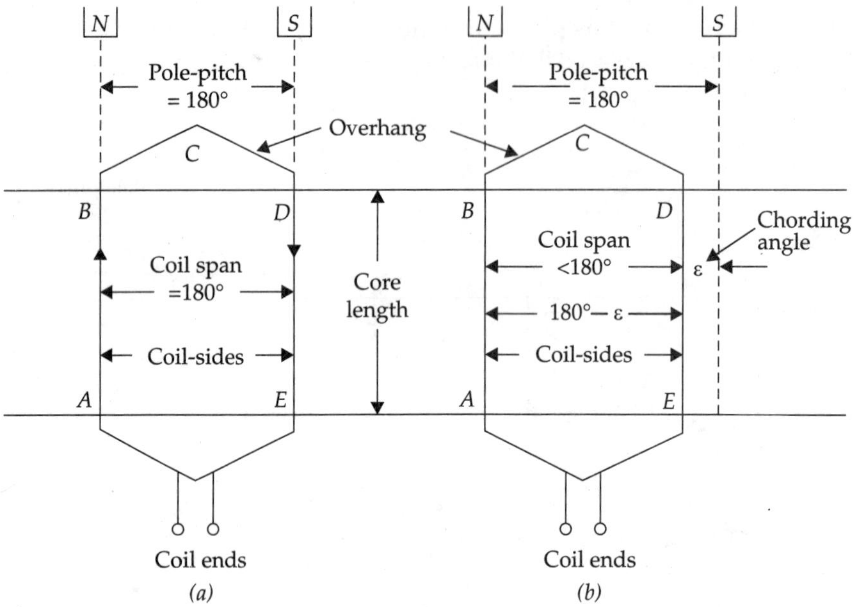

Fig 1.3: *(a)* Full-pitch coil and *(b)* short-pitched or chorded coil.

In case coil span is less than one pole-pitch, the coil is then called a chorded coil, short-pitched coil or fractional pitched coil as shown in Fig. 1.3 *(b)*.

Chording angle : The angle by which a coil-span of a coil differs from one pole-pitch is called chording angle. It is shown as ε (epsilon) in Fig. 1.3 *(b)*.

1.1.1. Active Portion and Overhang

The portion of a coil, where actual emf is generated, is called active portion of a coil. In Fig. 1.1, active portion of coil is coil side *AB* and coil-side *DE*. Induced emfs in *AB* is upward and is downward in *DE*, see Figs. 1.1 *(c)* and 1.3 *(a)*. In order to add these two emfs, back to back connection, called **overhang** is essential. In Fig. 1.1, back to back end connection *BCD*, is usually called **rear-end overhang**. Similarly, front end connection of coil-sides is called front-end overhang.

1.2. SLOTS FOR WINDINGS

A winding is made up of several coils inserted in slots along the air-gap periphery. These coils are then suitably interconnected to form armature winding. Fig. 1.4 *(a)* shows a stator with inner periphery slotted to house the stator coils.

The shape of **stator slots** is shown in Fig. 1.4 *(b)*. Open slots are used for high-voltage windings, because pre-fabricated coils can be easily inserted in these slots. Semiclosed slots are quite common for medium voltage stator windings. For power rated rotating machines, tapered slots shown in Fig. 1.4 *(b)* may be employed.

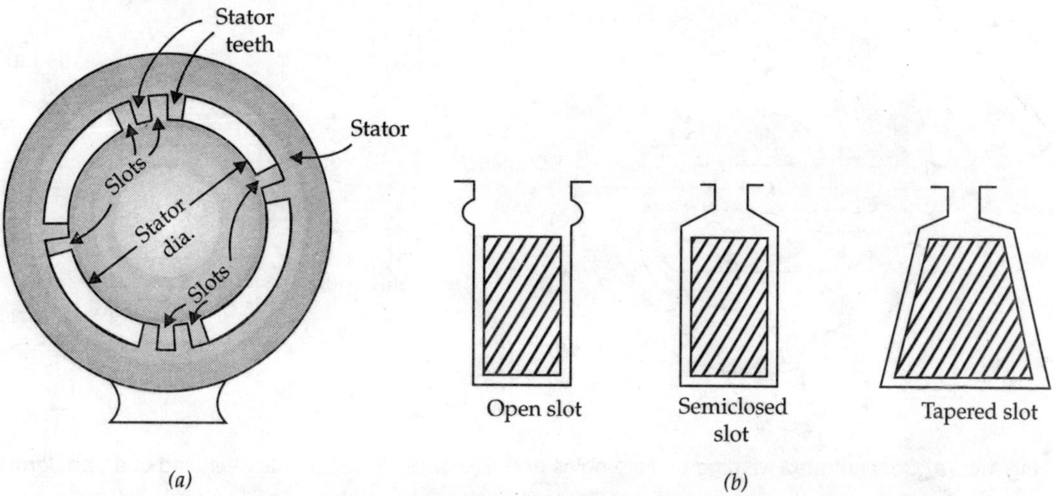

Fig 1.4: *(a)* Slots in the inner periphery of stator and *(b)* shape of stator slots.

The shape of rotor slots is shown in Fig. 1.5. Circular slot is quite often used for the cage rotors of induction machines. T-bar slots are also used in squirrel-cage induction machines.

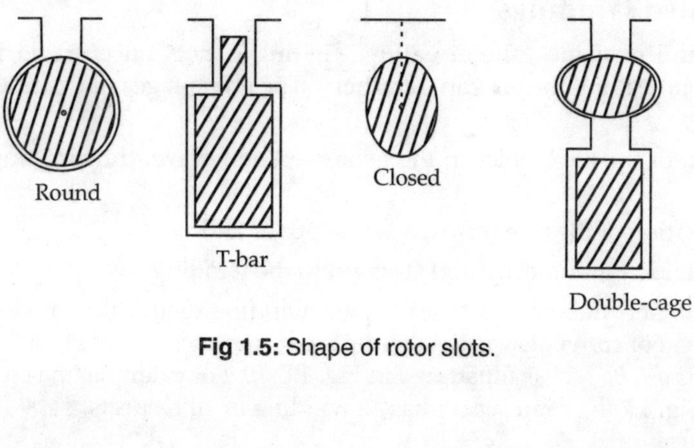

Fig 1.5: Shape of rotor slots.

Closed slots, as shown in Fig. 1.5, are sometimes used for induction machine rotors. In closed slots, sometimes bars and end-rings are cast directly in the rotor. Double-cage slots, shown in Fig. 1.5, are employed in double-cage three-phase induction motors.

1.3. ROTATING MACHINE WINDINGS AND WINDING AXIS

The windings used in rotating electrical machines can be classified as *(a)* concentrated windings and *(b)* distributed windings. These are now discussed briefly.

1.3.1. Concentrated Windings

In this winding, all the winding turns are wound together in series to form one multiturn coil. Field windings for salient-pole synchronous machines and dc machines are examples of concentrated windings on stator as shown in Fig. 1.6 *(a)*. When these windings are excited, current flows in windings and a magnetic flux is established. When current direction is as shown in Fig. 1.6 *(a)*, right-hand grip rule gives the direction of magnetic flux from left to right as indicated. This direction of flux is called the **magnetic axis** of the winding. In Fig. 1.6 (a), the **winding axis** or the **magnetic axis** of the concentrated winding is horizontal as shown.

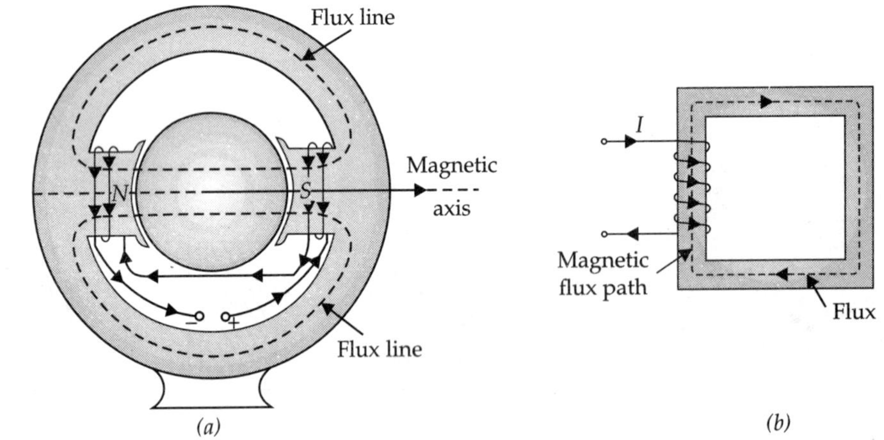

Fig 1.6: *(a)* Concentrated winding on field poles and *(b)* concentrated primary winding of a transformer.

Fig. 1.6 *(b)* shows the primary winding of a transformer. If a current flows in primary winding, magnetic flux along the vertical axis is established. The magnetic axis of all the primary turns is the same. Thus, the primary winding of a transformer also forms a concentrated winding.

1.3.2. Distributed Windings

In rotating electrical machines, the armature winding is not concentrated in a single slot, but distributed uniformly along the air-gap periphery. The advantages of distributing the winding in slots are :

(i) reduction of the harmonics in the generated emf wave, thus making it approach a sine wave,

(ii) full utilization of the armature iron and copper and

(iii) adding rigidity and mechanical strength to the winding.

Fig. 1.7 *(a)* shows 2-pole, 3-phase stator winding distributed in slots along the air-gap periphery. For convenience, the three-phase winding *a*, *b*, *c* of Fig. 1.7 *(a)* is represented by three coils *aa*′, *bb*′, *cc*′ as illustrated in Fig. 1.7 *(b)*. For example, the concentrated full-pitch coil *aa*′, Fig. 1.7 *(b)*, represents phase a winding in all respects.

A current in phase a winding establishes magnetic flux along the axis of coil aa'. When positive current, shown by cross in a' and dot in a flows, a horizontal flux is established. So the magnetic axis of phase a or the **winding axis of phase** a is as shown in Fig. 1.7 *(b)*. Similarly, the winding axes of phases b and c are shown. Note that the winding axis of phases a, b, c are spatially displaced from each other by a space angle of 120°.

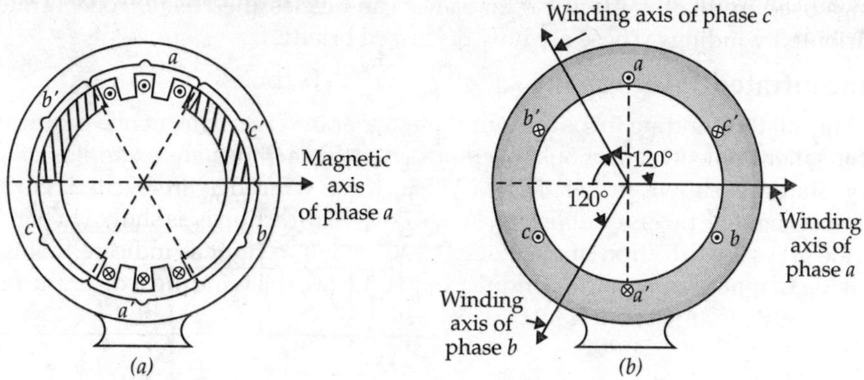

Fig 1.7: *(a)* A 3-phase 2-pole stator winding *(b)* magnetic of three-phase winding represented by three coils *aa'*, *bb'* and *cc'*.

1.4. AIR-GAP MMF DISTRIBUTION WITH FIXED CURRENT THROUGH WINDING

Here, we will examine the distribution of mmf and flux density waveforms produced by currents flowing in distributed windings. First of all, air-gap mmf produced by concentrated winding would be examined. Then, air-gap mmf produced by distributed winding would be described.

1.4.1. Air-gap MMF Produced by Concentrated Coil

Consider one full-pitched single N-turn coil on the stator of a 2-pole uniform air-gap machine as shown in Fig. 1.8 *(a)*. Each turn carries a current i. The magnetic field produced by this current is shown. As per right-hand grip rule, the field is clockwise for current indicated by cross (entering the page) in coil side a' and anticlockwise for current shown by dot (coming out of page) in coil side a. The mmf F for any closed path is Ni ampere turns enclosed by that path. Assuming infinite permeability for iron path, this mmf Ni is consumed in the air-gap only. Since each flux line crosses the air-gap twice, the mmf for each gap is 0.5 Ni.

$$\therefore \qquad \text{Air-gap mmf} = \frac{1}{2} Ni \qquad \text{...(1.1)}$$

Since any closed path around any coil-side satisfies Eq. (1.1), the variation of mmf along air-gap periphery is of rectangular waveform and of magnitude $\frac{1}{2} Ni$. The magnetic field leaving the rotor is considered positive, therefore, the variation of mmf along the air-gap periphery is as shown in Fig.1.8 *(b)*.

The rectangular mmf waveform of magnitude $\frac{1}{2} Ni$ can be decomposed by Fourier series into fundamental and higher order harmonic component. The fundamental component of rectangular wave is

$$F_{a1} = \frac{4}{\pi} \cdot \frac{Ni}{2} \cos \alpha = F_{1p} \cos \alpha \qquad \text{...(1.2)}$$

where α = electrical space angle measured from the magnetic axis of stator coil as shown in Fig. 1.8. In Eq. (1.2), peak value of sine mmf wave for a 2-pole machine is

$$F_{1p} = \frac{4}{\pi} \cdot \frac{Ni}{2} \text{ ATs/pole} \quad \text{...(1.3)}$$

This peak mmf F_{1p} is always along the magnetic axis of coil and its magnitude is proportional to the instantaneous value of current i. If $i = I_{max} = \sqrt{2}\,I$, then time maximum of peak mmf for a 2-pole machine is

$$F_{1pm} = \frac{4}{\pi} \frac{NI_m}{2} \text{ ATs/pole} \quad \text{...(1.4)}$$

and for a P-pole machine,

$$F_{1pm} = \frac{4}{\pi} \cdot \frac{NI_m}{P} \text{ ATs/pole} \quad \text{...(1.5)}$$

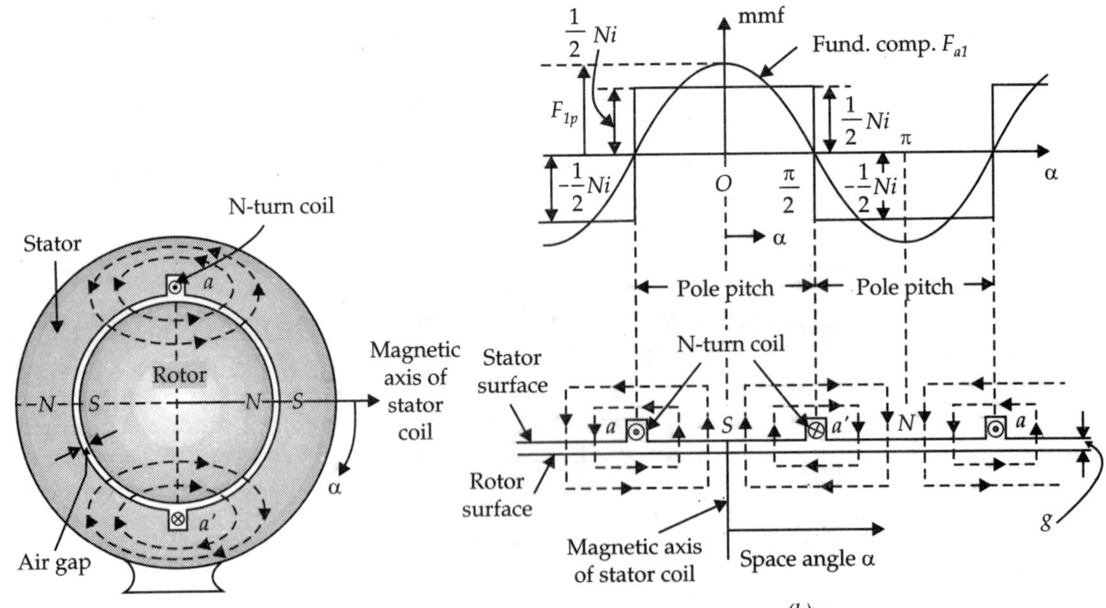

Fig 1.8: *(a)* Full-pitch coil on stator and *(b)* mmf distribution along the air-gap periphery.

1.4.2. Air-gap MMF Produced by Distributed Windings

The effect of distributing the winding in several slots is now examined. For this purpose, consider Fig. 1.9 *(a)*, where distributed winding of phase *'a'* in three adjacent slots for a 2-pole, 3-phase machine is shown. Six slots, for each phase b and c, are shown empty. Phase a winding is a two-layer winding. Each coil has N_c turns and its one coil-side is in top layer of one slot and its other coil-side is in the bottom layer of a slot nearly one pole-pitch apart.

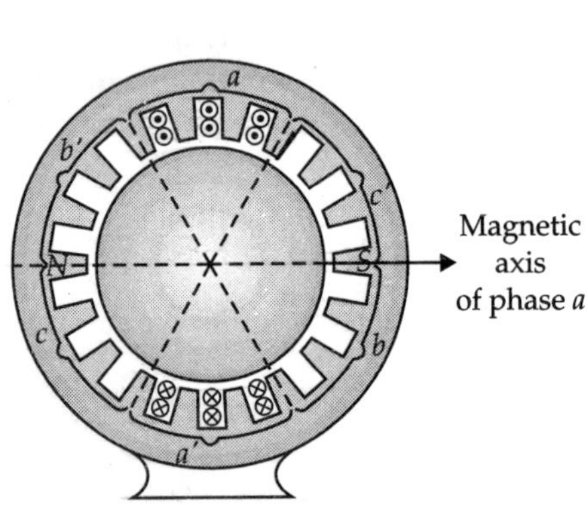

Fig 1.9: *(a)* Mmf of one phase of a 2-pole, 3-phase winding with full-pitch coils configuration.

In Fig. 1.9 *(b)* is shown the winding laid out flat. The mmf wave consists of series steps, each of height = ampere conductors in one slot = $2\,N_c\,i_c$, where i_c is the winding current. Comparing the mmf waveform in

Figs. 1.8 *(b)* and 1.9 *(b)*, it is seen that distributed winding produces mmf wave which is much closer to sine wave as compared to that produced by concentrated coil.

The resultant stepped wave of Fig. 1.9 *(b)* can be resolved into fundamental component and higher order harmonics. Mmf of each slot is displaced from adjacent slot by one slot angle. Therefore, resultant mmf wave obtained by the phasor sum of slot mmfs, would be less than the sum of individual coil mmfs. Thus the effect of winding distribution on mmf wave can be accounted for by introducing a multiplication factor k_d. Similarly, the effect of using chorded coils can be taken into consideration by using the multiplication factor k_p. Therefore, the fundamental component of mmf of phase *a*, obtained by modifying Eq. (1.2), is given by

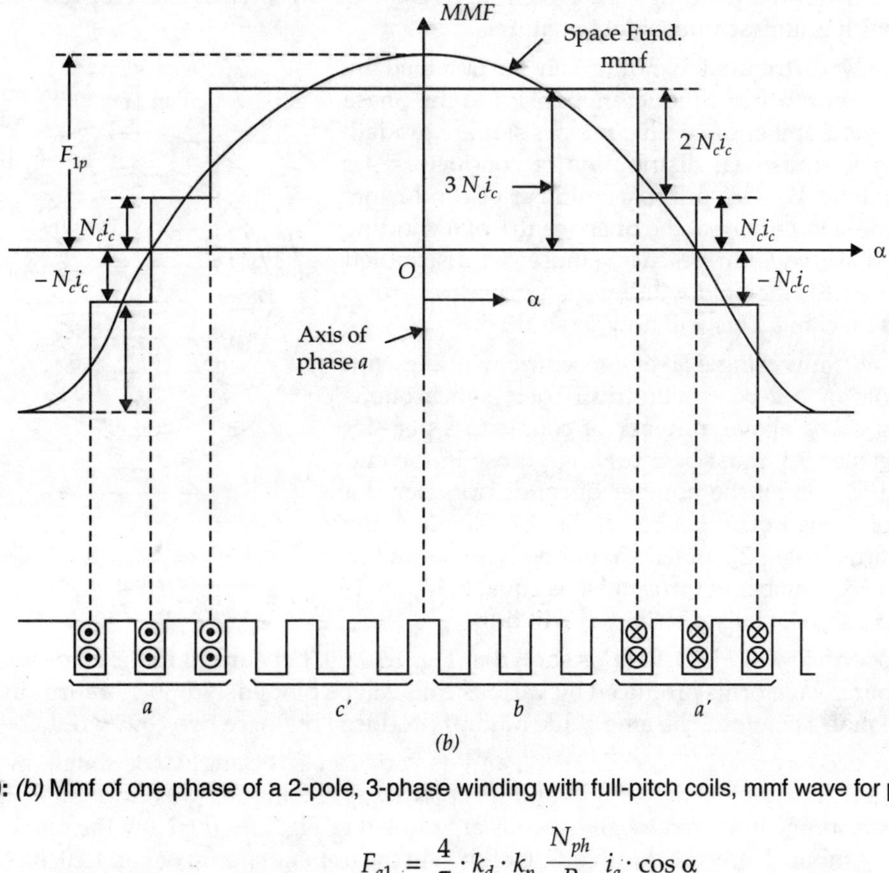

Fig 1.9: *(b)* Mmf of one phase of a 2-pole, 3-phase winding with full-pitch coils, mmf wave for phase *a*.

$$F_{a1} = \frac{4}{\pi} \cdot k_d \cdot k_p \frac{N_{ph}}{P} i_a \cdot \cos \alpha \qquad \text{...(1.6)}$$

where k_d = distribution or breadth factor,

k_p = pitch factor, N_{ph} = series turns per phase

i_a = current in phase *a*

P = number of poles

α = electrical space angle in degrees measured from the magnetic axis of phase *a*.

Eq. (1.6) can also be written as

$$F_{a1} = \frac{4}{\pi} \cdot k_w \cdot \frac{N_{ph}}{P} i_a \cos \alpha \qquad \text{...(1.7)}$$

where $k_w = k_d \cdot k_p$ = winding factor.

The mmf given by Eq. (1.7) is sinusoidally distributed along the air-gap periphery as described by cos α. Peak of F_{a1} is always along the magnetic axis of phase *a*. Its peak amplitude is proportional to the instantaneous value of current i_a. In case $i_a = I_m \cos \omega t$, then, the **time maximum** of peak of F_{a1} is given by

$$F_{1pm} = \frac{4}{\pi} \cdot k_w \cdot \frac{N_{ph} \cdot I_{max}}{P} \text{ ATs/pole} \qquad ...(1.8)$$

1.5. SINUSOIDALLY DISTRIBUTED WINDING

In order to reduce the space harmonics in the air-gap flux of rotating electrical machines, sinusoidally distributed windings are preferred. These windings, when excited produce mmf or flux wave which is almost sinusoidal in nature.

Sinusoidally distributed winding can be obtained by using different number of conductors per slot in the phase winding, *i.e.* the number of conductors per slot are **graded**. In other words, sinusoidal distribution of conductors per slot must be done. For this purpose, number of conductors per slot are more in the slot at the phase centre of a winding than at the phase ends. In practice, sinusoidal distributed winding is used for the field winding of a cylindrical-rotor synchronous machine. This will now be studied.

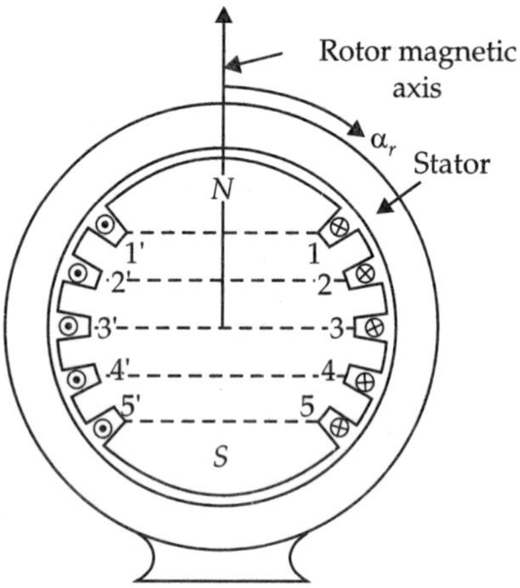

Fig 1.10: *(a)* Sinusoidally distributed winding on rotor.

Fig. 1.10 *(a)* shows single layer concentric winding with ten rotor slots of a 2-pole cylindrical rotor synchronous machine. As stated above, number of conductors per slot in the central slot 3,3′ must be more than those in the end slots 11′ and 55′. So lot the number of conductors per slot or number of turns in coil 33′ be N_3. For slot angle γ, the number of turns in coil 22′ or 44′ should be $N_3 \cos \gamma$ and in the coil 11′ or 55′, number of turns must be equal to $N_3 \cos 2\gamma$ for obtaining a sinusoidally distributed winding.

A developed view of Fig. 1.10 *(a)* is shown in Fig. 1.10 *(b)*. Let current in the rotor winding be I_r. Now the mmf waveforms produced by various coils can be plotted. Number of turns in coils 11′ and 55′ are equal. Therefore, the amplitude of mmf produced by these two coils would be equal.

Mmf produced by coil 11′ is $N'_1 I_r = N_1 I_r$ and its variation is rectangular as shown in Fig. 1.10 *(b)*. Further, coil 22′ mmf is $N_2' I_r = N_2 I_r$ and it is plotted as rectangular waveform in Fig. 1.10 (b). In this manner, mmfs produced by all the coils are plotted in Fig. 1.10 *(b)*. Now the resultant mmf wave, due to combined effect of these coils, is shown in the upper diagram of Fig. 1.10 *(b)*. Mmf $N_3 I_r$ is shown as $\frac{1}{2} N_3 I_r$ above the reference line and $-\frac{1}{2} N_3 I_r$ below the reference line for obtaining a symmetrical waveform.

Now $N_2 I_r$ and $N_1 I_r$ rectangular waveforms above $\frac{1}{2} N_3 I_r$ and $N_4 I_r$ and $N_5 I_r$ rectangular waveforms below $-\frac{1}{2} N_3 I_r$ are plotted. The three stepped resultant mmf waveform so obtained, shown at the top in Fig. 1.10 *(b)*, is seen to be more nearer to sine wave.

The three-stepped mmf waveform obtained in Fig. 1.10 *(b)* can be resolved into fundamental component and harmonics. The fundamental air-gap mmf, as per Eq. (1.7), is given by

$$F_{a1} = \frac{4}{\pi} \cdot \left[\frac{k_r \cdot N_r}{P}\right] \cdot I_r \cos \alpha_r \qquad ...(1.9)$$

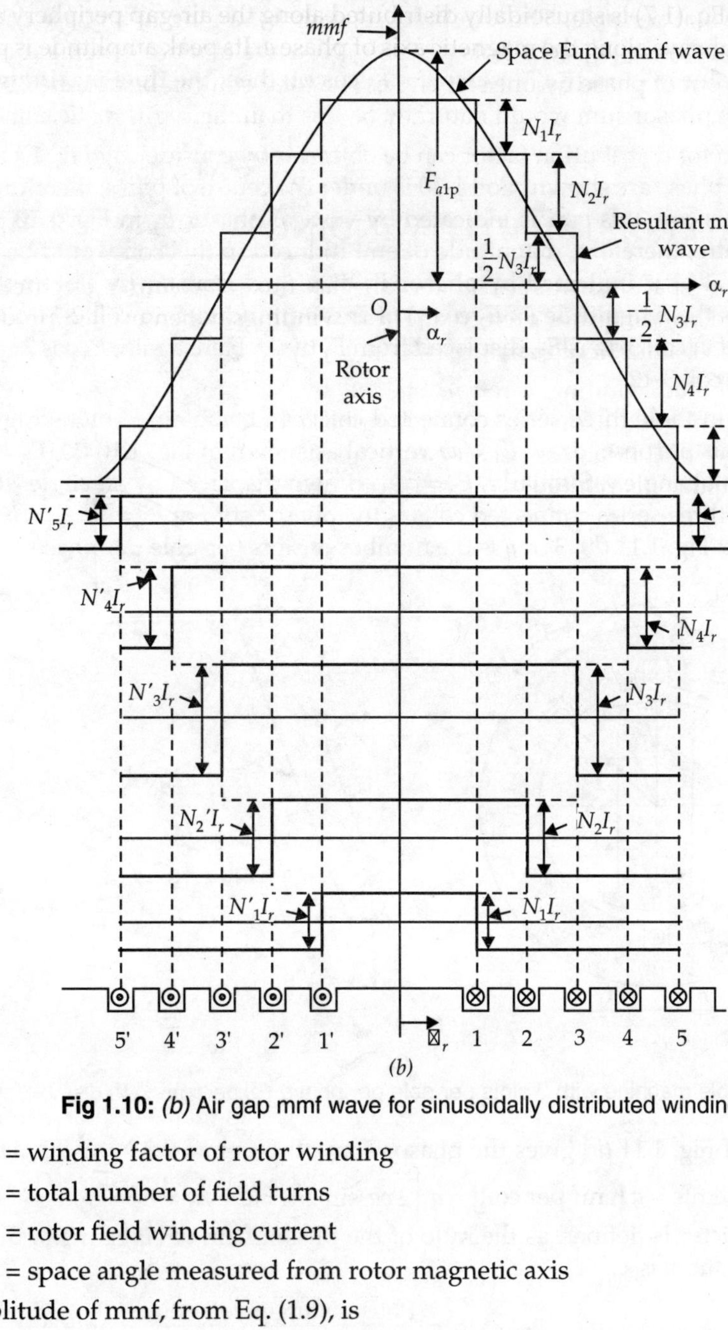

Fig 1.10: *(b)* Air gap mmf wave for sinusoidally distributed winding.

where k_r = winding factor of rotor winding

N_r = total number of field turns

I_r = rotor field winding current

α_r = space angle measured from rotor magnetic axis

Peak amplitude of mmf, from Eq. (1.9), is

$$F_{a1p} = \frac{4}{\pi} \cdot k_r \cdot \frac{N_r I_r}{P} \text{ ATs/pole} \qquad ...(1.10)$$

1.6. WINDING DISTRIBUTION FACTOR

If the coils belonging to a phase are housed in one slot per pole, then the emf generated in each of these coils would be equal in magnitude. The resultant emf generated by these coils can be obtained by simply taking their algebraic sum. In practice, however, it is not feasible to house one phase winding in one slot per pole. Thus, in practice, coils belonging to a phase of the winding are distributed in two or more adjacent slots per pole. Now the emf are generated in the coils in adjoining slots will be out of phase by one slot angle. The total emf can be obtained by the phasor sum of these emfs. The phasor sum would naturally be less than their arithmetic sum.

General expression for distribution factor can be obtained by considering Fig. 1.11 *(a)*, where 3 (= q) slots per pole per phase are shown. Coil 1-10 is under the centre of poles, therefore, maximum emf is generated in this coil, this emf is indicated by vertical phasor E_1 in Fig. 1.10 *(a)*. Coil 2-11 is away from pole centre, therefore, magnitude of emf induced in this coil would be less than E_1. Emf generated in coil 2-11 is indicated by phasor E_2 displaced from E_1 by slot angle γ. Vertical component of E_2 gives the magnitude (= $E_2 \cos \gamma$) of rms emf induced in coil 2-11. Similarly, rms value of emf generated in coil 3-12 is E_3, displaced from E_1 by 2γ. Here again, $E_3 \cos 2\gamma$ = magnitude of rms value of emf in coil 3-12.

The resultant emf in these three series connected coils can be obtained by taking phasor sum of E_1, E_2 and E_3. For this purpose, draw $E_1 = ab$ vertical as shown in Fig. 1.10 *(b)*, $E_2 = bc$ is drawn displaced from E_1 by slot angle γ. Similarly, $E_3 = cd$ is drawn displaced by an angle γ from E_2. The resultant emf in these three series connected coils is the phasor sum of $E_1 = ab$, $E_2 = bc$ and $E_3 = cd$ and it is given by ad. In Fig. 1.11 *(b)*, 3 or q is the number of slots per pole per phase.

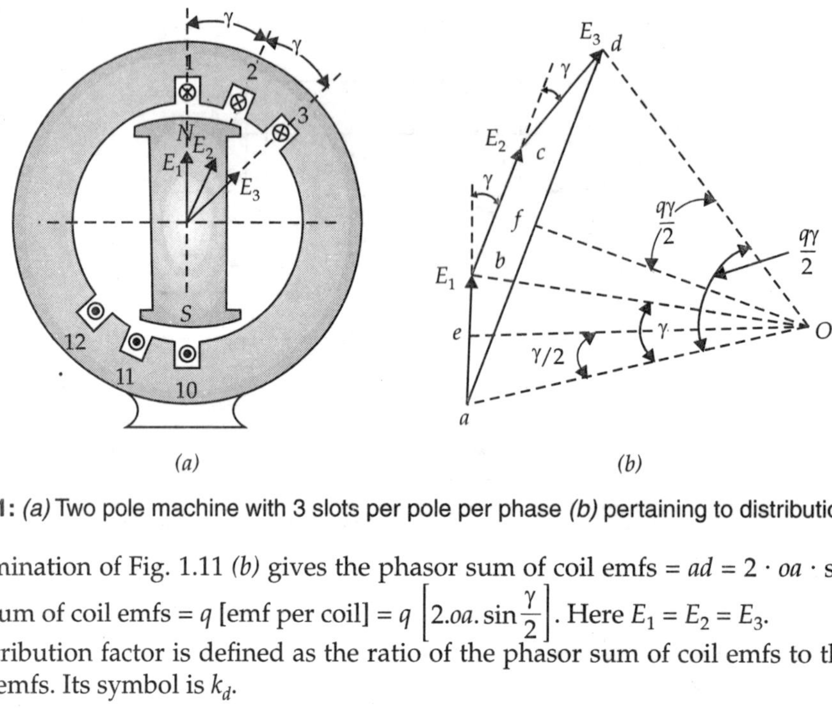

Fig 1.11: *(a)* Two pole machine with 3 slots per pole per phase *(b)* pertaining to distribution factor.

An examination of Fig. 1.11 *(b)* gives the phasor sum of coil emfs = $ad = 2 \cdot oa \cdot \sin \frac{q\gamma}{2}$. Also, arithmetic sum of coil emfs = q [emf per coil] = $q\left[2.oa.\sin\frac{\gamma}{2}\right]$. Here $E_1 = E_2 = E_3$.

The distribution factor is defined as the ratio of the phasor sum of coil emfs to the arithmetic sum of coil emfs. Its symbol is k_d.

$$\therefore \quad k_d = \frac{\text{Phasor sum of coil emfs}}{\text{Arithmetic sum of coil emfs}} = \frac{ad}{3 \cdot ab}$$

$$= \frac{ad}{q \cdot ab} \text{ in general}$$

$$= \frac{2 \cdot oa \cdot \sin\frac{q\gamma}{2}}{q\left[2 \cdot oa \cdot \sin\frac{\gamma}{2}\right]} = \frac{\sin\frac{q\gamma}{2}}{q\sin\frac{\gamma}{2}} \qquad \text{...(1.11)}$$

In Eq. (1.11), $q\gamma = \sigma$ is known as phase spread and is expressed in electrical degrees.

$$\therefore \quad k_d = \frac{\sin\frac{\sigma}{2}}{q\sin\frac{\sigma}{2q}} \qquad \text{...(1.12)}$$

Pitch Factor

In a full-pitched coil, the emfs E_1 and E_2 induced in the two coil sides are equal and in phase in the local circuit, Fig. 1.12 *(a)*. Therefore, net emf at the coil ends is $E_c = E_1 + E_2$. If $E_1 = E_2 = E$, then $AC = E_c = E + E = 2E$ = arithmetic sum of coil-side emfs of a coil, Fig. 1.12 *(a)*.

In short-pitch or chorded coil shown in Fig. 1.12 *(b)*, the emfs in the two coil sides are not in phase. For chording angle ε, the generated emf in coil-side 1 is $E_1 = AB$ but generated emf $E_2 = BC$ in coil-side 2 would be displaced from emf E_1 by chording angle ε. This is shown in the lower part of Fig. 1.12 *(b)*. In this figure, AC is the resultant emf obtained by the phasor sum of coil-side emfs E_1 and E_2. From Fig. 1.12 *(b)*, phasor sum of two coil-side emf is $E_c = AC = AD + DC = 2E\cos\varepsilon/2$.

Pitch factor is defined as the ratio of phasor sum of chorded coil emfs to the arithmetic sum of full-pitched coil emfs. Its symbol is k_p.

$$k_p = \frac{\text{phasor sum of chorded-coil emfs}}{\text{arithmetic sum of full-pitched coil emfs}}$$

$$= \frac{2E\cos\varepsilon/2}{2E} = \cos\frac{\varepsilon}{2} \qquad \text{...(1.13)}$$

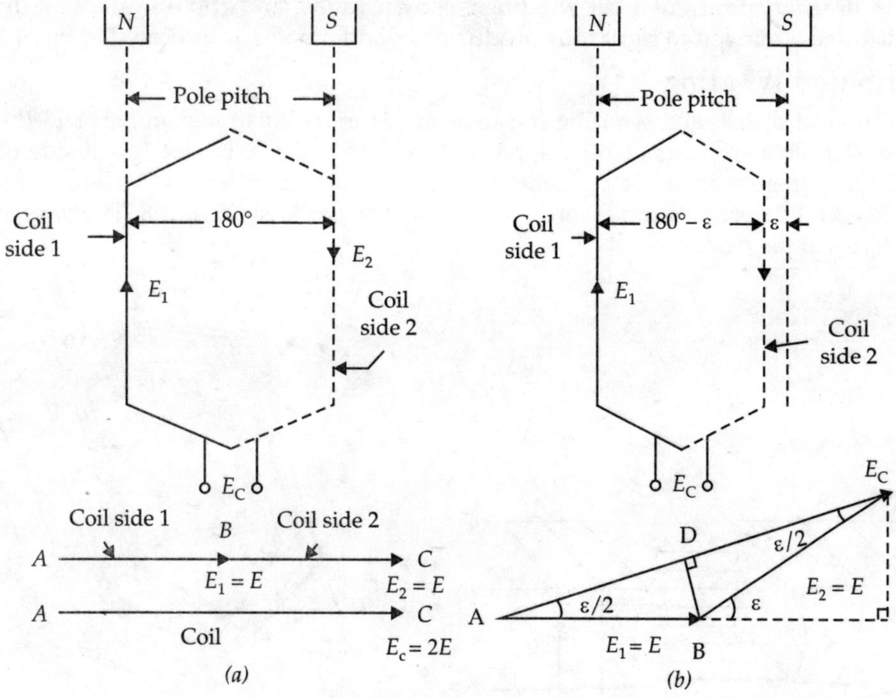

Fig 1.12: Pertaining to pitch factor *(a)* full-pitch coil *(b)* chorded coil.

The pitch factor given by Eq. (1.13) is for the fundamental frequency. If the field flux contains space harmonics, then pitch factor for *n*th harmonic is

$$k_{pn} = \cos\left(\frac{n\varepsilon}{2}\right) \qquad \text{...(1.14)}$$

For eliminating nth harmonic, $\cos \frac{n\varepsilon}{2} = 0 = \cos 90°$ or $\varepsilon = \frac{180}{n}$. Therefore, for eliminating 5th harmonic, the chording angle is $\frac{180}{5} = 36°$ and the coil span is $(180 - 36) = 144°$.

Advantages of chording the coil are

(i) overhang length of the coil is reduced and this leads to saving in the conductor material,

(ii) reduction of harmonics in the generated emf leads to output emf wave almost a sine wave.

Winding Factor : The product of distribution factor k_d and pitch factor k_p is called winding factor, symbol k_w.

$$\therefore \qquad \text{Winding factor, } k_w = k_d \times k_p \qquad \text{...(1.15)}$$

If the distributed winding uses full-pitch coils, then its winding factor would be k_d. In case the winding is concentrated in slots and uses short-pitched coil, then, for this winding, winding factor would be k_p.

1.7. 3D VISUALIZATION OF WINDING TYPES

Here an attempt is being made to give 3D visualization of concentrated and distributed windings.

1.7.1. Concentrated Winding

A 3D view of concentrated winding is shown in Fig. 1.13 *(a)*. Three dimensional visualization of two poles *N* and *S* is depicted. The concentrated winding wound over these two poles is also illustrated. The direction of current in the winding is shown. Right hand grip rule gives the direction of magnetic flux lines from left to right thus producing *N* and *S* poles as indicated in Fig. 1.13 *(a)*.

1.7.2. Distributed Winding

A 3D visualization of distributed winding for an *ac* armature is illustrated in Fig. 1.13 *(b)*. Here, only a total of four slots are taken. Coil 1 is housed in slots 1 and 7. In slot 1, coil side of coil 1 occupies top layer whereas its other coil-side occupies bottom layer in slot 7. Here coil span is 6 slots. Similarly, coil 2 occupies top layer in slot 2 and bottom layer in slot 8. The two coils are connected in series at the front end.

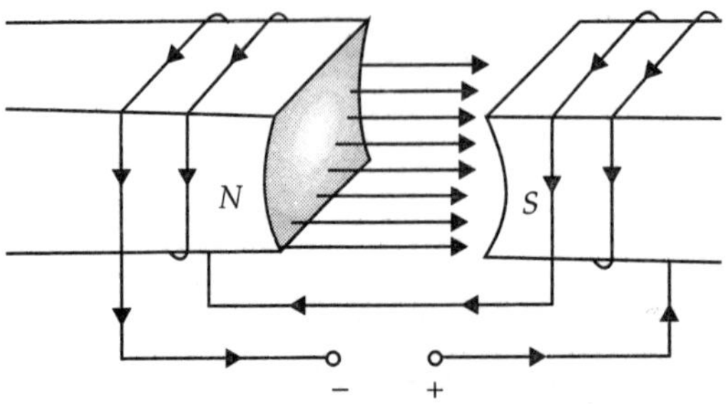

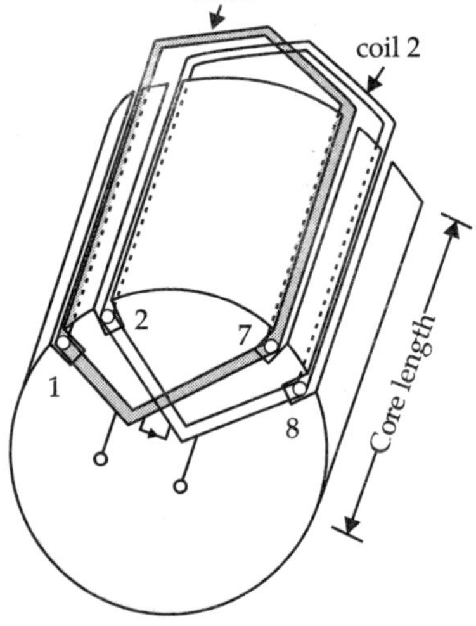

Fig 1.13: 3D visualization of *(a)* concentrated winding and *(b)* distributed winding.

Example 1.1. *(a) A uniform air-gap machine has one full-pitched coil having 20 turns. If each turn of this coil carries a current of 100 A, then calculate the magnitude of mmf along the air-gap periphery.*

(b) In part (a), the machine has four poles and each turn carries a current of 200 A. Calculate time maximum of peak fundamental mmf wave per pole.

(c) In part (b), calculate the time maximum of mmf at a space angle of 30° from the stator coil axis.

Solution. *(a)* Turns in full-pitched coil, $N = 20$; Current per turn, $I = 100$ A

∴ Magnitude of mmf along the air-gap periphery $= \frac{1}{2} NI = \frac{1}{2} \times 20 \times 100 = 1000$ ATs/pole

(b) From Eq. (1.5), time maximum of peak mmf is

$$F_{1pm} = \frac{4}{\pi} \frac{NI_m}{P} = \frac{4}{\pi} \times \frac{20 \times 200\sqrt{2}}{4} = 1800.4 \text{ ATs/pole}$$

(c) From Eqs. (1.2) and (1.5), time maximum of mmf at space angle of 30°

$$= \frac{4}{\pi} \cdot \frac{NI_m}{P} \cos\alpha = \frac{4}{\pi} \times \frac{20 \times 200\sqrt{2}}{4} \cos 30°$$

$$= 1559.16 \text{ ATs/pole.}$$

Example 1.2. *A 3-phase ac machine has 9 slots per pole. Calculate its breadth factor for (a) 60° phase spread and (b) 120° phase spread. Compare the two results.*

Solution. Slot angle, $\gamma = \frac{180°}{\text{slots per pole}} = \frac{180°}{9} = 20°$

(a) For a phase spread of $60° = q \times \gamma = 60°$

∴ Slots per pole per phase, $q = \frac{60°}{20°} = 3$

∴ Distribution factor, $k_d = \frac{\sin\frac{q\gamma}{2}}{q\sin\frac{\gamma}{2}} = \frac{\sin\frac{60}{2}}{3\sin\frac{20}{2}} = 0.9598$

(b) For a phase spread of 120°, $\sigma = q \times \gamma = 120°$

∴ $q = \frac{120°}{20°} = 6$

∴ Distribution factor, $k_d = \frac{\sin\frac{q\gamma}{2}}{q\sin\frac{\gamma}{2}} = \frac{\sin\frac{120}{2}}{6\sin\frac{20}{2}} = 0.831$

In rotating electrical machines, the generated voltage is proportional to distribution or breadth factor k_d. Therefore, a phase spread of 60° would give more output voltage than that obtained with 120° phase spread. In view of this, phase spread of 60° is preferred in all three-phase *ac* machines.

Example 1.3. *A 3-phase, 4 pole ac machine has 60 slots. Its coils are prepared with coil span* $= \frac{14}{15}$ *full pitch. Calculate pitch factor, distribution factor and winding factor.*

Solution. Pole pitch $= \frac{60}{4} = 15$ slots = full pitch

∴ Coil span $= \frac{14}{15} \times 15 = 14$ slots

Therefore, coil span is short of full pitch by one slot. Thus, the chording angle ε is

$$\varepsilon = \frac{4 \times 180}{60} = 12°$$

$\therefore$ Pitch factor, $k_p = \cos\frac{\varepsilon}{2} = \cos\frac{12}{2} = 0.9945$

Here slot angle, $\gamma = \frac{4 \times 180}{60} = 12°$

Slots/pole/phase, $q = \frac{60}{4 \times 3} = 5$

$\therefore$ Distribution factor, $k_d = \frac{\sin\frac{q\gamma}{2}}{q\sin\frac{\gamma}{2}} = \frac{\sin\frac{12\times 5}{2}}{5\sin\frac{12}{2}} = \frac{\sin 30°}{5\sin 6°} = 0.9567$

$\therefore$ Winding factor, $k_w = k_d \times k_p = 0.9567 \times 0.9945 = 0.9514.$

Example 1.4. *A 3-phase, 60 kw, 4-pole, delta-connected electric machine has 20 conductors per slot arranged in 72 slots. For a line current of 70 A, calculate the peak value of fundamental mmf wave of any phase. The winding is chorded by 1 slot.*

Solution. Slot angle, $\gamma = \frac{\text{Number of poles} \times 180°}{\text{Number of slots}} = \frac{4 \times 180°}{72} = 10°$

$\therefore$ Chording angle, ε = one slot angle $\gamma = 10°$

$\therefore$ Pitch factor, $k_p = \cos\frac{\varepsilon}{2}$

$= \cos\frac{10}{2} = 0.9962.$

Slots per pole per phase, $q = \frac{72}{3 \times 4} = 6$

$\therefore$ Distribution factor, $k_d = \frac{\sin\frac{q\gamma}{2}}{q\sin\frac{\gamma}{2}} = \frac{\sin\frac{6\times 10}{2}}{6\sin\frac{10}{2}} = 0.9561$

$\therefore$ Winding factor, $k_w = k_d \times k_p = 0.9561 \times 0.9962 = 0.9525.$

Turns per phase, $N_{ph} = \frac{\text{slots} \times \text{conductors per slot}}{2 \times \text{number of phases}}$

$\therefore$ $N_{ph} = \frac{72 \times 20}{2 \times 3} = 240$

Per-phase current, $I_{ph} = \frac{70}{\sqrt{3}}$ A

From Eq. (1.8), peak value of fundamental mmf wave of any one phase is given by

$$F_{1pm} = \frac{4}{\pi}\cdot k_w \frac{N_{ph}\cdot I_{max}}{P} \text{ ATs/pole}$$

$$= \frac{4}{\pi} \times 0.9525 \times \frac{240 \times 70 \times \sqrt{2}}{4 \times \sqrt{3}} = 4158.90 \text{ ATs/pole.}$$

Example 1.5. *A uniform air gap 2-pole machine is wound with 16 concentric field coils and with slot angle of 8°. Each coil has 12 turns. Field current is 120 A. Find the amplitude of the fundamental component of mmf produced by the field winding.*

Solution. All 16 coils, *i.e.* total 32 slots produce 2 poles.

$\therefore$ Phase spread, $\sigma = 16 \times 8 = 128°$

Slot angle $= 8° = \gamma$

There are 16 concentric coils for 2 poles. This can be taken as if 8 concentric coils distributed in slots create one pole. Therefore, take $q = 8$.

$$\therefore \quad k_d = \frac{\sin\frac{q\gamma}{2}}{q\sin\frac{\gamma}{2}} = \frac{\sin\frac{8\times 8}{2}}{8\sin\frac{8}{2}} = \frac{\sin 32^\circ}{8\sin 4^\circ} = 0.9496$$

Here $k_p = 1$, $\quad \therefore k_r = k_d \times k_p = 0.9496$

Total field turns, $\quad N_r = 16 \times 12 = 192$

From Eq. (1.10), peak amplitude of fundamental mmf wave is

$$F_{a1p} = \frac{4}{\pi}\cdot k_r \frac{N_r I_r}{P}$$

$$= \frac{4}{\pi} \times 0.9496 \times \frac{192 \times 120}{2} = 13928.47 \text{ ATs/pole.}$$

PROBLEMS

1.1. Explain, with suitable diagrams, the following terms pertaining to armature windings in rotating electrical machines :

Conductor, turn, coil, coil-side, pole-pitch, coil span, chorded coil, chording angle, full-pitch coil, active portion and overhang.

1.2. *(a)* Distinguish between single-layer and double-layer windings. Give the advantages of double-layer windings over single-layer windings.

(b) Draw the shape of various types of stator and rotor slots. Where are these types used?

1.3. What are concentrated windings? Give at least two examples of these windings with appropriate diagrams. Hence define the term winding-axis.

1.4. What are distributed windings? Give their advantages.

Draw a diagram showing phase '*a*' winding for a 2-pole 3-phase winding distributed in stator slots. Hence show winding axis of the three phases of a rotating electrical machine.

1.5. A uniform air-gap machine has one full-pitch *N* turn coil on the stator. If current in each turn is *i* amperes, show that the mmf along the air-gap periphery is of rectangular waveform of magnitude $\frac{1}{2}\cdot Ni$.

Show that peak value of fundamental mmf produced by this *N*-turn coil is given by

$$F_{1p} = \frac{4}{\pi}\cdot\frac{Ni}{2} \text{ ATs/pole}$$

1.6. A 2-pole, 3-phase ac machine has two-layer winding in 18 stator slots. Each coil has N_c turns and current in each turn is i_c. Sketch mmf wave produced by phase '*a*' alone.

Hence, derive an expression for the peak value of fundamental component of mmf wave.

[Ans. $\frac{4}{\pi}\, k_w \cdot \frac{N_{ph}\cdot I_{max}}{P}$ ATs/pole]

1.7. What is sinusoidally distributed winding? Where is it used?

Sketch air-gap mmf wave for a sinusoidally distributed winding by taking a total of 8 slots on the cylindrical rotor of an alternator.

Hence show that peak amplitude of fundamental mmf wave is

$$F_{a1p} = \frac{4}{\pi}\cdot k_r \cdot \frac{N_r I_r}{P} \text{ ATs/pole}$$

1.8. Define distribution factor. Show that its expression for fundamental frequency component is given by $k_d = \dfrac{\sin\dfrac{q\gamma}{2}}{q\sin\dfrac{\gamma}{2}}$ where q = slots/pole/phase and γ = slot angle.

1.9. *(a)* Define pitch factor. Derive an expression for it.

(b) What should be the coil-span for eliminating fifth harmonic components?

[**Ans.** *(b)* 144°]

1.10. Sketch 3D visualization of concentrated winding and distributed winding.

1.11. A uniform air-gap machine has one full-pitch coil on the stator with 30 turns. Each turn of this coil carries a current of 120 A. Calculate time maximum of mmf per pole, produced at a space angle of *(a)* 60° *(b)* 90° and *(c)* 120° from the axis of stator coil.

[**Ans.** *(a)* 1620.57 ATs/pole *(b)* zero *(c)* – 1620.57 ATs/pole]

1.12. A 3-phase, 6 pole star-connected electric machine has single layer winding arranged in 90 slots. Coils are short-pitched by 1 slot and turns per coil are 6. For a line current of 30 A, calculate the peak value of fundamental mmf for any one phase.

[**Hint.** Number of coils = $\frac{1}{2}$ (number of slots in single layer winding)]

[**Ans.** 770.905 ATs/pole]

Objective Type Questions

1. One turn consists of

(a) two coil sides *(b)* two conductors *(c)* four conductors *(d)* four turns

2. One coil consists of

(a) two conductors *(b)* two turns *(c)* two coil-sides *(d)* four turns

3. A multiturn coil has

(a) multi-coil sides *(b)* one coil-side *(c)* two coil-sides *(d)* four coil-sides

4. A pole pitch in rotating electrical machines is

(a) = 180° electrical *(b)* = 180° mechanical

(c) > 180° electrical *(d)* < 180° electrical

5. Read the following statements about the chorded coils :

1. chorded coils lead to reduction in harmonics,
2. chorded coils require more conductor material,
3. in chorded coils, coil span < 180° electrical,
4. in chorded coils, coil span may be less or more than 180° electrical.

From these, the correct statements are

(a) 1, 2, 3 *(b)* 1, 2, 4 *(c)* 1, 3 *(d)* 2, 4

6. Read the following statements :

1. active portion of a coil is where actual emf is generated,
2. overhang is back to back connection of two conductors,
3. chording angle = 180° – coil span in electrical degrees,
4. chorded coils require less conductor material.

From above, the correct statements are

(a) 1, 2, 3 *(b)* 1, 2, 3, 4 *(c)* 2, 3, 4 *(d)* 1, 3, 4

7. Read the following statements :
   1. open slots for stator are used for medium voltage machines,
   2. closed slots are used for induction motor rotors,
   3. double-cage slots are used for 3-phase induction motors,
   4. tapered slots on stator are used for medium power-rated in duction machines.

   From above, the correct statements are

   (*a*) 1, 2, 3, 4 (*b*) 2, 3 (*c*) 1, 3, 4 (*d*) 1, 2, 3

8. Read the following statements :
   1. concentrated windings are not used in rotating electrical machines,
   2. distributed winding adds rigidity and mechanical strength to the winding,
   3. transformer primary winding is a concentrated winding,
   4. dc machine stator uses concentrated windings.

   From these, the correct statements are

   (*a*) 1, 2, 3 (*b*) 2, 3, 4 (*c*) 1, 3, 4 (*d*) 1, 2, 4

9. Air-gap mmf produced by concentrated coil is

   1. one step wave, 2. two-stepped wave,
   3. of rectangular waveshape, 4. of square waveform,

   From above, the correct statements are

   (*a*) 1, 3, 4 (*b*) 2, 3, 4 (*c*) 3, 4 (*d*) 1, 2, 3

10. Mmf produced by 2-pole, 3-phase winding with 3 slots per phase has

    (*a*) sinusoidal waveform, (*b*) three-stepped waveform,
    (*c*) two-stepped waveform (*d*) rectangular wave shifted by one slot angle

11. In sinusoidally distributed windings
    1. number of conductors in all the slots are equal,
    2. number of conductors in the middle of phase winding are maximum,
    3. number of conductors at the end of phase winding are minimum,
    4. number of conductors near the pole are minimum,
    5. these are used in 3-phase windings.

    From above, the correct statements are

    (*a*) 1, 3, 5 (*b*) 2, 3, 4, 5 (*c*) 1, 3, 4 (*d*) 2, 3, 4

12. The distribution factor is defined as the ratio of

    (*a*) arithmetic sum of coil emfs to the phasor sum of coil emfs,
    (*b*) phasor sum of emf per coil to the arithmetic sum of emf per coil,
    (*c*) phasor sum of coil emfs to the arithmetic sum of coil emfs,
    (*d*) phasor sum of coil emfs to the per phase voltage.

13. In rotating electrical machines, pitch factor is defined as the ratio of resultant emf of a

    (*a*) full pitched coil to that of chorded coil,
    (*b*) full pitched coil to the phase emf,
    (*c*) chorded coil to phase emf,
    (*d*) chorded coil to that of a full-pitched coil.

14. A 3-phase, 4-pole ac machine has 60 stator slots carrying a 3-phase distributed winding. Each coil of the winding is short chorded by one slot pitch. The winding factor is given by

(a) $\frac{\cot 6°}{20}$ (b) $\frac{\cot 6°}{10}$ (c) $\frac{1}{10 \sin 6°}$ (d) $\frac{\cos 6°}{10}$

15. In 48 slots, 4-pole, 3-phase ac machine, the coil span is 10. Its pitch factor is

(a) 0.9659 (b) 0.9671 (c) 0.9814 (d) 0.9695

16. In rotating electrical machines, which of the following coils will have mmf closer to sine waveform?

(a) concentrated winding with full-pitched coils,

(b) concentrated winding with short-pitched coils,

(c) distributed winding with full pitch coils,

(d) distributed winding with short pitch coils.

17. In 36 slots, 4-pole, 3-phase ac machine, the coil pitch is 7. The electrical angle by which the winding is chorded is

(a) 40° (b) 30° (c) 60° (d) 15°

Answers

1. (b)	**2.** (c)	**3.** (c)	**4.** (a)	**5.** (c)
6. (d)	**7.** (b)	**8.** (b)	**9.** (a)	**10.** (c)
11. (d)	**12.** (c)	**13.** (d)	**14.** (b)	**15.** (a)
16. (d)	**17.** (a)			

Chapter

2

Pulsating and Revolving Magnetic Fields

In rotating electrical machines, presence of pulsating and revolving magnetic fields is quite common. Therefore, a study of these two types of magnetic fields is essential for understanding the theory and operation of rotating electrical machines.

2.1. CONSTANT MAGNETIC FIELD

In Fig. 2.1 *(a)*, two coils are wound, one on each pole, as shown. Now dc voltage is applied to the two coils in series with terminal B positive and terminal A negative. The current flows in the two coils as indicated. Right-hand grip rule gives the direction of magnetic flux lines from right to left. As a result, poles N and S are created on the stator. Since current is constant dc current, the magnetic flux produced by this current is also constant.

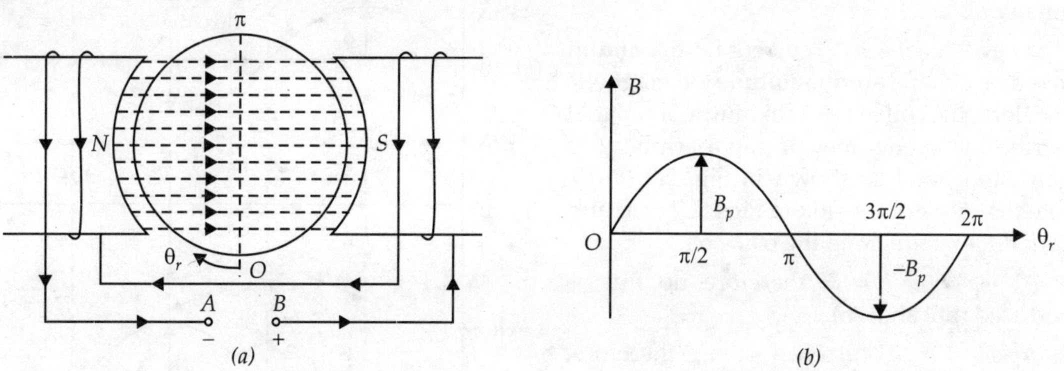

Fig 2.1: *(a)* Production of constant magnetic field and *(b)* variation of flux density waveform with space angle θ_r along air-gap periphery.

If variation of flux density along the air-gap periphery is plotted, Fig. 2.1 *(b)* is obtained. The flux density B at $\theta_r = 0$ is zero, at $\theta_r = \frac{\pi}{2}$, B is maximum positive, at $\theta_r = \pi$, B is zero and so on. This variations of B along air-gap periphery is assumed sinusoidal.

Thus, when dc is applied to two coils on stator in Fig. 2.1 (*a*), it is observed from the magnetic flux lines that

(i) a constant magnetic field is produced,

(ii) magnetic field is distributed sinusoidally in space (*i.e.* along the air-gap periphery),

(iii) magnitude of magnetic field strength does not change with time,

(iv) axis of magnetic field remains fixed in position along the coil axis.

Thus, in Fig. 2.1, a constant magnetic field is produced which is time invariant (does not vary with time), but sinusoidally distributed in space. Its magnetic axis remains fixed.

In short, a **constant magnetic field** does not change with time and its magnetic axis remains the same.

2.2. PULSATING MAGNETIC FIELD

Let us consider Fig. 2.1 *(a)* again. Now, we apply an alternating current $i = I_m \sin \omega t$, shown in Fig. 2.2 *(a)*, at the terminals A, B of the two coils in Fig. 2.1 *(a)*. The type of magnetic field produced at different instants of time is now investigated.

At instant $\omega t = 0$, current $i = 0$, therefore no magnetic field is produced at this instant, see Fig. 2.2 *(b i)*.

At instant $\omega t = 0a$, current $i = ab$ in Fig. 2.2 *(a)*, therefore, magnetic field, proportional to current ab is produced $\left(\text{flux} = \dfrac{\text{coil turns} \times \text{coil current}}{\text{reluctance}}\right)$. The plot of this flux, along the air-gap periphery is plotted in Fig. 2.2 *(b ii)*. Note that amplitude of flux ϕ_{ab} is proportional to current ab, but spatial distribution along air-gap periphery is sinusoidal.

At instant $\omega t = \pi/2$, current i = maximum current I_m, therefore magnitude of magnetic flux along the coil axis is maximum. Its spatial distribution along the air-gap periphery is again sinusoidal as shown in Fig. 2.2 *(b iii)*. Note that peak of the flux in Figs. 2.2 *(b ii)* and 2.2 *(b iii)* is again along the coil axis.

At $\omega t = \pi$, $i = 0$, therefore no flux is produced (not shown).

At $\omega t = 3\pi/2$, current i = $-I_m$, therefore, amplitude of flux along the coil axis is again maximum but negative, *i.e.* it is now $-\phi_m$. Spatial distribution of flux at $\omega t = 3\pi/2$ is shown in Fig. 2.2 *(b iv)*.

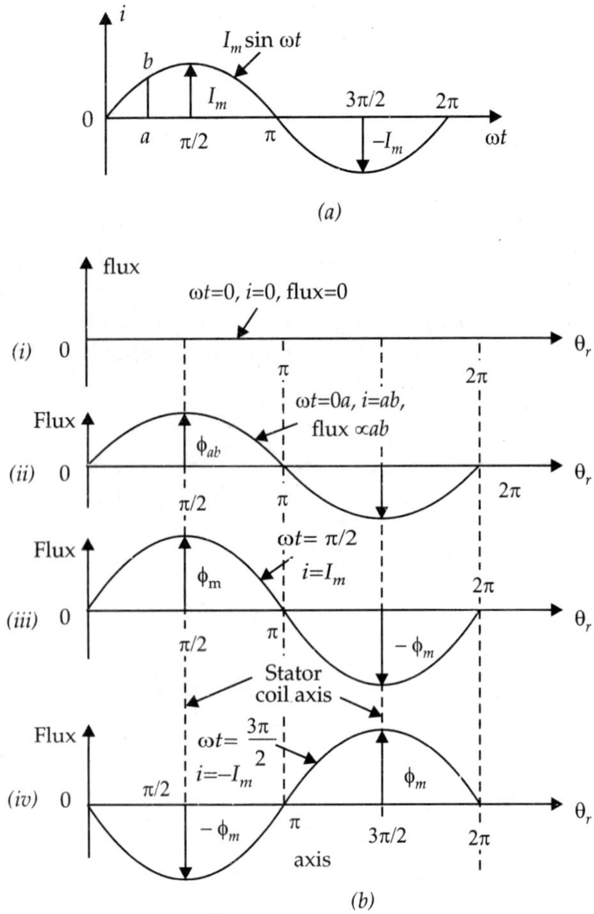

Fig 2.2: *(a)* Plot of current $i = I_m \sin \omega t$ and *(b)* plot of flux as current in coils varies.

Note from above that when concentrated coil on stator are excited with alternating current, an alternating or pulsating magnetic flux is set up such that

(i) axis of stator field remains fixed along the stator coil axis at all instants of time and

(ii) magnitude of magnetic field strength varies from zero, ϕ_m, zero, $-\phi_m$, zero and so on, *i.e.* stator field strength pulsates in magnitude as the exciting current $i = I_m \sin \omega t$ varies sinusoidally with time.

When stator coil is excited with dc, magnetic flux is set up along the stator coil axis. If stator coil is excited with ac, the magnetic field would be alternating or pulsating in nature, but its magnetic axis would always remain along the stator coil axis. For such a field, we say, "stator field or mmf is stationary in space."

Thus a pulsating field may be defined as one whose mmf wave is stationary in space but stator field strength is alternating in polarity and varying sinusoidally with time.

2.3. PULSATING FIELDS PRODUCED BY SPATIALLY DISPLACED WINDINGS

In Fig. 2.3 *(a)*, three full-pitched coils distributed on the stator are shown. If current flows in these coils, a magnetic flux is set up. In case the coils carry alternating current, a pulsating magnetic field is produced. Axis of this field remains horizontal, but the strength of the magnetic field would change with time as explained in Fig. 2.2 *(b)*. For convenience, the three full-pitched coils can be represented by one coil $\alpha'\alpha$ as shown in Fig. 2.3 *(b)*.

Let us now consider two windings spatially displaced from each other by 90° as shown in Fig. 2.4 *(a)*. These two windings can be taken to represent a two-phase winding of a rotating electrical machine. For convenience, the two-phase winding α, β can be represented by two full-pitched coils $\alpha\alpha'$, $\beta\beta'$ as illustrated in Fig. 2.4 *(b)*. The concentrated full-pitch coil $\alpha\alpha'$ represents phase α winding of a 2-phase machine in all respects. Similarly, full-pitched coil $\beta\beta'$ represents second phase β winding.

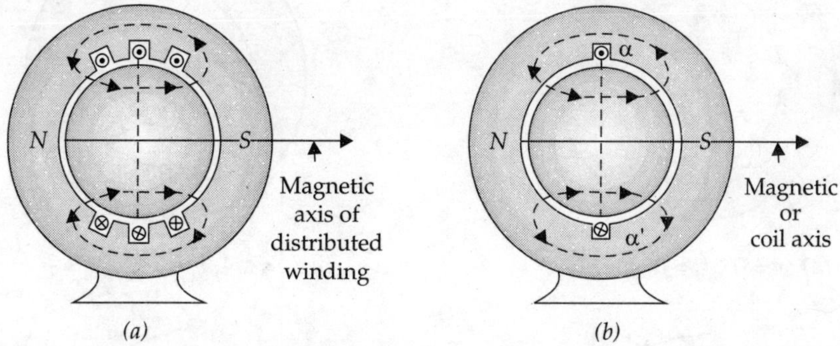

Fig 2.3: *(a)* Pertaining to flux produced by distributed winding and *(b)* its representation by one coil.

A current in phase α winding produced pulsating magnetic field directed along the magnetic axis of coil $\alpha\alpha'$. Positive currents are assumed to flow as indicated by cross in coil-sides α', β', Fig. 2.4 *(b)*. It means that when phase α alone carries positive current, the flux produced by this phase is directed horizontally from right to left. If phase α current is negative, the flux produced would be directed horizontally from right to left.

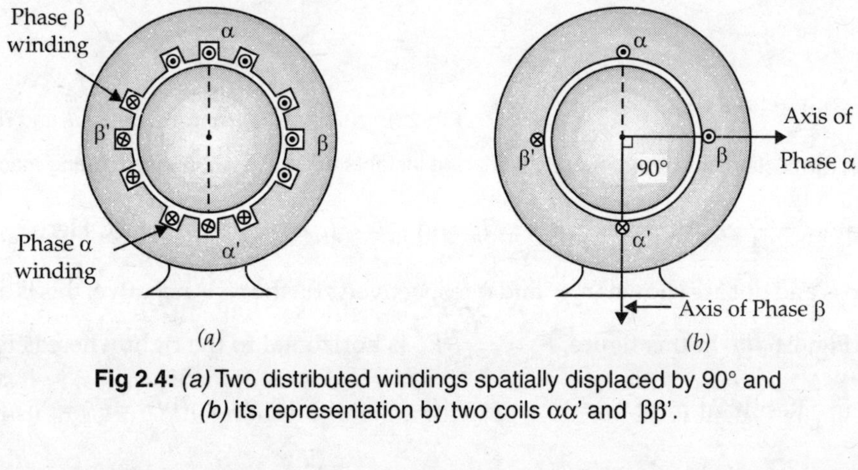

Fig 2.4: *(a)* Two distributed windings spatially displaced by 90° and *(b)* its representation by two coils αα' and ββ'.

Now consider that 2-phase currents are flowing in the two-phase winding of Fig. 2.4 *(b)*. These currents vary sinusoidally with time as shown in Fig. 2.5 *(a)*. The mmf produced by these currents in the two windings spatially displaced by 90° is now investigated.

At instant $\omega t = 0$, $i_\alpha = 0$ and $i_\beta = -I_m$. In Fig. 2.6, these currents are shown by dot and cross. Since $i_\alpha = 0$, nothing is shown in coil $\alpha\alpha'$ in Fig. 2.6 *(a)*. Current i_β is negative, therefore, it is indicated by dot in coil-side β and cross in coil-side β in Fig. 2.6 *(a)*. No flux is produced by phase α but flux produced by phase β winding is maximum but negative, *i.e.* $-\phi_m$.

In Fig. 2.6 *(a)*, right-hand rule gives phase β mmf vertically up and equal to F_m. Therefore, resultant mmf at $\omega t = 0$ is $F_R = \bar{F}_\alpha + \bar{F}_\beta = 0 + F_m = F_m = N.\ I_m$.

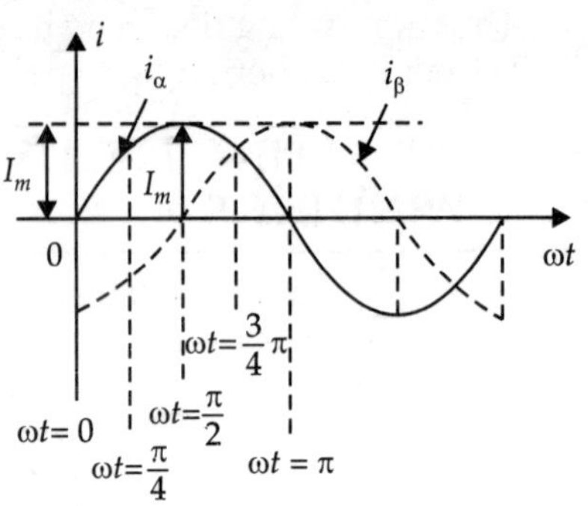

Fig 2.5: Two-phase currents i_α and i_β .

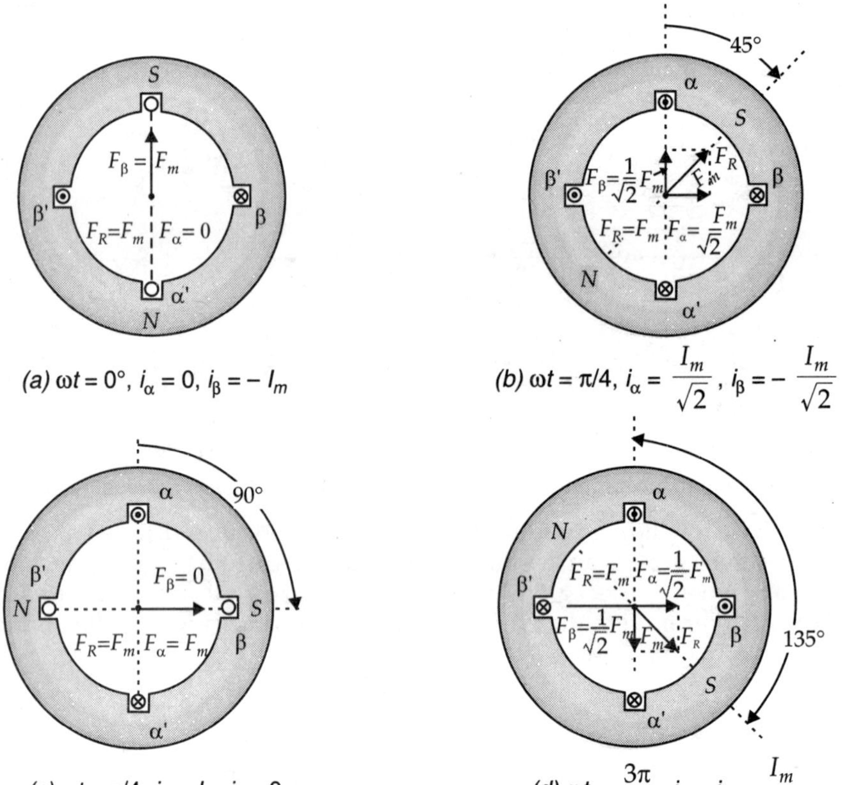

(a) $\omega t = 0°$, $i_\alpha = 0$, $i_\beta = -I_m$

(b) $\omega t = \pi/4$, $i_\alpha = \frac{I_m}{\sqrt{2}}$, $i_\beta = -\frac{I_m}{\sqrt{2}}$

(c) $\omega t = \pi/4$, $i_\alpha = I_m$, $i_\beta = 0$

(d) $\omega t = \frac{3\pi}{4}$, $i_\alpha = i_\beta = \frac{I_m}{\sqrt{2}}$

Fig 2.6: Production of field produced at different instants of time in a 2-phase rotating machine.

At instant $\omega t = \frac{\pi}{4}$, $i_\alpha = I_m \sin\frac{\pi}{4} = \frac{1}{\sqrt{2}} I_m$ and $i_\beta = -I_m \cos\frac{\pi}{4} = -\frac{1}{\sqrt{2}} I_m$. Here i_α is positive, therefore, cross and dot are shown in α′ and α respectively; further i_β is negative, this is accordingly indicated in Fig. 2.6 *(b)*. In this figure, $F_\alpha = \frac{1}{\sqrt{2}} F_m$ is horizontal to the right whereas $F_\beta = \frac{1}{\sqrt{2}} F_m$ is vertically up. Resultant mmf $F_R = \bar{F}_\alpha + \bar{F}_\beta = [(F_m/\sqrt{2})^2 + (F_m/\sqrt{2})^2]^{1/2} = F_m = N\ I_m$. Note that resultant mmf at $\omega t = \frac{\pi}{4}$ is equal to that instant $\omega t = 0°$, but F_R has rotated through a space angle of 45° clockwise, equal to time angle $\omega t = \pi/4$.

At instant $\omega t = \pi/2$, $i_\alpha = I_m$ and $i_\beta = 0$. Therefore, mmf $F_\alpha = F_m$ and $F_\beta = 0$. Resultant mmf $F_R = F_m$ is now along phase α axis, Fig. 2.6 *(c)*. So resultant mmf F_R has not changed from its magnitude at $\omega t = 0$ and $\omega t = \pi/4$; but has rotated through 45° from its orientation at $\omega t = \pi/4$. Here also, space angle rotation = time angle $\pi/4$.

At instant $\omega t = \frac{3\pi}{4}$, $i_\alpha = I_m \sin 135 = \frac{1}{\sqrt{2}} I_m$ and $i_\beta = I_m \sin 45° = \frac{1}{\sqrt{2}} I_m$, Fig. 2.5. Both currents are equal and positive. Therefore, $F_\alpha = F_m/\sqrt{2}$ is along phase α-axis and mmf $F_\beta = F_m/\sqrt{2}$ is along the phase β-axis, see Fig. 2.6 *(d)*. The resultant mmf $F_R = F_m$ as in Fig. 2.6 *(b)*. Note also that resultant mmf has not altered from its previous values but has travelled through a space angle of 45° from its position at $\omega t = \pi/2$.

At other instants of time beyond $\omega t = \frac{3}{4}\pi$, it would be observed that resultant mmf revolves further but its amplitude remains constant at $F_m = N I_m$. An elapse of certain angle ωt in time, results in rotation of mmf by the space angle (α) equal to time angle. Thus, when two-phase balanced currents are applied to two phase windings, a rotating magnetic field of constant amplitude is produced. The amplitude of this mmf, $F_m = N.I_m$, remains constant.

The two poles produced by rotating field are shown on stator in Fig. 2.6. It is seen that for a 2-pole machine, the rotating field travels a distance of one revolution in one cycle. This distance is equal to two pole-pitches (= 360° electrical) in one cycle. For a 4-pole machine, the rotating field will travel a distance covered by two pole pitches, *i.e.* $\frac{1}{2}\left(=\frac{1}{4/2}\right)$ revolution in one cycle. For a P pole machine, rotating field speed is $\frac{1}{P/2}$ revolutions in one cycle, or $\frac{f}{P/2}$ revolutions in f cycles or speed $\frac{2f}{P}$ revolutions per second in f cycles per second. But f cycles per second is the supply frequency in Hz. Therefore, speed of rotating field, called synchronous speed is given by

$$n_r = \frac{2f}{P} \text{ revolutions per sec.} \quad ...(2.1)$$

or

$$N_s = \frac{120f}{P} \text{ revolutions per minute} \quad ...(2.2)$$

where f = supply frequency in Hz and P = number of poles in the machine.

2.4. THREE WINDINGS SPATIALLY SHIFTED BY 120° DEGREES

Consider a 2-pole, 3-phase winding distributed in 18 slots on stator as shown in Fig. 2.7 *(a)*. These three windings are spatially shifted from each other by 120° electrical. For convenience, the three-phase distributed winding can be represented by three full-pitched coils *aa'*, *bb'*, *cc'* as illustrated in Fig. 2.7 *(b)*. For instance, the concentrated full pitch coil *aa'* represents phase *a* winding in all respects. Positive phase currents are assumed to be flowing as indicated by crosses in coil sides *a'*, *b'*, *c'*. When phase *a* alone carries positive current, mmf produced by this phase is directed horizontally from left to right as shown in Fig. 2.7 *(b)*. In case phase *a* current is negative, the mmf produced by this phase would be directed horizontally from right to left in Fig. 2.7 *(b)* (not shown).

Consider Fig. 2.8 *(a)* where current in phase *a* is taken as maximum positive I_m. Then currents in both phases *b* and *c* would be $-\frac{1}{2} I_m$. These currents are indicated by cross in *a'* and dot in *a* for

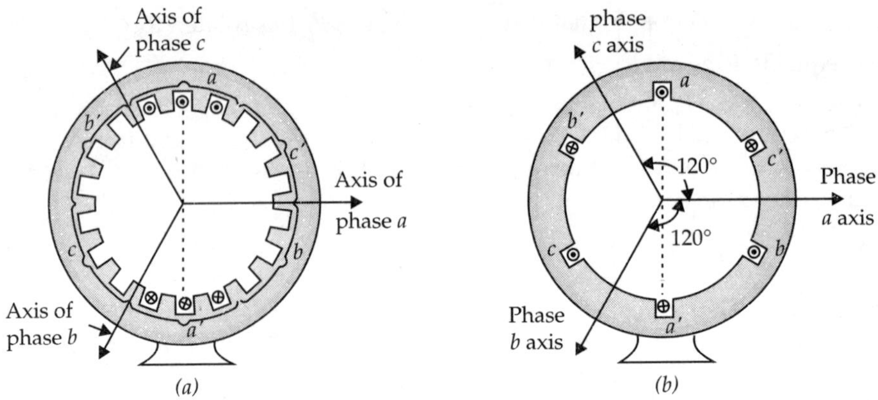

Fig 2.7: *(a)* Three-phase distributed winding and *(b)* its representation by three coils *aa*', *bb*', *cc*'.

positive phase a current. For negative phase currents, dots in b', c' and crosses in b, c are shown in Fig. 2.8 *(a)*. Mmf F_a produced by I_m is maximum mmf F_m. Mmf produced by $\frac{I_m}{2}$ is $\frac{F_m}{2}$. Mmf F_a is along the phase a axis. Mmf F_b and F_c are shown reversed because both currents I_b and I_c are negative. The magnitudes of mmfs are $F_a = F_m$ ($\because i_a = I_m$) and $F_b = F_c = F_m/2$. The resultant of mmfs F_a, F_b, F_c in Fig. 2.8 *(a)* is

$$F_R = F_m + F_b \cos 60° + F_c \cos 60°$$

$$= F_m + \frac{F_m}{2} \cdot \cos 60 + \frac{F_m}{2} \cdot \cos 60°0 = \frac{3}{2} F_m$$

Fig. 2.8 *(b)* shows the conditions at an instant 30° (= ωt) later. Here current $i_b = 0$, $\therefore$ $F_b = 0$; current $i_a = \frac{\sqrt{3}}{2} I_m$ and positive, therefore mmf $F_a = \frac{\sqrt{3}}{2} F_m$ is shown along the axis of phase a. Current $i_c = -\frac{\sqrt{3}}{2} \cdot I_m$, $\therefore$ mmf $F_c = -\frac{\sqrt{3}}{2} F_m$ is shown reversed along the phase-c axis. The resultant of mmfs F_a, F_b, F_c in Fig. 2.8 *(b)* is $F_R = \overline{F}_a + \overline{F}_b + \overline{F}_c = \frac{\sqrt{3}}{2} F_m \cos 30° + 0 + \frac{\sqrt{3}}{2} F_m \cos 30° = \frac{3}{2} F_m.$

It is seen from Fig. 2.8 *(b)* that F_R has rotated clockwise through a space angle of 30°, equal to time angle $\omega t = 30°$.

Fig. 2.8 *(c)* shows that conditions 30° later in time with respect to those shown in Fig. 2.8 *(b)*. Here $i_a = i_b = +\frac{1}{2} I_m$ but $i_c = -I_m$. Crosses and dots are accordingly put in coil sides and mmf $F_a = \frac{1}{2} F_m$ $F_b = \frac{1}{2} F_m$ and $F_c = -F_m$ are depicted in Fig. 2.8 *(c)*. The resultant mmf $F_R = \overline{F}_a + \overline{F}_b + \overline{F}_c = \frac{F_m}{2} \cos 60 + \frac{F_m}{2} \cos 60 + F_m = \frac{3}{2} F_m$. Here also, F_R is seen to rotate clockwise further by a space angle of 30°.

Now compare Figs. 2.8 *(a)*, *(b)*, *(c)*. In Fig. 2.8 *(b)*, resultant mmf F_R has rotated through 30° as compared to its position in Fig. 2.8 *(a)*. Similarly, mmf F_R in Fig. 2.8 *(c)* has further advanced by 30° as compared to its orientation in Fig. 2.8 *(b)*. This shows that an angle of 30°electrical in time causes a rotation of F_R by a space angle 30°. Thus, for every time angle of 30°, the mmf F_R rotates through a space angle of 30°, but its amplitude remains constant at $\frac{3}{2} F_m$. At other instants, *i.e.* as the time passes, mmf F_R revolves further through a space angle, equal to time angle.

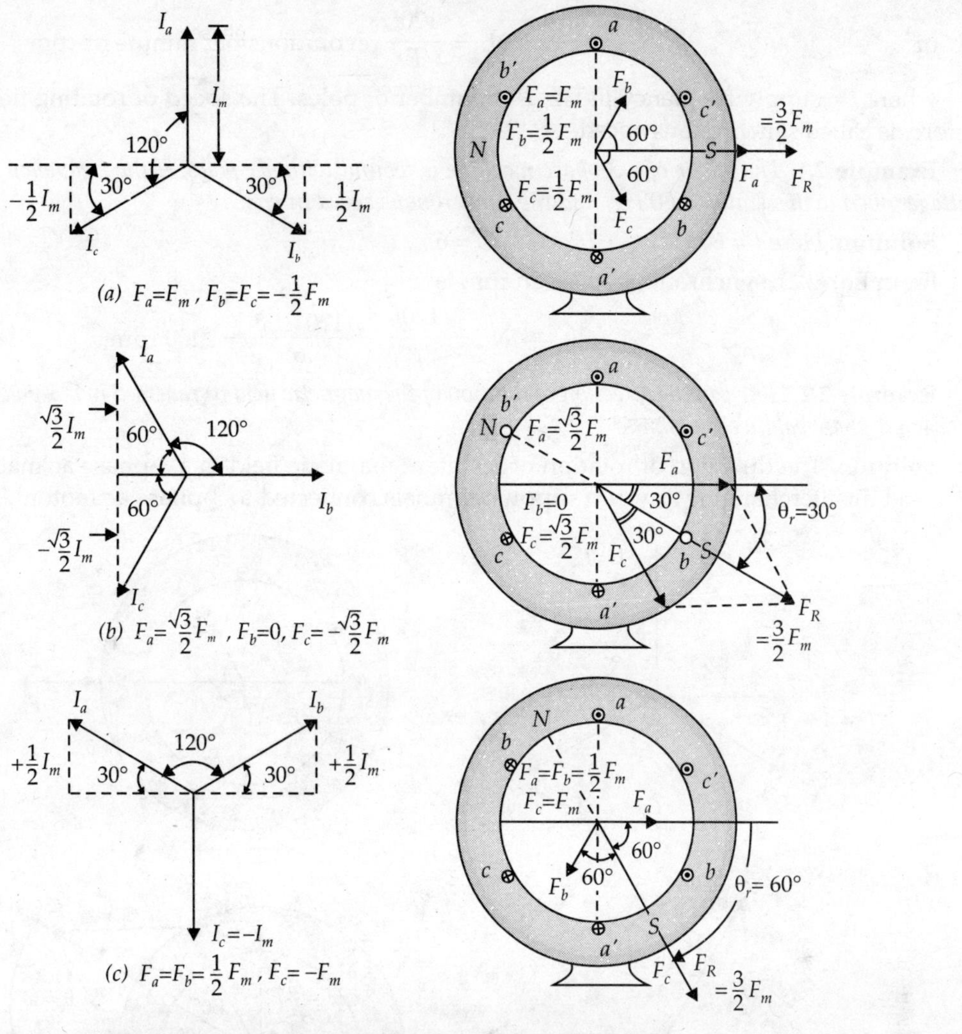

Fig 2.8: Production of rotating magnetic field illustrated by space phasor mmfs F_a, F_b, F_c and resultant mmf F_R.

It is seen from above that three-phase windings spatially shifted by 120° and carrying three-phase balanced currents would produce a rotating magnetic field of constant amplitude $\frac{3}{2}F_m$.

For every 30° time interval, the axis of magnetic flux in a 2-pole stator rotates through 30° in space. Consequently, in one cycle of 360°, the flux rotates through a space of angle 360°, *i.e.* one revolution or two pole-pitch. For a P pole stator, rotating field speed is $\frac{2}{P}$ or $\frac{1}{\frac{P}{2}}$ revolution in one cycle and therefore $\frac{f}{P/2}$ or $\frac{2f}{P}$ revolutions in f cycles. In other words, rotating field speed is $\frac{2f}{P}$ revolutions per second in f cycles per second. But f cycles per second is the supply frequency. Therefore, rotating field speed is

$$n_s = \frac{2f}{P} \text{ revolutions per second or rps} \qquad ...(2.1)$$

or $$N_s = \frac{120f}{P} \text{ revolutions per minute or rpm} \qquad ...(2.2)$$

where f = supply frequency in Hz, P = number of poles. The speed of rotating field, as stated before, is called synchronous speed.

Example 2.1. *The stator of a 3-phase machine is wound with six poles. If the frequency of the supply voltage given to this stator is 60 Hz, find the synchronous speed in rpm.*

Solution. Here $f = 60$ Hz, $P = 6$.

From Eq. (2.2), synchronous speed in rpm is

$$N_s = \frac{120f}{P} = \frac{120 \times 60}{6} = 1200 \text{ rpm.}$$

Example 2.2. *How can the direction of rotation of the magnetic field be reversed in a 3-phase ac machine fed from 3-phase balanced currents?*

Solution. The direction of rotation of resultant magnetic field in a 3-phase ac machine can be reversed by interchanging any two supply terminals connected to 3-phase ac motor.

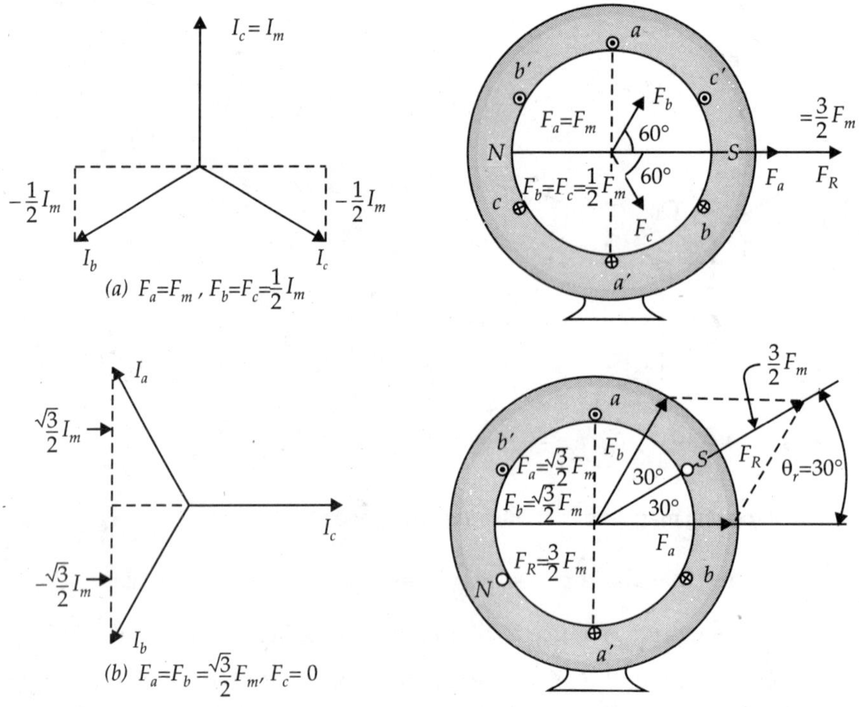

Fig 2.9: Direction of rotating field reversed pertaining to Example 2.2.

Out of three supply terminals a, b, c ; let us interchange two supply terminals b and c. With this change, phasor diagram of Fig. 2.8 *(a)* gets modified to that shown in Fig. 2.9 (*a*), where now the phase sequence is *acb*. Here again $I_b = I_c = -\frac{1}{2} I_m$ and $I_a = I_m$. For I_a, cross in a' and dot in a, are shown in Fig. 2.9 (*a*). For I_b and I_c, dots in b', c' and crosses in b, c aree shown. Mmfs produced by three windings are shown as $F_a = F_m$ and $F_b = F_c = -\frac{1}{2} F_m$ and the resultant mmf F_R is given by $F_R = F_m + \frac{F_m}{2} \cos 60° + \frac{F_m}{2} \cos 60 = \frac{3}{2} F_m$. Orientation of mmf F_R here in Fig. 2.9 *(a)* is the same as it is in Fig. 2.8 *(a)*.

Now consider the instant 30° later (now ωt = 30°). Fig. 2.9 *(b)* shows the phasor diagram of 3-phase currents. Here $I_a = \frac{\sqrt{3}}{2} I_m$, $I_b = -\frac{\sqrt{3}}{2} I_m$ and $I_c = 0$. Fig. 2.9 *(b)* shows cross in *a′* and dot in *a* for I_a. For I_b, cross in *b* and dot in *b′* are shown. Current $I_c = 0$, there nothing is shown in coil *cc′*. The mmfs are $F_a = \frac{\sqrt{3}}{2} F_m$, $F_b = -\frac{\sqrt{3}}{2} F_m$ and $F_c = 0$. Mmf F_b and F_c are displaced from each other by 60° as shown in Fig. 2.9 *(b)*. The resultant mmf F_R is given by

$$F_R = \bar{F}_a + \bar{F}_b + \bar{F}_c = \frac{\sqrt{3}}{2} F_m \cos 30 + \frac{\sqrt{3}}{2} F_m \cos 30 + 0 = \frac{3}{2} F_m.$$

Now in Fig. 2.9 (*b*), F_R is seen to have rotated through a space angle of 30° (equal to time angle of 30°) in the anticlockwise direction. But in Fig. 2.8 *(b)*, resultant mmf F_R is shown to rotate clockwise by a space angle of 30°.

This shows that direction of rotation of rotating magnetic flux in a 3-phase machine can be reversed by interchanging any two supply terminals connected to 3-phase ac motor terminals.

Example 2.3. *If single-phase distributed winding is excited by an alternating current, a pulsating mmf wave is produced. Derive an expression for this pulsating mmf wave.*

Solution. When one phase of a 3-phase distributed winding is excited, the fundamental component of mmf wave, sinusoidally distributed along the air-gap periphery, given by Eq. (1.7), is

$$F_{a1} = \frac{4}{\pi} \cdot k_w \cdot \frac{N_{ph}}{P} i_a \cdot \cos \alpha \qquad ...(i)$$

If single-phase winding is energised by sinusoidally varying alternating current $i_a = I_m \cos \omega t$, then mmf distribution, given by Eq. *(i)* is

$$F_{a1} = \frac{4}{\pi} k_w \frac{N_{ph}}{P} I_m \cos \omega t \cos \alpha = F_m \cos \omega t \cdot \cos \alpha \qquad ...(2.3)$$

where
$$F_m = \frac{4}{\pi} \cdot k_w \cdot \frac{N_{ph} \cdot I_m}{P} \qquad ...(2.4)$$

In Eq. (2.4), mmf F_m is the same as given by Eq. (1.8). Here F_m is the mmf per pole corresponding to maximum current I_m.

In Eq. (2.3), cos α indicates that mmf is sinusoidally distributed along the air-gap periphery and the term cos ω*t* implies that mmf amplitude varies sinusoidally with time at frequency ω as shown in Fig. 2.2 *(b)*. This shows that Eq. (2.3) gives an expression for the pulsating mmf wave.

Example 2.4. *Derive an expression for the resultant rotating mmf wave produced in (a) a two-phase balanced machine and (b) a 3-phase balanced machine.*

Solution. *(a)* It is seen from Fig. 2.6 that amplitude of resultant rotating mmf wave is $F_R = F_m$. But F_m is given by Eq. (2.4). Therefore, in a two phase machine, with balanced windings and balanced currents, expression for the resultant rotating mmf wave is given by

$$F_R = \frac{4}{\pi} k_w \frac{N_{ph}}{P} I_m \qquad ...(2.4)$$

(*b*) It is observed from Fig. 2.8 that resultant amplitude of rotating mmf wave is

$$F_R = \frac{3}{2} F_m$$

Substituting the value of F_m from Eq. (2.4), we get an expression for the resultant mmf F_R as

$$F_R = \frac{3}{2} \times \frac{4}{\pi} kw \frac{N_{ph} \sqrt{2} I}{P} = 2.7\, kw \frac{N_{ph} I}{P} \text{ ATs/pole} \qquad ...(2.5)$$

PROBLEMS

2.1. What is constant magnetic field? How can it be produced? Give the properties of constant magnetic field.
What do you understand by the statement, "magnetic field is time invariant."

2.2. Two series connected coils are wound, one on each pole. If an alternating current is applied to these coils, discuss the type of magnetic field produced at different instants of time. Hence, define the pulsating magnetic field.
What do you understand by the statement, "stator field is stationary in space."

2.3. *(a)* Two windings spatially displaced by 90° are energised from 2-phase ac balanced currents. Discuss about orientation of the fields produced on at least four instants of sinusoidal supply currents. Hence, discuss about the nature of the magnetic field produced.
(b) Derive an expression for the speed of rotating magnetic field produced in part *(a)*.

2.4. Describe, with suitable diagrams, how revolving magnetic field is produced when three windings spatially shifted by 120 degrees are carrying three-phase balanced currents.
Derive an expression for the speed of this revolving magnetic field. What is this speed called?

2.5. Two concentric coils on stator are connected in series. Discuss about the type of field produced and its properties in case these two coils are excited from *(a)* dc source and *(b)* ac source.

2.6. Explain how pulsating magnetic field can be produced. Derive an expression for this field.

Objective Type Questions

1. If F_m is the maximum mmf due to any one phase, then the resultant mmf in 2-phase and 3-phase ac machines would respectively be given by

(a) F_m and 1.5 F_m ; both rotating, *(b)* F_m and 1.5 F_m; both standstill,
(c) F_m, standstill and 1.5 F_m rotating *(d)* 1.5 F_m and 2 F_m; both rotating.

2. A single coil is wound over an electromagnetic bar. If this coil is excited with

1. dc, pulsating magnetic field is produced, 2. dc, constant magnetic field is produced,
3. ac, pulsating magnetic field is produced, 4. ac, constant magnetic field is produced.

From above, the correct statements are

(a) 1, 3 *(b)* 2, 4 *(c)* 2, 3 *(d)* 1, 4

3. Consider the following statements about pulsating magnetic field.

1. stator magnetic axis remains unchanged, 2. stator mmf is stationary in space,
3. stator field strength remains constant, 4. polarity of stator field is alternating.

From above, the correct statements are

(a) 1, 2, 3 *(b)* 1, 2, 3, 4 *(c)* 2, 3, 4 *(d)* 1, 2, 4

4. Two distributed windings are spatially displaced by 90°. When two phase balanced currents $i_\alpha = I_m \sin \omega t$, $i_\beta = I_m \sin (\omega t - 90°)$ are applied to these windings, clockwise rotating field *(RF)* is produced. Read the following statements. If

1. $i_\alpha = I_m \sin \omega t$, $i_\beta = I_m \cos \omega t$, *RF* rotates clockwise,
2. $i_\alpha = I_m \cos \omega t$, $i_\beta = I_m \sin \omega t$, *RF* rotates clockwise,
3. $i_\alpha = I_m \cos \omega t$, $i_\beta = I_m \cos (\omega t - 90°)$, *RF* rotates clockwise,
4. $i_\alpha = I_m \sin \omega t$, $i_\beta = I_m \cos \omega t$, *RF* rotates anticlockwise.

From above, the correct statements are

(a) 1, 2, 3 *(b)* 2, 3, 4 *(c)* 3, 4 *(d)* 2, 4

5. When three-phase ac supply, with phase sequence *a, b, c* is applied to 3-phase induction motor, clockwise rotating field *(RF)* is produced. If the supply phase sequence is changed to
   1. *b, c, a* ; *RF* would rotate clockwise,
   2. *b, a, c* ; *RF* would rotate clockwise,
   3. *c, b, a* ; *RF* would rotate anticlockwise,
   4. *a, c, b* ; *RF* would rotate anticlockwise.

   From above, the correct statement is

   (a) 1, 3, 4 *(b)* 2, 3, 4 *(c)* 1, 2, 3 *(d)* 1, 2, 4

Answers

1. *(a)*	**2.** *(c)*	**3.** *(d)*	**4.** *(b)*	**5.** *(a)*

Chapter 3

Induction Machines

Induction machines consist of both motors and generators. Primarily, induction machines of three-phase type are more common.

Three-phase induction motors are the most popular type in industry. It is because these motors are simply, rugged, cheap and reliable. At the same time, maintenance of these motors is easy. In this chapter, operation of three-phase induction machines as induction motors and also as induction generators is described.

3.1. CONSTRUCTION

A three-phase induction motor consists of two main parts : a stator and a rotor. The stator is stationary part and rotor is revolving part. Rotor is separated from stator by a small air gap.

3.1.1. Stator

The stator consists of stator frame, stator core, three-phase winding, two end-covers and bearings. The stator core made from steel laminations fits in the stator frame made from cast-iron or steel. The laminations are slotted along the inner periphery to house the insulated stator conductors. These stator conductors are suitably connected to form three-phase winding. The phasor winding is either star-connected or delta-connected. The two end-covers made from cast-iron and stator frame provide mechanical support to stator core.

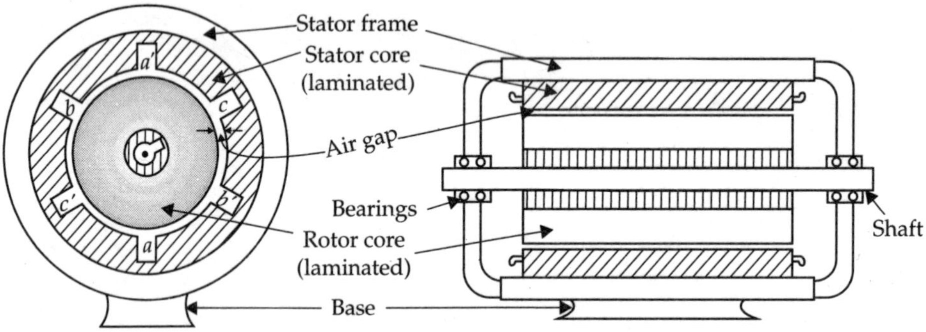

Fig 3.1: Constructional features of polyphase induction motors.

The essential features of a 3-phase induction motor are shown in Fig. 3.1. Stator core is shown to have six slots for simplicity. Actually, the number of stator slots is far more than six.

3.1.2. Rotor

The rotor is made from thin circular laminations of the same material as used in stator core.

Rotor core is mounted directly on the shaft or on the cast-iron spider carried by the shaft. Rotor laminations are slotted on their other periphery to house the rotor conductors.

Three-phase induction motors have two types of rotors:

(*a*) Squirrel-cage rotor or cage rotor. Motors using this type of rotor are called squirrel-cage induction motors or cage induction motors.

(*b*) Wound-rotor or phase-wound rotor. Motors using this type of rotor are usually called wound-rotor induction motors *(WRIMs)* or slip-ring induction motors *(SRIMs)*.

3.1.2.1. *Squirrel-cage rotor*

It consists of circular laminated core with slots on the outer periphery of rotor. These rotor slots are skewed (*i.e.* not parallel to the shaft axis) for obtaining a quiet and smooth operation of three-phase induction motor.

Each rotor slot contains an un-insulated bar conductor of copper or aluminum. At each end of the rotor, rotor bars are short-circuited by two thick end rings of the same material. The bar conductors and the two end rings form a cage of the type which had been in common use for keeping the squirrels; hence the name squirrel-cage rotor. A cage rotor is shown in Fig. 3.2.

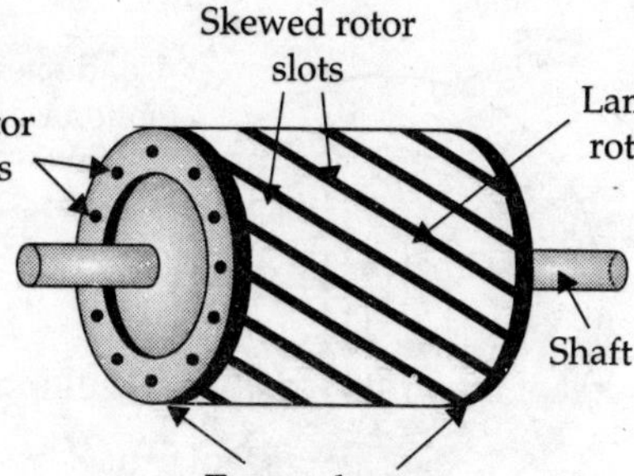

Fig 3.2: Constructional details of a squirrel-cage rotor.

3.1.2.2. *Wound rotor or slip-ring rotor*

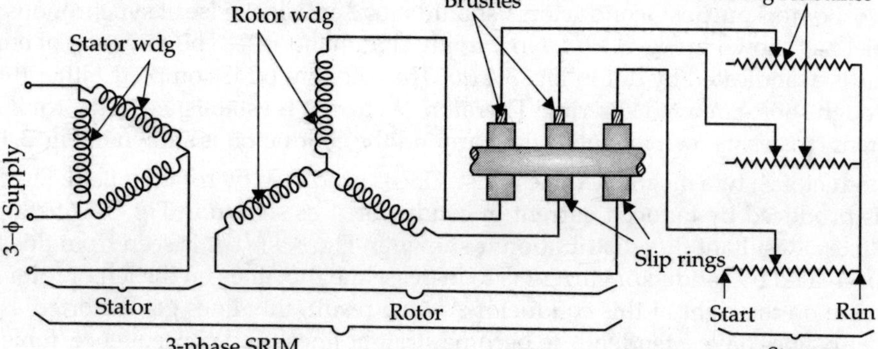

Fig 3.3: Three-phase slip-ring induction motor (SRIM) with starter.

The wound-rotor consists of laminated rotor core with slots on its outside periphery. Insulated conductors are placed in the rotor slots. These conductors are suitably connected to form a three-phase distributed winding similar to that used on the stator. The rotor winding is connected in star. Other three ends of the star-connected winding are connected to three slip rings mounted on but insulated from the shaft. Carbon brushes resting on the slip rings allow external star-connected resistors to be inserted in series with the rotor winding. External resistors allow the control of resistance in each rotor phase and serve the following two purposes:

(*a*) for speed control of the motor and

(*b*) for increasing the motor starting torque and reduce the starting current taken from the supply.

A three-phase slip-ring induction motor, along with its starter, is shown in Fig. 3.3.

3.2. PRINCIPLE OF OPERATION

When three-phase supply is given to three-phase winding on the stator of a 3-phase induction motor, a rotating magnetic field is produced as explained in Art. 2.4. In Fig. 3.4 *(a)*, two poles *N*, *S* produced by rotating flux are shown. These poles are assumed to rotate clockwise at synchronous speed. Rotor is at standstill. Therefore, rotor conductors are being cut by rotating flux and emfs and emfs are induced in rotor conductors as per Faraday's law. This emf is maximum in rotor conductors *A* and *B*, because these are under the influence of maximum flux density.

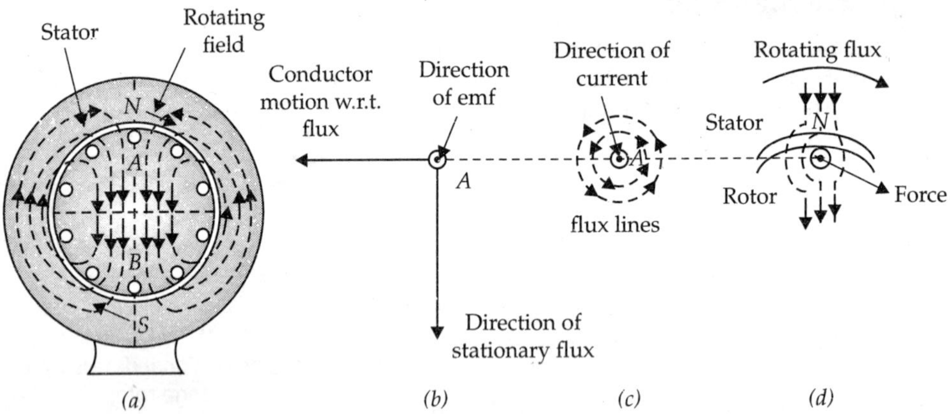

Fig 3.4: Production of force on conductor in a three-phase induction motor.

Here, we consider only one conductor *A* on the rotor for the sake of simplicity. In order to determine the direction of induced emf in this conductor, field must be stationary and conductor *A* should move. For this purpose, conductor *A* should move anticlockwise at synchronous speed in a stationary field as shown in Fig. 3.4 *(b)*. Now apply right hand rule. The direction of emf is found to be outwards as indicated by dot in Fig. 3.4 *(b)*. The rotor circuit is complete either through end rings or through short-circuited slip ring. Therefore, a current is established in the rotor conductor *A*. This current creates its own magnetic field around the conductor as shown in Fig. 3.4 *(c)*.

Near conductor *A*, two magnetic fluxes exist. One is produced by rotating field, Fig. 3.4 *(a)*. The other flux is produced by induced current in conductor *A* as shown in Fig. 3.4 *(c)*. Superimpose these two fluxes. Resultant flux distribution is shown in Fig. 3.4 *(d)*. It is seen from this figure that effect of flux created by conductor current is to increase the flux lines on the left of rotor conductor *A* and decrease on the right of this conductor *A*. As a result, flux lines get distorted as shown in Fig. 3.4 *(d)*. Flux lines have a tendency to become straight lines. As a consequence, force is exerted on the rotor conductor *A* tending to move it in the direction of rotating flux. Similarly, forces are developed on other rotor conductors. Sum of forces on all the rotor conductors produce a torque in the direction of rotating flux.

It may be concluded from above that when 3-phase supply is given to three-phase stator winding, rotor begins to rotate in the direction of revolving magnetic flux. It shows that a three-phase induction motor is a self starting motor.

3.3. ROTOR SPEED AND SLIP

At standstill, speed of rotating field with respect to stationary rotor is synchronous speed N_s. As the motor accelerates, relative speed between rotating flux and rotor decreases. For rotor speed N_r in the direction of rotating field, the relative speed between rotating field and rotor decreases to $(N_s - N_r)$. This difference between synchronous speed and actual rotor speed is called **slip speed**.

If N_s and N_r are in rpm, then

$$\text{slip speed} = (N_s - N_r) \text{ rpm} \quad ...(3.1)$$

It is usual to express slip speed as a fraction of synchronous speed. This ratio is called **per-unit slip** or **slip** and is denoted by s.

$$\therefore \quad s = \frac{N_s - N_r}{N_s} \text{ per unit} \quad ...(3.2\,a)$$

$$\text{Percentage slip} = \text{per-unit slip} \times 100 = \frac{N_s - N_r}{N_s} \times 100 \quad ...(3.2\,b)$$

The rotor of a 3-phase induction motor cannot rum at synchronous speed. Let us assume that rotor is running at synchronous speed. Under this condition, relative speed between rotating flux and rotor would be zero. As a result, there would be no flux cutting action by rotor ; thus no rotor emf, no rotor current and therefore no rotor torque is produced to drive the load. The rotor, in a 3-phase induction motor, therefore, always rotates at a speed less than synchronous speed. A 3-phase induction motor is also called asynchronous motor since it cannot run at synchronous speed.

From Eq. (3.2 *a*), slip speed, $s\,N_s = N_s - N_r$

$\therefore$ Rotor speed, $\quad N_r = N_s - s\,N_s = N_s\,(1 - s)$ rpm $\quad$ ...(3.3 *a*)

or $\quad n_r = n_s\,(1 - s)$ rpm $\quad$ ...(3.3 *b*)

where $\quad n_s$ = synchronous speed in rps

$\quad n_r$ = rotor speed in rps.

Also, rotor speed, $\quad \omega_r = \omega_s\,(1 - s)$ rad/sec. $\quad$ ...(3.4)

where ω_s = synchronous speed in rad/sec = $2\,\pi\,n_s = \dfrac{4\pi f_1}{P}$ rad/sec.

and ω_r = rotor speed in rad/sec = $2\,\pi\,n_r$

The vaue of full-load slip varies from about 6% for small motors to about 2% for large motors.

3.4. FREQUENCY OF ROTOR EMF AND CURRENT

Frequency of the emf generated in rotor circuit is given by rotor frequency,

$$f_2 = \frac{\text{poles}[\text{relative speed between rotating flux and rotor} = (N_s - N_r)\text{rpm}]}{120}$$

Note that number of poles on rotor and stator are equal.

$$\therefore \quad f_2 = \frac{P(N_s - N_r)}{120} \quad ...(3.5)$$

At standstill, $\quad N_r = 0, \ \therefore f_2 = \dfrac{P \cdot N_s}{120} = f_1$ (stator frequency in Hz)

From Eq. (3.2 *a*), slip speed $s\,N_s = (N_s - N_r)$. Substituting this value in Eq. (3.5), we get

$$f_2 = \frac{P \cdot s \cdot N_s}{120} = s\,\frac{P \cdot N_s}{120} = s\,f_1 \quad ...(3.6)$$

$\therefore$ Frequency of rotor emf (or current) f_2 = slip × stator frequency f_1.

At standstill, $N_r = 0$; from Eq. (3.2 *a*), $s = 1$ and $f_2 = f_1$. At synchronous speed, $s = 0$ and $f_2 = 0$.

Example 3.1. *A prime-mover, coupled to a 3-phase, 6-pole alternator, drives it at 1000 rpm. When this alternator delivers power to a three-phase induction motor, it runs at a full load speed of 1450 rpm. Calculate the slip and number of poles on the induction motor.*

Solution. Frequency of alternator emf $f = \dfrac{P \cdot N_s}{120} = \dfrac{6 \times 1000}{120} = 50$ Hz.

Alternator delivers power to 3-phase induction motor. Therefore, $f_1 = 50$ Hz. Note that a 3-phase induction motor runs at a speed slightly less than synchronous speed. For $f_1 = 50$ Hz, the possible synchronous speeds $\left(= \frac{120 f_1}{P}\right)$ are 3000, 1500, 1000, 750 rpm etc. Therefore, possible synchronous speed, a little above 1450 rpm, is 1500 rpm = N_s.

$\therefore$ Number of poles on the induction motor, $P = \frac{120 f_1}{N_s} = \frac{120 \times 50}{150} = \mathbf{4}$

Example 3.2. *A 6-pole, 50 Hz, 3-phase induction motor has no-load slip of 1% and full-load slip of 4%. Calculate (a) no-load and full-load speeds (b) frequency of rotor emf at standstill, at no load and at full load.*

Solution. Synchronous speed, $N_s = \frac{120 \cdot f_1}{P} = \frac{120 \times 50}{6} = 1000$ rpm

(a) No-load speed, $N_{ro} = N_s\,[1 - \text{no-load slip}] = 1000\,[1 - 0.01] = 990$ rpm

Full-load speed, $N_r = N_s\,[1 - \text{full load slip}] = 1000\,[1 - 0.04] = 960$ rpm

(b) Frequency of rotor emf at standstill, $f_2 = s\,f_1 = 1 \times 50 = 50$ Hz

Frequency of rotor emf at no-load, $f_2 = s_o \cdot f_1 = 0.01 \times 50 = 0.5$ Hz

Frequency of rotor emf at full load, $f_2 = s_{fl} \cdot f_1 = 0.04 \times 50 = 2$ Hz

3.5. ROTOR EMF AND CURRENT

(a) **Standstill conditions :** At standstill, emfs induced in each phase of stator and rotor windings are given by

$$\left.\begin{aligned} E_1 &= \sqrt{2}\ \pi f_1 \cdot \phi \cdot k_{w1} \cdot N_1 \\ E_2 &= \sqrt{2}\ \pi f_1 \cdot \phi \cdot k_{w2} \cdot N_2 \end{aligned}\right\} \quad ...(3.7)$$

where E_1, E_2 = per-phase induced emfs at standstill in stator and rotor windings respectively,

f_1 = supply frequency, Hz

ϕ = flux per pole, Wb

N_1, N_2 = per-phase series turns in stator and rotor windings respectively, and k_{w1}, k_{w2} = winding factors for stator and rotor windings respectively.

Emf expressions in Eq. (3.7) are similar to a transformer, except the introduction of winding factors. It is because stator and rotor windings in a 3-phase induction motor are distributed.

Rotor resistance per phase = r_2

Rotor leakage reactance at standstill = $2\pi f_1 \cdot l_2 = x_2$

Rotor leakage impedance at standstill = $\sqrt{r_2^2 + x_2^2}$

Rotor current per phase at standstill = $\frac{E_2}{\sqrt{r_2^2 + x_2^2}} = \frac{E_2}{z_2}$

Rotor power factor at standstill = $\frac{r_2}{\sqrt{r_2^2 + x_2^2}} = \frac{r_2}{z_2}$

(b) **Running at slip s :** When the rotor revolves at any slip s, emf induced in rotor = $\sqrt{2} \cdot \pi$ (rotor frequency, f_2) $\cdot k_{w2} \cdot \phi \cdot N_2 = \sqrt{2} \cdot \pi\,(s f_1) \cdot k_{w2} \cdot \phi \cdot N_2$

$$= s \cdot [\sqrt{2} \cdot \pi f_1\,k_{w2} \cdot \phi \cdot N_2] = s\,E_2$$

$\therefore$ At any slip s, rotor emf per phase = $s \cdot E_2$

Rotor leakage reactance per phase at any slip s = $2\pi f_2\,l_2$

$$= 2\pi\,(s f_1)\,l_2 = s\,[2\pi f_1 \cdot l_2] = s \cdot x_2$$

Rotor leakage impedance per phase at any slip $s = \sqrt{r_2^2 + (sx_2)^2}$

$\therefore$ Rotor current per phase at any slip s, $I_2 = \dfrac{sE_2}{\sqrt{r_2^2 + (sx_2)^2}}$ ...(3.8 *a*)

$$= \frac{E_2}{\sqrt{\left(\frac{r_2}{s}\right)^2 + x_2^2}} \quad \text{...(3.8 } b\text{)}$$

Rotor power factor at any slip $s = \dfrac{r_2}{z_2 \text{ at } s} = \dfrac{r_2}{\sqrt{r_2^2 + (sx_2)^2}}$ ...(3.9)

Example 3.3. *A 3-phase, 6-pole, 50 Hz, three-phase induction motor has rotor resistance of 0.4 Ω per phase and standstill rotor leakage reactance of 1.2 Ω per phase. Determine rotor power factor (a) at standstill and (b) at motor speed of 960 rpm.*

Solution. Synchronous speed $N_s = \dfrac{120 \cdot f_1}{P} = \dfrac{120 \times 50}{6} = 1000$ rpm

(a) Leakage impedance per phase at standstill, $z_2 = \sqrt{r_2^2 + x_2^2} = \sqrt{0.4^2 + 1.2^2}$

$\therefore$ Rotor pf at standstill $= \dfrac{r_2}{z_2 \text{ at stand still}} = \dfrac{r_2}{\sqrt{r_2^2 + x_2^2}} = \dfrac{0.4}{\sqrt{0.4^2 + 1.2^2}} = 0.3162$ lag

(b) Slip, $s = \dfrac{1000 - 960}{1000} = 0.04.$

Rotor leakage impedance per phase at slip $s = \sqrt{r_2^2 + (sx_2)^2} = \sqrt{0.4^2 + (0.04 \times 1.2)^2}$ Ω

$\therefore$ Rotor power factor at slip $s = \dfrac{r_2}{\sqrt{r_2^2 + (sx_2)^2}} = \dfrac{0.4}{\sqrt{0.4^2 + (0.04 \times 1.2)^2}} = 0.9928$ lag.

This example shows that power factor of a 3-phase induction motor at starting (*i.e.* at standstill) is very low but it improves under normal running conditions.

Example 3.4. *A 3-phase, 4-pole, delta-connected 3-phase induction motor is supplied with three-phase rated voltage. With the rotor at rest, a voltage of 80 V is recorded at any two slip rings of star-connected rotor. Rotor leakage impedance is (0.6 + j 4.8) Ω per phase. Calculate rotor current and rotor power factor with the motor (a) at standstill and with star-connected impedance of (4 + j 4) Ω inserted in the rotor circuit and (b) running normally with a slip of 4%.*

Solution. Induced rotor emf per phase at standstill, $E_2 = \dfrac{80}{\sqrt{3}} = 46.19$ V

(a) Total rotor circuit impedance per phase at standstill = rotor circuit impedance per phase at standstill + starting impedance per phase,

$$Z = (0.6 + j\,4.8) + (4 + j\,4) = 4.6 + j\,8.8 = 9.9298\ \angle 62.4^\circ\ \Omega$$

$\therefore$ Per phase rotor current at standstill,

$$I_2 = \frac{E_2}{Z} = \frac{46.19}{9.9298\ \angle 62.4^\circ} = 4.652\ \angle -62.4^\circ \text{ A}$$

Rotor power factor at starting = cos 62.4° = 0.4633 lag.

(*b*) Slip $s = 0.04$. Under normal running conditions, starting impedance is completely cut out.

$$\therefore \quad \text{Rotor current for slip } (= 0.04) = \frac{sE_2}{r_2 + jsx_2} = \frac{0.04 \times 46.19}{0.6 + j\,0.04 \times 4.8}$$

$$= \frac{1.848}{0.6 + j\,0.192} = \frac{1.848}{0.63\angle 17.745^\circ} = 2.933\angle -17.745^\circ \text{ A}$$

Rotor power factor under normal running = cos 17.745° = 0.9524 lag.

3.6. ROTOR INPUT AND DEVELOPED TORQUE

From Eq. (3.8 *b*), rotor current is given by

$$I_2 = \frac{E_2}{\sqrt{\left(\frac{r_2}{s}\right)^2 + x_2^2}} \quad \text{...(3.8 } b)$$

The above equation can be represented by a simple series circuit shown in Fig. 3.5. This circuit represents per-phase rotor equivalent circuit of a 3-phase induction motor. From Fig. 3.5, per-phase power input to rotor is given by

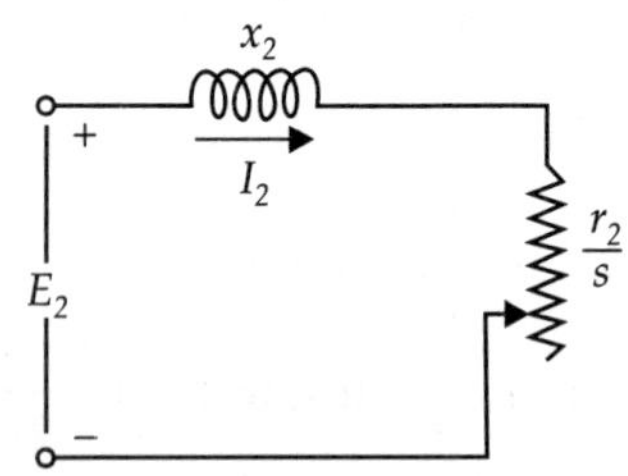

Fig 3.5: Per phase equivalent circuit for rotor of a 3-phase induction motor.

$$P_g = E_2 I_2 \cos\theta_2$$

But $$\cos\theta_2 = \frac{r_2/s}{\sqrt{\left(\frac{r_2}{s}\right)^2 + x_2^2}}$$

Substituting this value of $\cos\theta_2$, we get

$$P_g = \left[\frac{E_2}{\sqrt{\left(\frac{r_2}{s}\right)^2 + x_2^2}}\right] \cdot I_2 \cdot \frac{r_2}{s} = I_2^2 \frac{r_2}{s} \quad \text{...(3.10)}$$

Here P_g is the power transferred from stator to rotor across the air gap. Therefore, P_g is called **air-gap power**. Also

P_g = air-gap power = stator power output = rotor power input = $I_2^2 \frac{r_2}{s}$

Expression for power P_g can also be written as under :

$$P_g = I_2^2 \frac{r_2}{s} = I_2^2 r_2 \left[\frac{1}{s}\right] = I_2^2 r_2 \left[\frac{s + (1-s)}{s}\right]$$

$$= I_2^2 r_2 \left[1 + \frac{1-s}{s}\right]$$

$$= I_2^2 r_2 + I_2^2 r_2 \left(\frac{1-s}{s}\right)$$

= (Rotor ohmic loss)

+ (total mechanical power developed in rotor, P_m)

or $$P_g = sP_g + (1-s) P_g \quad \text{...(3.11)}$$

Total or internal mechanical power developed in rotor P_m is given by

$$P_m = (1-s) P_g$$

= power input to rotor, P_g – rotor I^2R loss, sP_g.

Also, rotor ohmic loss $= s\,P_g = \left[\frac{s}{1-s}\right] P_m = I_2^2 r_2 = s$ (power input to rotor) ...(3.12)

Rotor ohmic loss is equal to slip times the air gap power. The term $s P_g$ is therefore called **slip power**, because it is proportional to slip. From above,

$$\left.\begin{aligned} P_g : \text{rotor ohmic loss} : P_m &= P_g : s P_g : (1-s) P_g \\ &= 1 : s : (1-s) \end{aligned}\right\} \quad \text{...(3.13)}$$

The internal or total torque developed is due to the electromechanical process in the motor. It is also called electromagnetic torque T_e. The shaft torque is equal to T_e minus the torque lost due to friction and windage.

The internal torque developed is given by

$$T_e = \frac{\text{mechanical power developed in rotor, } P_m}{\text{rotor speed in mechanical rad per sec, } \omega_r}$$

$$= \frac{P_m}{\omega_r} = \frac{(1-s)P_g}{(1-s)\omega_s} = \frac{P_g}{\omega_s} \quad \text{...(3.14)}$$

Here $\omega_s = 2\,\pi\, n_s = \frac{4\pi f_1}{P}$ = synchronous speed in mechanical rad/sec.

Also, electromagnetic torque is

$$T_e = \frac{P_g}{\omega_s} = \frac{1}{\omega_s} \cdot I_2^2\, \frac{r_2}{s}$$

$$= \frac{\text{Rotor ohmic loss}}{\omega_s\,(\text{slip})} = \frac{1}{2\pi n_s} \times I_2^2\, \frac{r_2}{s} \quad \text{...(3.15)}$$

Shaft power P_{sh} can be obtained from air-gap power P_g as under.

$$P_{sh} = P_m - \text{friction and windage } (F \text{ and } W) \text{ losses}$$

$$= P_g - \text{rotor ohmic loss} - F \text{ and } W \text{ losses}$$

$$= \text{power output}$$

Output or shaft torque, $$T_{sh} = \frac{P_{sh}}{\omega_r} = \frac{P_{sh}}{\omega_s(1-s)} \quad \text{...(3.16)}$$

If stator input is known, then air-gap power is given by

P_g = stator power input – stator ohmic loss – stator core loss

Example 3.5. *The power input to a 3-phase, 50 Hz, 6-pole induction motor is 50 kW. Total stator losses are 1 kW. The rotor emf makes 90 complete alterations in one minute. Calculate (a) slip (b) motor speed (c) mechanical power developed (d) rotor ohmic loss and (e) developed torque.*

Solution. *(a)* One complete alteration means one cycle of rotor frequency.

∴ Rotor frequency, $$f_2 = \frac{90}{60} = 1.5 \text{ Hz}$$

Slip, $$s = \frac{f_2}{f_1} = \frac{1.5}{50} = 0.03 \text{ or } 3\%$$

(b) Motor speed, $$N_r = N_s(1-s) = \frac{120 \times 50}{6}\,[1 - 0.03] = 970 \text{ rpm}$$

(c) Stator input = 50 kW, Total stator losses = 1 kW

∴ Stator output = rotor input = air-gap power = 50 – 1 = 49 kW

Mechanical power developed, $P_m = (1-s)\,P_g = (1 - 0.03) \times 49 = 47.53$ kW

(d) Developed torque, $$T_e = \frac{P_g}{\omega_s} = \frac{P_g}{2\pi n_s} = \frac{47530 \times 60}{2\pi \times 1000} = 453.88 \text{ Nm}$$

Example 3.6. *A 400 V, 50 Hz, 20 kW, 6-pole, 3-phase induction motor develops rated power at power factor 0.88 and at a speed of 950 rpm. Mechanical losses are 1 kW. Calculate (a) slip (b) rotor I^2R loss (c) total power input if stator losses are 1.5 kW and (d) line current.*

Solution. $$N_s = \frac{120\, f_1}{P} = \frac{120 \times 50}{6} = 1000 \text{ rpm}$$

(*a*) Slip, $$s = \frac{N_s - N_r}{N_s} = \frac{1000 - 950}{1000} = 0.05 \text{ pu}$$

(*b*) Shaft power, $P_{sh} = 20$ kW

∴ Mechanical power developed, $P_m = P_{sh}$ + Mechanical, or friction and windage, losses
$= 20 + 1 = 21$ kW

From Eq. (3.12), rotor ohmic losses $$= \frac{s}{1-s} \times P_m = \frac{0.05}{1-0.05} \times 21000 = 1105.3 \text{ W}$$

Also, from Eq. (3.12), air-gap power, $$P_g = \frac{\text{rotor ohmic losses}}{\text{slip}}$$
$$= \frac{1105.3}{0.05} = 22106 \text{ W}$$

Total power input = air-gap power + stator losses
= 22106 + 1500 = 23606 W

(*d*) Line current $$= \frac{23606}{\sqrt{3} \times 400 \times 0.88} = 38.72 \text{ A}$$

3.7. LOSSES AND EFFICIENCY

Power input to a 3-phase induction motor is given by $3\, V_1\, I_1 \cos \cos \theta_1$, where V_1, I_1 are the per-phase stator voltage and current respectively and $\cos \theta_1$ is the stator power factor.

Stator losses :

(*i*) I^2R loss in stator winding $= 3\, I_1^2\, r_1$ = stator ohmic loss

(*ii*) Stator core losses = sum of hysteresis and eddy current losses in stator core.

Stator power output is transferred from stator to rotor through an air-gap of a 3-phase induction motor. Therefore, stator power output is also called air-gap power P_g of the motor.

∴ Stator power output = rotor power input = air-gap power, P_g

Rotor losses :

(*i*) Rotor ohmic loss $= 3\, I_2^2\, r_2$

(*ii*) Rotor core losses are usually neglected. Under normal running conditions, rotor frequency is very low. Rotor core losses, almost proportional to rotor frequency squared, are therefore neglected.

(*iii*) Friction and windage (*F* and *W*) loss.

(*iv*) Stray load loss : These are taken into consideration by taking motor efficiency 0.5% less than that calculated at rated load.

Internal mechanical power developed : The power $(P_g - 3\, I_2^2\, r_2)$ is converted from electrical to mechanical. This power is, therefore, called **internal mechanical power developed,** P_m.

∴ P_m = rotor power input, P_g – rotor ohmic losses $3\, I_2^2\, r_2$

Output power or shaft power, $P_{sh} = P_m$ – *F* and *W* losses – stray load losses

This P_{sh} is also called useful power or motor output power.

Fixed losses or **no-load rotational losses** occur only when the motor is running. It is given by

No-load rotational losses = stator core loss + F and W losses

No-load rotational losses or fixed losses are usually treated constant. These losses can be determined from no-load test on a 3-phase induction motor.

$\therefore$ No-load rotational losses = power input to stator at no load – stator I^2R loss at no load

Sum of no-load rotational losses and stray load losses is called **rotational loss**.

In case stray load losses are ignored, then there is no difference between rotational losses and no-load rotation losses.

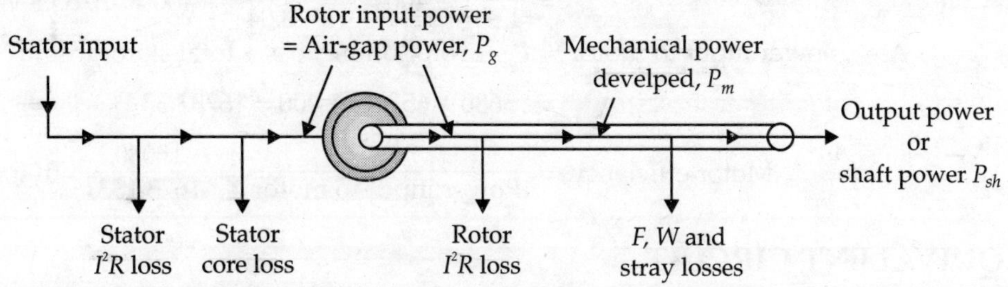

Fig 3.6: Power flow diagram for a 3-phase induction motor.

Power flow diagram for a 3-phase induction motor gives the distribution of power as the power input to stator flows to the shaft. Fig. 3.6 gives the power flow diagram for a 3-phase induction motor.

Efficiency of a 3-phase induction motor is given by

$$\eta = \frac{P_{sh}}{P_{sh} + P_f + P_{oh}} \quad \text{...(3.17)}$$

where P_{sh} = shaft power or motor rating in W or kW

P_f = fixed or no-load rotational losses

= F and W losses + stator core loss

P_{oh} = stator and rotor ohmic losses.

Example 3.7. *A 400 V, 4-pole, 50 Hz, 3-phase induction motor develops shaft torque of 100 Nm at a rotor frequency of 2 Hz. Calculate (a) shaft power and mechanical power developed if friction and windage losses are 600 W (b) rotor ohmic loss (c) power input to rotor and (d) motor efficiency in case total stator loss is 400 W. Neglect stray losses.*

Solution. Shaft torque, $T_{sh} = 100 \text{ Nm}, N_s = \frac{120 \times 50}{4} = 1500 \text{ rpm}$

Slip, $s = \frac{f_2}{f_1} = \frac{2}{50} = 0.04$

Rotor speed $N_r = N_s(1-s) = 1500(1-0.04) = 1440 \text{ rpm}$

Also, rotor speed, $\omega_r = \omega_s(1-s) = \frac{4\pi f_1}{P}(1-s)$

$$= \frac{4\pi \times 50}{4}(1-0.04) = 150.8 \text{ rad/sec.}$$

(a) Shaft power, $P_{sh} = T_{sh} \times \omega_r = 100 \times 150.8 = 15080$ W

Mechanical power developed, $P_m = P_{sh} + F$ and W losses

$= 15080 + 600 = 15680$ W

(b) From Eq. (3.12), rotor ohmic loss $= \left[\frac{s}{1-s}\right] P_m$

$= \left[\frac{0.04}{1-0.04}\right] \times 15680 = 653.33$ W

(c) Power input to motor $= P_g +$ total stator loss

$= \frac{P_m}{1-s} + 400 = \frac{15680}{(1-0.04)} + 400 = 16733.3$ W

Also, power input to motor $= P_m +$ rotor ohmic loss + total stator loss

$= 15680 + 653.33 + 400 = 16733.33$ W

(d) Motor efficiency $= \frac{P_{sh}}{\text{Power input to motor}} = \frac{15080}{16733.33} \times 100 = 90.12\%$

3.8. EQUIVALENT CIRCUIT

Stator of a 3-phase induction motor is directly connected to three-phase ac source. Its rotor winding receives energy from stator by means of induction, *i.e.* transformer action. Thus, three-phase induction motor equivalent circuit must be similar to transformer equivalent circuit.

For obtaining three-phase induction motor equivalent circuit, first develop circuit model for stator and then for rotor. Further, combine these two circuit models to obtain the required equivalent circuit of a three-phase induction motor.

The equivalent circuit helps in obtaining the performance characteristics of three-phase induction motors.

3.8.1. Stator Circuit Model

When a voltage V_1 is applied to stator terminals of a 3-phase induction motor, a rotating magnetic field is produced. This flux generates emf E_1 in stator winding. The stator terminal voltage has to overcome emf E_1 and stator leakage impedance drop $\overline{I}_1\ (r_1 + j\,x_1)$. Therefore, just like a transformer, the stator voltage is given by

$$\overline{V}_1 = \overline{E}_1 + \overline{I}_1\ (r_1 + j\,x_1)$$

As in a transformer, stator current I_1 has two components. One component I_1' is the load component and other is the no-load component I_o. Current I_o has further two components, I_c and I_m. The component I_c takes into account core loss. The other component I_m represents the magnetizing component for setting up the flux ϕ. In stator circuit model, core loss is represented by core loss resistance R_c and flux ϕ is represented by magnetizing reactance X_m, in parallel with R_c. Fig. 3.7 gives the stator circuit model of a 3-phase induction motor.

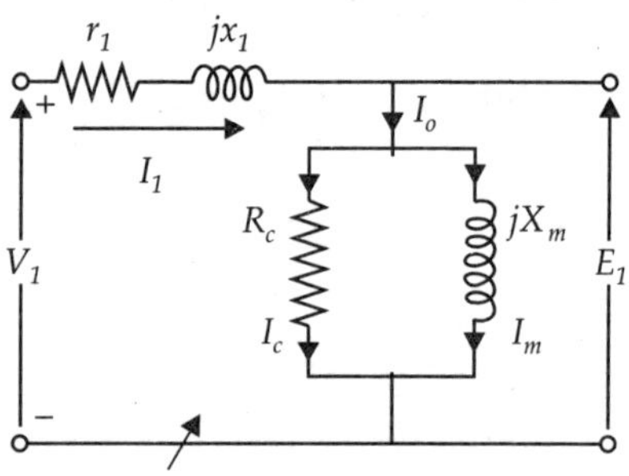

Fig 3.7: Stator circuit model for a 3-phase induction motor.

3.8.2. Rotor Circuit Model

From Eq. (3.8 *a*), rotor current is given by

$$I_2 = \frac{s E_2}{\sqrt{r_2^2 + (s x_2)^2}} \quad ...(3.18)$$

From Eq. (3.8 *b*), rotor current is

$$I_2 = \frac{E_2}{\frac{r_2}{s} + jx_2} \quad ...(3.19)$$

The magnitude and phase of rotor current I_2 obtained from Eqs. (3.18) and (3.19) are the same. However, there is a difference in their interpretation.

In Eq. (3.18), the rotor emf is of slip frequency. The magnitude of rotor emf under running condition is *s* times the magnitude of rotor emf at standstill conditions. Rotor circuit has constant resistance r_2 and variable leakage reactance sx_2. This interpretation agrees with actual physical facts under running conditions. Current I_2 is at slip frequency. Therefore, Eq. (3.18) gives the rotor circuit model at slip frequency *sf* as shown in Fig. 3.8 *(a)*.

As per Eq. (3.19), under running conditions, the rotor emf and current are at line frequency. The magnitude of rotor emf is equal to that at standstill. Rotor leakage reactance is constant at x_2 but rotor resistance is variable and equal to r_2/s. This interpretation is useful in drawing the equivalent circuit and also for analysing the behaviour of 3-phase induction motor. Therefore, Eq. (3.19) gives the rotor circuit model at line frequency *f* as shown in Fig. 3.8 *(b)*.

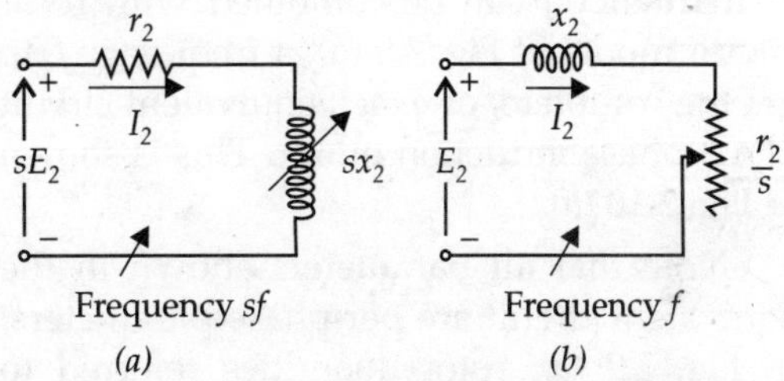

Fig 3.8: Rotor circuit model *(a)* at slip frequency *sf* and *(b)* at line frequency *f*.

Stator circuit model of Fig. 3.7 is at line frequency *f*. The stator and rotor circuit models can be combined only if these are at the same frequency. This means that rotor circuit model at frequency *f*, shown in Fig. 3.8 *(b)*, is only to be considered for obtaining complete circuit model of a 3-phase induction motor.

3.8.3. Complete Circuit Model

The complete per-phase equivalent circuit for a 3-phase induction motor can be obtained only if rotor circuit parameters are referred to stator side.

In a transformer, secondary parameters are referred to primary by means of turns ratio of the transformer. Same is true in case of 3-phase induction motor.

$$\text{Rotor voltage referred to} = \frac{E_2}{N_2'} \times N_1' = E_1$$

where $N_1' = k_{w1} \cdot N_1$ = effective stator turns per phase

$N_2' = k_{w2} \cdot N_2$ = effective rotor turns per phase.

$$\text{Rotor leakage impedance when referred to stator} = \left[\frac{r_2}{s} + jx_2\right]\left[\frac{N_1'}{N_2'}\right] = \frac{r_2'}{s} + jx_2'$$

$$\text{Rotor current } I_2 \text{ referred to stator is } I_2\left[\frac{N_2'}{N_1'}\right] = I_2'$$

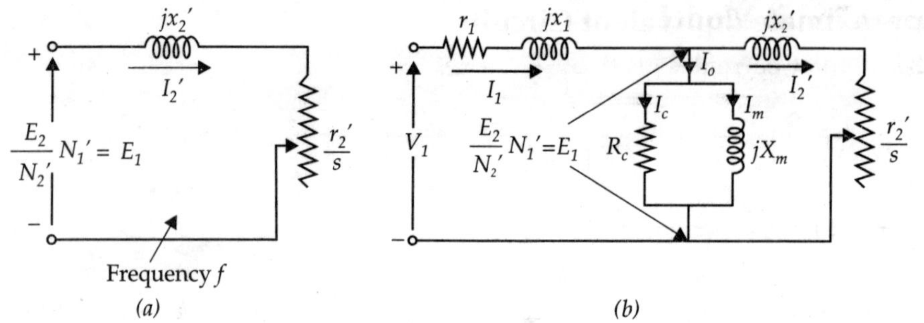

Fig 3.9: *(a)* Rotor circuit referred to stator and *(b)* complete (or exact) equivalent circuit for a 3-phase induction motor.

Rotor circuit model referred to stator is shown in Fig. 3.9 *(a)* above.

Now the stator circuit model of Fig. 3.7 at frequency f can be combined with rotor circuit model of Fig. 3.9 *(a)* at frequency f, to get the complete, or exact, equivalent circuit of a 3-phase induction motor. This is shown in Fig. 3.10 *(b)*.

Note that all parameters shown in the equivalent circuit are per phase parameters. In Fig. 3.9 *(b)*, rotor quantities referred to stator have been primed [′].

For simplicity and convenience, a more general equivalent circuit of a 3-phase induction motor is shown in Fig. 3.10 *(a)*, where

(i) prime notation, used for referred quantities, have been dropped and

(ii) the complex notation (*j* with reactances) has been dropped.

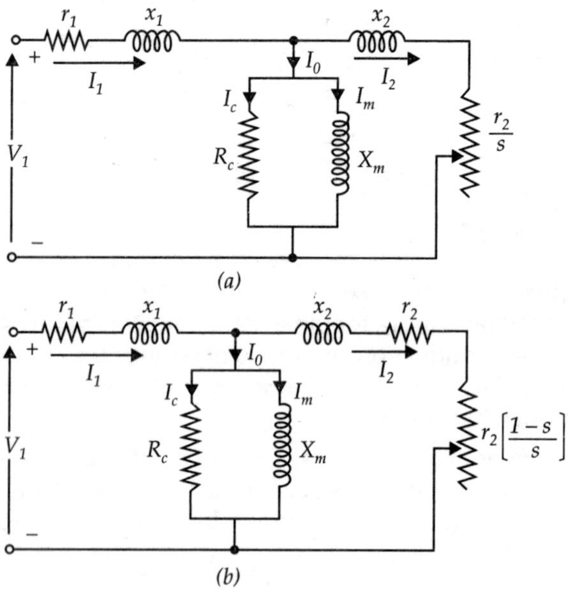

Fig 3.10: *(a)* Exact equivalent circuit of a 3-phase induction motor and *(b)* its modified form.

But one must keep in mind that all parameters are referred to stator side and are at stator frequency.

The resistance $\frac{r_2}{s}$ can be expressed as $\frac{r_2}{s} = r_2 + r_2\left(\frac{1-s}{s}\right)$

Therefore, equivalent circuit of Fig. 3.10 *(a)* can be redrawn as shown in Fig. 3.10 *(b)*. This exact equivalent circuit brings out the similarity between transformer and induction motor equivalent circuit. For example, at standstill, $s = 1$ circuit of Fig. 3.10 *(b)* becomes the equivalent circuit of a short-circuited two winding transformer. Similarly, at $s = 0$, the circuit becomes the equivalent circuit of an open-circuited transformer.

In Fig. 3.10 *(b)*, r_2 represents the actual rotor winding resistance (referred to stator). Variable resistance $r_2\left[\frac{1-s}{s}\right]$ represents the **variable mechanical load** on the 3-phase induction motor.

3.8.4. Approximate Equivalent Circuit

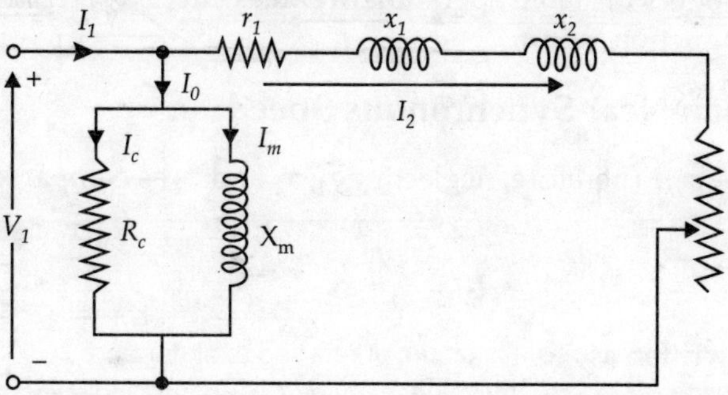

Fig 3.11: Approximate equivalent circuit of a 3-phase induction motor.

If the shunt branch (R_c in parallel with X_m) of the exact equivalent circuit of Fig. 3.10 *(a)* is shifted to input stator terminals, an approximate equivalent circuit of a 3-phase induction motor is obtained. This circuit is shown in Fig. 3.11. In a transformer, no-load current I_o is about 2 to 6% of full load primary current. But in a 3-phase induction motor, no-load current is about 30 to 50% of full load current. Therefore, use of the approximate equivalent circuit of an induction motor may result in considerable error. However, use of the circuit of Fig. 3.11 leads to simpler computational work for the analysis of a 3-phase induction motor.

3.9. TORQUE SLIP CHARACTERISTICS

From the approximate equivalent circuit of Fig. 3.11,

Rotor current

$$I_2 = \frac{V_1}{\sqrt{\left(r_1 + \frac{r_2}{s}\right)^2 + (x_1 + x_2)^2}} \quad ...(3.20)$$

From Eq. (3.15), the developed torque per phase is

$$T_e = \frac{1}{2\pi n_s} \cdot I_2^2 \frac{r_2}{s}$$

$$= \frac{1}{\omega_s} \cdot \frac{V_1^2}{\left(r_1 + \frac{r_2}{s}\right)^2 + (x_1 + x_2)^2} \cdot \frac{r_2}{s}$$

Total torque developed is

$$T_e = \frac{3}{\omega_s} \cdot \frac{V_1^2}{\left(r_1 + \frac{r_2}{s}\right)^2 + (x_1 + x_2)^2} \cdot \frac{r_2}{s} \quad ...(3.21)$$

The variation of torque with slip or speed of a 3-phase induction motor can be plotted from Eq. (3.21) for different values of slips. A general shape of the torque-speed or torque-slip characteristic is shown in Fig. 3.12.

The rotor revolves in the direction of rotating field. Therefore, slip varies from 1 at standstill to zero at synchronous speed. Likwise, speed varies from zero at standstill to synchronous speed N_s. In this figure, T_{est} = starting torque, T_{em} = maximum torque and s_{mT} = slip at which maximum torque occurs are indicated.

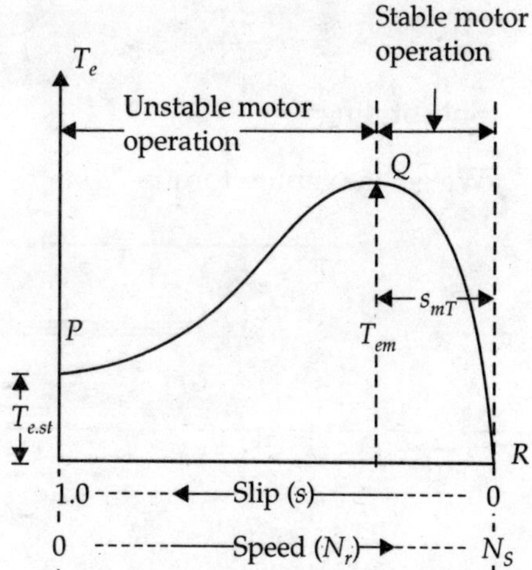

Fig 3.12: Torque-slip characteristics of a 3-phase induction motor.

The maximum torque is also called **breakdown torque** or **pull-out torque**. Also, curve *PQ* of the torque-slip characteristic offers unstable operation, whereas curve *QR* represents stable operating region of a three-phase induction motor.

3.9.1. Motor Operation Near Synchronous Speed

At small slips, $\frac{r_2}{s} >> (x_1 + x_2)$. Therefore, neglecting r_1, x_1 and x_2 as compared to $\frac{r_2}{s}$ at small slips, Eq. (3.20) gives

$$I_2 = \frac{sV_1}{r_2}$$

and Eq. (3.21) can be written as

$$T_e = \frac{3}{\omega_s} \cdot \frac{sV_1^2}{r_2} \quad ...(3.22)$$

Eq. (3.22) shows that at small slips, $T_e \propto s$. This is the reason torque-slip characteristic is nearly a straight line at small values of slips.

It is seen from Fig. 3.12 that in stable region, the motor speed varies from about 0.95 N_s to very near to synchronous speed. This is the reason a 3-phase induction motor is said to possess shunt characteristics.

3.9.2. Maximum Developed Torque

The condition for maximum torque can be obtained by applying maximum power transfer theorem to approximate equivalent circuit of Fig. 3.11. Torque is maximum when power delivered to load $\frac{r_2}{s}$ is maximum. Applying this theorem to Fig. 3.12, power transfer to load $\frac{r_2}{s}$ would be maximum when $\frac{r_2}{s}$ = impedance seen by $\frac{r_2}{s}$ towards voltage source V_1.

$$\therefore \quad \frac{r_2}{s_{mT}} = \sqrt{r_1^2 + (x_1 + x_2)^2} = \sqrt{r_1^2 + X^2}$$

where s_{mT} = slip at maximum torque

and $X = x_1 + x_2$

$$\therefore \quad s_{mT} = \frac{r_2}{\sqrt{r_1^2 + X^2}} \quad ...(3.23)$$

Substituting $\frac{r_2}{s_{mT}} = \sqrt{r_1^2 + X^2}$ in place of $\frac{r_2}{s}$ in Eq. (3.21)

We get maximum torque T_{em} as

$$T_{em} = \frac{3 \cdot V_1^2}{\omega_s} \cdot \frac{\sqrt{r_1^2 + X^2}}{[r_1 + \sqrt{r_1^2 + X^2}]^2 + X^2}$$

$$= \frac{3 \cdot V_1^2}{\omega_s} \cdot \frac{\sqrt{r_1^2 + X^2}}{r_1^2 + r_1^2 + X^2 + 2r_1\sqrt{r_1^2 + X^2} + X^2}$$

$$= \frac{3 \cdot V_1^2}{\omega_s} \cdot \frac{\sqrt{r_1^2 + X^2}}{2\sqrt{r_1^2 + X^2}[r_1 + \sqrt{r_1^2 + X^2}]}$$

$$= \frac{3 \cdot V_1^2}{\omega_s} \cdot \frac{1}{2[r_1 + \sqrt{r_1^2 + X^2}]} \quad ...(3.24)$$

It is seen from Eq. (3.23) that slip at which maximum torque occurs is directly proportional to rotor resistance r_2. Eq. (3.24) shows that maximum torque is independent of rotor resistance. It is also seen from Eq. (3.24) that

(i) T_{em} is directly proportional to square of applied voltage,

(ii) T_{em} is reduced by an increase in stator resistance,

(iii) T_{em} is reduced by an increase in stator and rotor leakage reactances respectively, because $X = x_1 + x_2$ and

(iv) T_{em} does not depend on rotor circuit resistance.

In Fig. 3.13, torque-slip characteristic for rotor resistance r_2 is plotted. In case rotor circuit resistance is increased to $r_2' > r_2$, by inserting external resistance in rotor circuit as shown in Fig. 3.13, then s_{mT} increases but T_{em} remains the same. This is plotted in Fig. 3.13 and is indicated by r_2'. For $r_2'' > r_2'$, torque-slip characteristic is also shown in Fig. 3.13. It is seen from this figure that by varying rotor circuit resistance in a slip-ring induction motor,

(i) motor speed can be controlled and

(ii) motor starting torque can be varied.

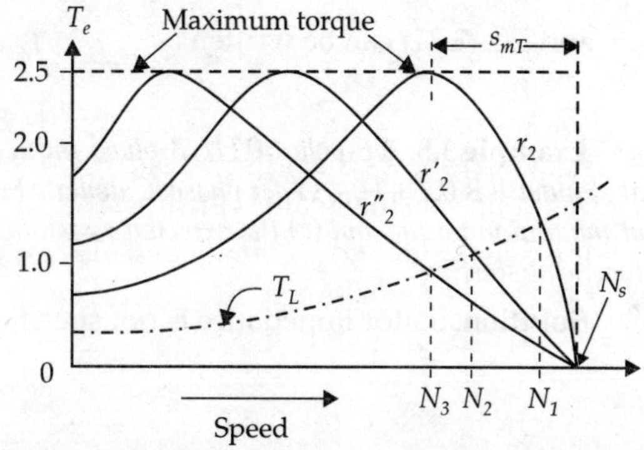

Fig 3.13: Effect of rotor resistance on torque-slip characteristics of a 3-phase induction motor.

3.9.3. Motor Starting Torque

At starting, slip $s = 1.0$. From Eq. (3.21), the starting torque is given by

$$T_{e \cdot st} = \frac{3}{\omega_s} \cdot \frac{V_1^2}{(r_1 + r_2)^2 + X^2} \cdot r_2 \qquad ...(3.25)$$

Eq. (3.25) shows that starting torque can be controlled by varying rotor circuit resistance. Maximum torque at starting would occur when $s_{mT} = 1.0$, *i.e.* when [from Eq. (3.23)], $R_2 = \sqrt{r_1^2 + X^2}$. Here R_2 is the total rotor circuit resistance to get maximum torque at starting.

$\therefore$ External resistance to be inserted in rotor circuit to get maximum torque at starting $= R_2 - r_2 = \sqrt{r_1^2 + X^2} - r_2$. It is seen from Fig. 3.13 that for obtaining more starting torque, extra resistance should be added in the rotor circuit and cut out gradually as the rotor accelerates.

3.9.4. Motor Torque in Terms of Maximum Torque, T_{em}

The motor developed torque T_e at any slip s can be expressed in terms of maximum torque T_{em} from Eqs. (3.21) and (3.24). In order to get a simpler expression, stator resistance r_1 is neglected.

From Eq. (3.21),
$$T_e = \frac{3V_1^2}{\omega_s} \cdot \frac{1}{\left(\frac{r_2}{s}\right)^2 + X^2} \cdot \frac{r_2}{s}$$

From Eq. (3.24),
$$T_{em} = \frac{3V_1^2}{\omega_s} \cdot \frac{1}{2X} \qquad ...(3.26)$$

$$\therefore \quad \frac{T_e}{T_{em}} = \frac{2X}{\left(\frac{r_2}{s}\right)^2 + X^2} \cdot \frac{r_2}{s}$$

From Eq. (3.23), with $r_1 = 0$, we get $r_2 = s_{mT} X$

Substituting this value of r_2 in the above expression, we get

$$\frac{T_e}{T_{em}} = \frac{2X}{\left[\frac{s_{mT}\cdot X}{s}\right]^2 + X^2} \cdot \frac{s_{mT}\cdot X}{s}$$

$$= \frac{2}{\frac{s_{mT}}{s} + \frac{s}{s_{mT}}} = \frac{2\cdot s\, s_{mT}}{s^2 + s_{mT}^2} \qquad \text{...(3.27 a)}$$

or

$$T_e = \frac{2T_{em}}{\frac{s}{s_{mT}} + \frac{s_{mT}}{s}} \qquad \text{...(3.27 b)}$$

Example 3.8. *A 6-pole, 50 Hz, 3-phase induction motor has full-load speed of 950 rpm. Rotor impedance at standstill is 0.1 + j 0.4 Ω per phase. Calculate (a) maximum torque in terms of full load torque (b) the speed at maximum torque and (c) the external resistance per phase to be inserted in rotor circuit to get maximum torque at starting.*

Solution. Stator impedance is not specified, therefore take $r_1 = x_1 = 0$.

$$N_s = \frac{120\times 50}{6} = 1000 \text{ rpm} ; s_{fl} = \frac{1000-950}{1000} = 0.05.$$

$$r_2 = 0.1\ \Omega,\ x_2 = 0.4\ \Omega$$

(*a*) From Eq. (3.23),

$$s_{mT} = \frac{r_2}{x_2} = \frac{0.1}{0.4} = 0.25$$

From Eq. (3.27 a),

$$\frac{T_{e\cdot fl}}{T_{e\cdot m}} = \frac{2}{\frac{s_{mT}}{s_{fl}} + \frac{s_{fl}}{s_{mT}}} = \frac{2}{\frac{0.25}{0.05} + \frac{0.05}{0.25}} = \frac{2}{5.2} = \frac{1}{2.6}$$

∴

$$T_{em} = 2.6\ T_{efl}$$

(b) Speed at maximum torque

$$= N_s(1 - s_{mT})$$

$$= 1000\ (1 - 0.25) = 750 \text{ rpm}$$

(c) Maximum torque at starting requires

$$s_{mT} = 1.0 = \frac{R_2}{x_2}$$

∴ R_2 = total rotor circuit resistance = $x_2 = 0.4\ \Omega$

Per-phase external resistance to be inserted in the rotor circuit

$$= 0.4 - r_2 = 0.4 - 0.1 = 0.3\ \Omega$$

Example 3.9. *A 400 V, 4-pole, 50 Hz, 3-phase delta-connected wound-rotor induction motor has star-connected rotor. When stator is connected to rated voltage, the voltage between two slip rings is 200 at standstill. The stator leakage impedance per phase is 0.3 + j 1.0 Ω and rotor leakage impedance at standstill is 0.04 + j 0.20 Ω per phase. Calculate (a) the slip at maximum torque (b) the maximum torque (c) torque, slip and power output at full load in case maximum torque is twice the full load torque.*

Solution. Stator voltage per phase = 400 V = E_1

Rotor voltage per phase

$$E_2 = \frac{200}{\sqrt{3}}\ \text{V}$$

∴

$$\frac{E_1}{E_2} = \frac{N_1'}{N_2'} = \frac{400}{200} \times \sqrt{3} = 2\sqrt{3}$$

Rotor impedance per phase referred to stator = $(0.04 + j\,0.20)\,[2 \times \sqrt{3}\,]^2$

$$= r_2 + j\,x_2 = 0.48 + j\,2.4\,\Omega$$

Stator leakage impedance $\quad r_1 + j\,x_1 = 0.3 + j\,1.0\,\Omega$

(a) From Eq. (3.23), the slip at maximum torque is

$$s_{mT} = \frac{r_2}{\sqrt{r_1^2 + (x_1 + x_2)^2}} = \frac{0.48}{\sqrt{0.3^2 + (1 + 2.4)^2}} = 0.1406$$

(b) Synchronous speed $\quad \omega_s = \dfrac{4\pi\, f_1}{P} = \dfrac{4\pi \times 50}{4} = 50\,\pi$ rad/sec

From Eq. (3.24), maximum torque is

$$T_{em} = \frac{3 \cdot V_1^2}{\omega_s} \cdot \frac{1}{2\left[r_1 + \sqrt{r_1^2 + (x_1 + x_2)^2}\right]}$$

$$= \frac{3 \times 400^2}{50\pi} \cdot \frac{1}{2\left[0.3 + \sqrt{0.3^2 + 3.4^2}\right]} = 411.473 \text{ Nm}$$

(c) Full load torque, $\quad T_{efl} = \dfrac{1}{2} \cdot T_{em} = \dfrac{411.473}{2} = 205.74$ Nm

From Eq. (3.21), full load torque is

$$205.74 = \frac{3 \times 400^2}{50\pi} \cdot \frac{1}{\left[0.3 + \frac{0.48}{s}\right]^2 + 3.4^2} \times \frac{0.48}{s}$$

$$s\left[\left(0.3 + \frac{0.48}{s}\right)^2 + 3.4^2\right] = 7.13$$

$$11.65\, s^2 - 6.842\, s + 0.2304 = 0$$

$$\therefore s = \frac{6.842 \pm \sqrt{6.842^2 - 4 \times 11.65 \times 0.2304}}{2 \times 11.65} = 0.03588 \text{ or } 0.5514$$

Since $\quad s_{mT} = 0.1406$, slip $s = 0.5514$ lies in unstable region.

Therefore, full-load slip, $\quad s_{fl} = 0.03588$

Full load power output $= \omega_r \times T_{e\cdot fl}$

$$= 50\,\pi\,[1 - 0.03588] \times 205.74 = 31158 \text{ W}$$

Example 3.10. *A 3-phase, 50 Hz induction motor has a starting torque which is 1.1 times the full load torque and a maximum torque which is 2.2 times the full load torque. Calculate (a) slip at maximum torque (b) full load slip and (c) rotor current at starting in terms of full-load rotor current.*

Solution. *(a)* Here $\quad T_{est} = 1.1\, T_{efl}$ and $T_{e\cdot m} = 2.2\, T_{efl}$

$$\therefore \quad \frac{T_{est}}{T_{e\cdot m}} = \frac{1.1\, T_{e\cdot fl}}{2.2\, T_{efl}} = \frac{2}{\frac{s_{mT}}{1} + \frac{1}{s_{mT}}} = \frac{1}{2} \text{ or } \frac{s_{mT}}{1 + s_{mT}^2} = \frac{1}{4}$$

or $\quad s_{mT}^2 - 4\, s_{mT} + 1 = 0$

Its solution gives $\quad s_{mT} = 3.732$ or 0.268

$\therefore$ Slip at maximum torque, $\quad s_{mT} = 0.268$

(b) $$\frac{T_{efl}}{T_{e \cdot m}} = \frac{1\, T_{e \cdot fl}}{2.2\, T_{e \cdot fl}} = \frac{2}{\dfrac{s_{mT}}{s_{fl}} + \dfrac{s_{fl}}{s_{mT}}} = \frac{1}{2.2}$$

$$\frac{0.268}{s_{fl}} + \frac{s_{fl}}{0.268} = 4.4$$

or $$s_{fl}^2 - 1.1792\, s_{fl} + 0.071824 = 0$$

Its solution gives $s_{fl} = 0.0644$ or 1.1148

∴ Full-load slip, $s_{fl} = 0.0644$

(c) $$T_{est} = \frac{3}{\omega_s} \cdot I_{2 \cdot st}^2 \cdot \frac{r_2}{1} \text{ and } T_{e\ fl} = \frac{3}{\omega_s}\, I_{2 \cdot fl}^2 \cdot \frac{r_2}{s_{fl}}$$

∴ $$\frac{T_{est}}{T_{e \cdot fl}} = \left[\frac{I_{2st}}{I_{2 \cdot fl}}\right]^2 \cdot s_{fl}$$

or $$I_{2st} = \left[\frac{T_{est}}{T_{e \cdot fl}} \frac{1}{s_{fl}}\right]^{1/2} \cdot I_{2fl} = \left[\frac{1.1\, T_{e \cdot fl}}{T_{ef}} \times \frac{1}{0.0644}\right]^{1/2} \cdot I_{2f}$$

$$= \left[\frac{1}{0.0644}\right]^{1/2} \cdot I_{2fl} = 4.133\, I_{2fl}.$$

3.10. INDUCTION MOTOR PHASOR DIAGRAM

Phasor diagram of a 3-phase induction motor is almost similar to the transformer phasor diagram.

First draw flux ϕ horizontal. This flux induces emfs E_1 and E_2 lagging ϕ by 90° as in a transformer. Here E_1 and E_2 are per-phase emfs generated in stator and standstill rotor windings respectively. These emfs E_1 and E_2 are due to rotating field running at synchronous speed.

For rotor running at a slip s, rotor emf equation, from Fig. 3.8 (*a*) is $s\, E_2 = r_2\, I_2 + j\, s\, x_2\, I_2$.

Draw I_2 lagging E_2 by rotor power factor angle θ_2, where

$$\theta_2 = \tan^{-1}\left(\frac{sx_2}{r_2}\right)$$

Now $I_2 r_2$, $js\, x_2\, I_2$ and sE_2 are drawn as shown in Fig. 3.14.

Rotor current I_2 is reflected as current I_2' in stator. Here I_2' is given by $I_2'\, N_1' = I_2\, N_2'$

or $$I_2' = I_2 \frac{N_2'}{N_1'} = I_2 \times \frac{N_2 \cdot k_{w2}}{N_1 \cdot k_{w1}}.$$

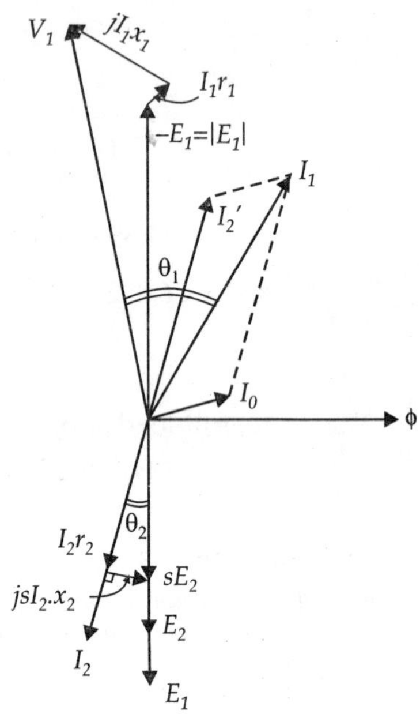

Fig 3.14: Phasor diagram for a 3-phase induction motor.

No load current I_o is shown leading flux ϕ as in transformer. Phasor sum of I_o and I_2' gives the stator current I_1.

Add stator leakage impedance drop to $|E_1| = -\overline{E}_1$ to get stator applied voltage $V_1 = I_1\,(r_1 + j\, x_1) + E_1$, Fig. 3.14. Here θ_1 is the stator power factor angle by which I_1 lags V_1. Stator power factor is $\cos\theta_1$. All quantities shown in the phasor diagram have per-phase values.

At standstill, $\theta_2 = \tan^{-1}\left(\dfrac{x_2}{r_2}\right)$ is fairly large. As a consequence, angle θ_1 would be large indicating that stator power factor at starting is quite low.

3.11. EFFECT OF PARAMETER VARIATION ON TORQUE-SPEED CHARACTERISTICS

Here the effect of variation of the following parameters on the torque-speed characteristics of a 3-phase induction motor is examined.

(*a*) Stator resistance variation

(*b*) Rotor resistance variation

(*c*) Star voltage variation and

(*d*) Stator frequency variation.

Now the effect of parameter variation on the torque-speed characteristics of a 3-phase induction motor is briefly described.

3.11.1. Stator Resistance Variation

In case per-phase resistance r_1 of stator is increased, it would affect torque-speed characteristics. It is seen from Eq. (3.21) that if stator resistance r_1 is increased, magnitude of torque decreases. Therefore, torque speed characteristics shifts downward with increased stator resistance as shown in Fig. 3.15. In this figure, it is assumed that stator resistance is increased to r_1' where r_1' is more than normal stator resistance r_1. Its effect is now investigated as under.

(*a*) Eq. (3.24) shows that maximum torque T_{em} gets reduced.

(*b*) Eq. (3.23) reveals that s_{mT}, the slip at which maximum torque occurs, is also reduced.

(*c*) Eq. (3.25) shows that starting torque $T_{e\ st}$ is reduced.

The effects listed above for increased resistance $r_1' > r_1$ are shown in Fig. 3.15. For load torque T_L as shown, motor speed with increased stator resistance r_1' is N_2 which is more than normal speed N_1 with stator resistance r_1.

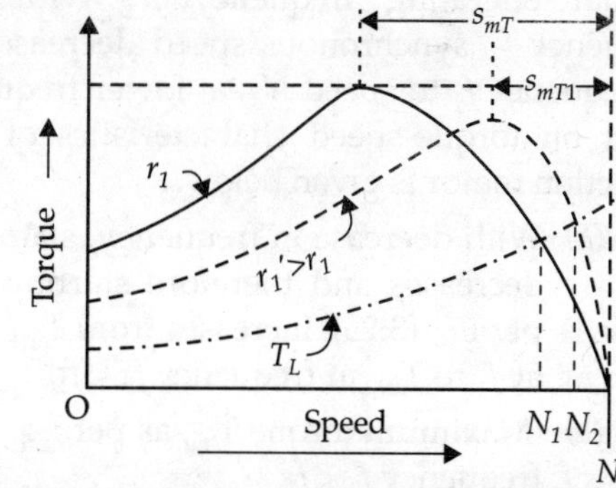

Fig 3.15: Effect of increase in stator resistance.

3.11.2. Rotor Resistance Variation

In order to examine the effect of rotor resistance variation on torque-speed characteristics of a 3-phase induction motor, observe Fig. 3.13 carefully. This figure reveals as under.

(*a*) If rotor circuit resistance is increased, starting torque T_{est} increases. Eq. (3.25) also proves this fact.

(*b*) Magnitude of maximum torque developed T_{em} is not affected by rotor resistance variation as per Fig. 3.13. It is also seen from Eq. (3.24), that T_{em} does not depend on rotor circuit resistance r_2.

(*c*) Slip at which maximum torque T_{em} occurs increases as rotor circuit resistance is increased, see Fig. 3.13 and Eq. (3.23).

(*d*) By varying rotor circuit resistance, motor speed can be controlled. Fig. 3.13 shows that for load torque T_L speed for r_2 is N_1, speed for $r_2' > r_2$ is $N_2 < N_1$ and so on.

(*e*) It is seen from Eq. (3.20) that starting current gets reduced if rotor circuit resistance is increased.

3.11.3. Stator Voltage Variation

It is seen from Eq. (3.21) that in a 3-phase induction motor, torque $T_e \propto V_1^2$ or torque $\propto$ (supply voltage)^2. Therefore, if supply voltage decreases, torque T_e decreases and torque-speed curve shifts bodily downward as a whole. It is seen from Fig. 3.16 that if supply voltage decreases, then

(a) maximum torque T_{em} decreases, see Eq. (3.24),

(b) starting torque T_{est} decreases, see Eq. (3.25),

(c) slip s_{mT}, at which maximum torque T_{em} occurs, remains the same, see Eq. (3.23),

(d) for load torque T_L, motor speed decreases from N_1 at voltage V_1 to lower speed N_2 at voltage $V_2 < V_1$, see Fig. 3.16,

(e) full-load slip has increased, its value is s_{fl1} for voltage V_1 and $s_{fl2} > s_{fl1}$ at lower voltage $V_2 < V_1$, see Fig. 3.16.

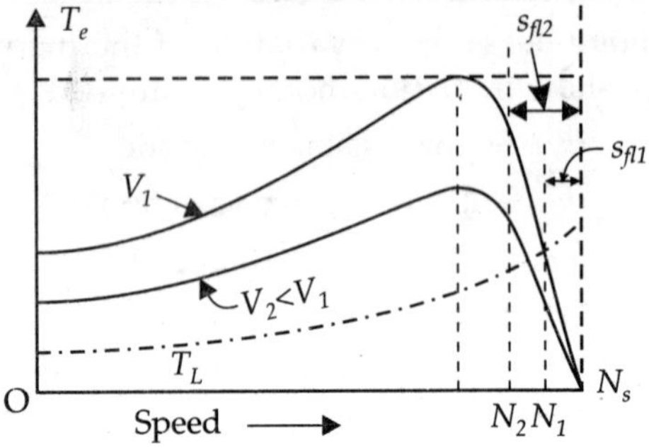

Fig 3.16: Effect of stator voltage variation.

3.11.4. Stator Frequency Variation

If supply frequency varies, the magnitude of rotating flux and its synchronous speed change. Let us consider the effect of supply frequency variation below the normal operating frequency f_1. With decreased frequency f_2, synchronous speed decreases from N_{s1} at frequency f_1 to speed N_{s2} at lower frequency f_2. Its effect on torque-speed characteristics of a 3-phase induction motor is given below.

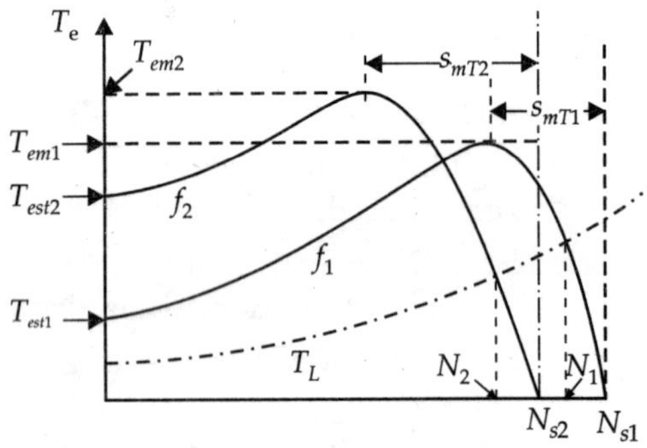

Fig 3.17: Effect of stator frequency variation.

(a) With decrease in frequency, stator reactance decreases and therefore starting torque, as per Eq. (3.25), increases from T_{est1} at frequency f_1 to T_{est2} at frequency $f_2 < f_1$.

(b) Maximum torque T_{em}, as per Eq. (3.24), also increases from T_{em1} at frequency f_1 to T_{emt2} at frequency $f_2 < f_1$.

(c) Slip s_{mT}, at which maximum torque occurs, also increases from s_{mT1} at frequency f_1 to s_{mT2} at frequency $f_2 < f_1$.

(d) For load torque T_L, motor speed decreases from N_1 at frequency f_1 to speed N_2 at frequency $f_2 < f_1$.

3.12. METHODS OF STARTING

Torque-slip characteristic of Fig. 3.12 shows that a 3-phase induction motor has positive finite starting torque at slip $s = 1$. Therefore, a 3-phase induction motor is a self starting motor and begins to rotate when fed from a 3-phase source.

At standstill, a 3-phase induction behaves like a transformer with its secondary short-circuited. Therefore, it takes a high starting current (5 to 8 times the full load current) if started at full voltage. This large starting current at low power factor is objectionable, because it causes drop in the supply line voltage. As a consequence, performance of other equipment connected to this line is affected considerably.

3.12.1. Starting of Cage Motors

The following three methods are used for the starting of 3-phase squirrel cage induction motors:

(i) Direct-on-line starting (ii) Auto-transformer starting (iii) Star-delta starting.

3.12.1.1. Direct-on-line (D.O.L.) starting

This method of starting a squirrel cage induction motor is simple and inexpensive. In this method, the motor is directly switched on to the supply mains as shown in Fig. 3.18. The motor takes 5 to 8 times the full load current at starting. This large current of short duration may not harm the rugged and robust squirrel cage motor. But this high starting current, as stated before, may cause objectionable voltage drop in the supply line voltage. If the 3-phase supply system is strong enough, then direct-on-line starting is preferred.

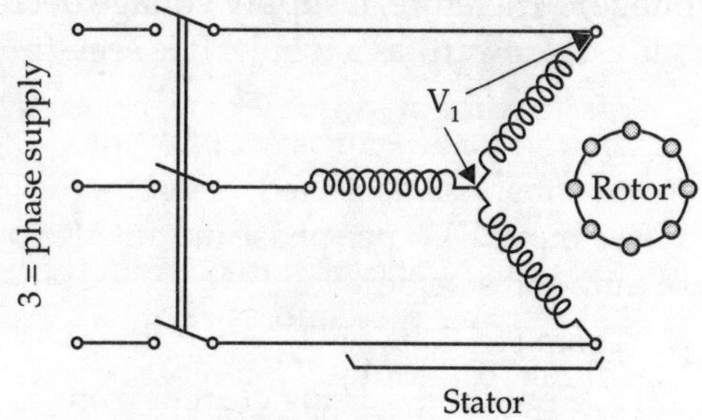

Fig 3.18: Direct-on-line starting.

Let I_{st} = per-phase starting current taken from supply,

I_{fl} = per-phase full load current taken from supply.

From Eq. (3.15), $$T_e = \frac{1}{\omega_s} \cdot I_2^2 \frac{r_2}{s}$$

$$\therefore \quad \frac{T_{e \cdot st}}{T_{e \cdot fl}} = \frac{I_{2st}^2 \frac{r_2}{1}}{I_{2fl}^2 \frac{r_2}{s_{fl}}} = \left[\frac{I_{2 \cdot st}}{I_{2 \cdot fl}}\right]^2 \times s_{fl} \qquad \text{...(3.28)}$$

If no-load current is neglected, then

I_{st} × effective stator turns = $I_{2 \cdot st}$ × effective rotor turns and

I_{fl} × effective stator turns = $I_{2 \cdot fl}$ × effective rotor turns.

From above, $$\frac{I_{st}}{I_{fl}} = \frac{I_{2 \cdot st}}{I_{2 \cdot fl}}$$

From Eq. (3.28), we get $$\frac{T_{e \cdot st}}{T_{e \cdot fl}} = \left[\frac{I_{st}}{I_{fl}}\right]^2 \times s_{fl} \qquad \text{...(3.29)}$$

If V_1 = stator voltage per phase and Z_{sc} = total motor leakage impedance per phase referred to stator at standstill, then starting current with direct switching $I_{st} = \frac{V_1}{Z_{sc}} = I_{sc}$, short circuit current at starting.

This means that starting current is equal to short circuit current.

$$\therefore \quad \frac{T_{e \cdot st}}{T_{e \cdot fl}} = \left[\frac{I_{sc}}{I_{fl}}\right]^2 \times s_{fl} \qquad \text{...(3.30)}$$

3.12.1.2. Auto-transformer starting

In this method, at the time of starting, a fraction xV_1 of the supply voltage V_1 is applied to stator terminals with the help of an auto-transformer as shown in Fig. 3.19. This reduces the motor current and current drawn from the supply mains. As the motor accelerates, the voltage applied to stator terminals is gradually increased. When the motor has accelerated near to its steady speed, auto-transformer is disconnected from the supply. Now full voltage is applied to the motor terminals by connecting it directly across the supply mains. In voltage xV_1, x is the ratio of output voltage to input voltage of auto-transformer. In other words, x is the transformation ratio of auto-transformer and is less than one.

Now, per-phase starting current in motor winding

$$= \frac{xV_1}{Z_{sc}} = x\,I_{sc} \qquad ...(3.31)$$

If no-load current of auto-transformer is neglected, then per-phase input *VA* = per-phase output *VA* of auto-transformer.

From Fig. 3.19, $I_{st} \cdot V_1 = x\,V_1\,(x\,I_{sc})$

$\therefore$ Per-phase starting current from the supply mains

$$I_{st} = x^2 \cdot I_{sc} \qquad ...(3.32)$$

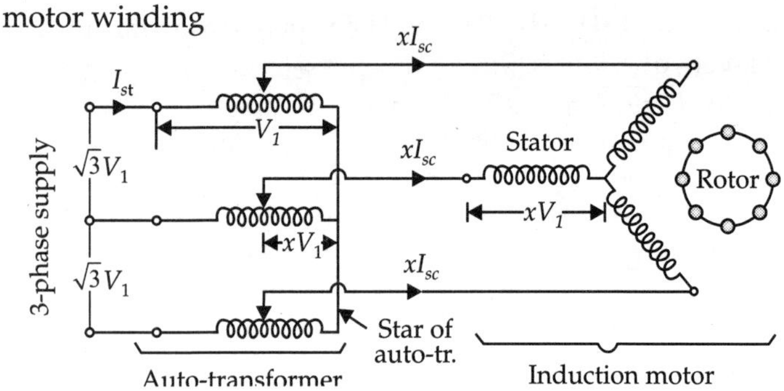

Fig 3.19: Auto-transformer starting.

From Eq. (3.19), $\frac{T_{e\cdot st}}{T_{e\cdot fl}} = \left[\frac{\text{Per-phase starting current in motor winding}}{\text{Per-phase motor full load current}}\right]^2 \times s_{fl}$

$$= \left[\frac{x \cdot I_{sc}}{I_{fl}}\right]^2 \cdot s_{fl} = x^2 \left[\frac{I_{sc}}{I_{fl}}\right]^2 \cdot s_{fl} \qquad ...(3.33)$$

For an induction motor, torque $\propto$ (voltage)^2

$$\therefore \quad \frac{T_{est} \text{ with auto-transformer starting}}{T_{est} \text{ with D.O.L. starting}} = \left[\frac{xV_1}{V_1}\right]^2 = x^2 \qquad ...(3.34)$$

It is seen from Eqs. (3.32) and (3.34) that with auto-transformer starting, the starting line (not motor) current and starting torque are reduced to x^2 times their corresponding values with D.O.L. starting.

3.12.1.3. Star-delta starting

This method of starting is applicable to motors designed to run normally with delta-connected stator windings. Fig. 3.20 gives the connection diagram for star-delta starting of a 3-phase squirrel cage induction motor. The stator terminals are marked A_1, A_2 for phase A; B_1, B_2 for phase B and C_1, C_2 for phase C.

For starting the motor, switch *S* is thrown to position 1. Terminals A_2, B_2, C_2 get short circuited and supply is connected to terminals A_1, B_1, C_1. This connects the stator winding in star. After the motor has reached steady state speed, triple pole switch *S* is thrown to position 2. Now terminals A_2, B_2, C_2 get connected to terminals C_1, A_1, B_1 respectively. In position 2, stator winding, therefore, gets connected in delta as per Fig. 3.20 *(a)*.

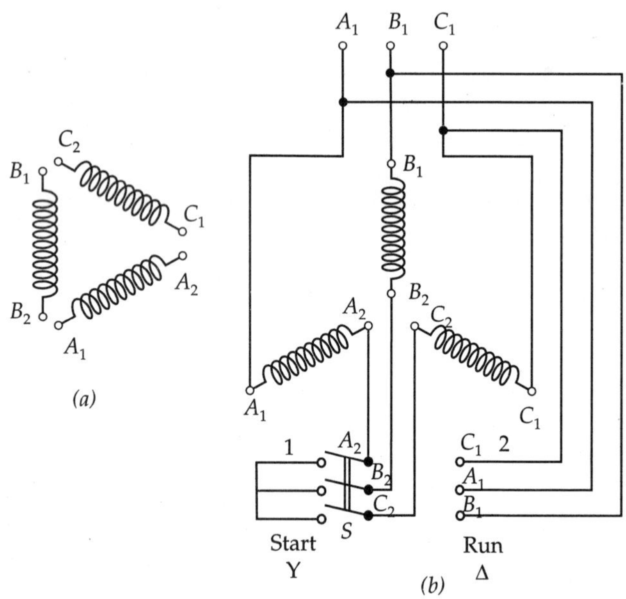

Fig 3.20: Star-delta starting of a 3-phase induction motor.

Let V_L = line voltage. Then, per-phase starting current $I_{st\cdot y}$, with stator winding in star, is given by

$$I_{sty} = \frac{V_L}{\sqrt{3} \cdot Z_{sc}} \qquad \text{...(3.35)}$$

With stator in star, I_{sty} is also the starting line current with star-delta starting.

With delta-connected stator winding, the motor starting current per phase would be

$$I_{std} = \frac{V_L}{Z_{sc}} = I_{scd}$$

and the line-current at starting = $\sqrt{3}\ I_{std} = \dfrac{\sqrt{3}\,V_L}{Z_{sc}} = \sqrt{3}\ I_{scd}$ ...(3.36)

From above, note that $I_{sty} = \dfrac{1}{\sqrt{3}}\left[\dfrac{V_L}{Z_{sc}}\right] = \dfrac{1}{\sqrt{3}}\ [I_{std}] = \dfrac{1}{\sqrt{3}} \cdot I_{scd}$

From Eqs. (3.35) and (3.36), we get

$$\frac{\text{starting line current with star-delta starting}}{\text{starting line current with direct-switching in delta}} = \frac{I_{st\cdot y}}{\sqrt{3} \cdot I_{st\cdot d}} = \frac{\dfrac{1}{\sqrt{3}} \cdot \dfrac{V_L}{Z_{sc}}}{\sqrt{3} \cdot \dfrac{V_L}{Z_{sc}}} = \frac{1}{3} \qquad \text{...(3.37)}$$

Thus, with star-delta starting, starting line current from the supply mains is one-third of that with direct switching in delta. As per Eq. (3.25), motor starting torque is proportional to per-phase voltage squared. Therefore,

$$\frac{\text{starting torque with star-delta starting}}{\text{starting torque with direct switching in delta}} = \frac{\left(\dfrac{V_L}{\sqrt{3}}\right)^2}{V_L^2} = \frac{1}{3} \qquad \text{...(3.38)}$$

This shows that star-delta starting also reduces the starting torque to one-third of that obtained with direct switching in delta.

In an auto-transformer, if (output voltage/input voltage) = $\dfrac{1}{\sqrt{3}}$ = x, then Eqs. (3.32) and (3.34) show that both starting line current and motor starting torque are reduced to one-third of their corresponding values with direct switching in delta. This also happens in star-delta starter. From this, it can be concluded that with star-delta starter, a motor behaves as if it is started by an auto-transformer with transformation ratio $x = \dfrac{1}{\sqrt{3}} = 0.58$, *i.e.* with 58% tapping. Also,

$$\frac{\text{starting torque with star-delta starting, } T_{est}}{\text{full-load torque with stator winding in delta, } T_{efl}} = \frac{\dfrac{1}{\omega_s} \cdot \left(I_{st\cdot y}\right)^2 \dfrac{r_2}{1}}{\dfrac{1}{\omega_s}\left(I_{fld}\right)^2 \cdot \dfrac{r_2}{s_{fl}}} = \left[\frac{I_{sty}}{I_{fld}}\right]^2 \cdot s_{fl} \qquad \text{...(3.39)}$$

where I_{sty} = starting phase current with stator in star

I_{fld} = full-load phase current with stator in delta.

After Eq. (3.36), it is proved that $I_{sty} = \dfrac{1}{\sqrt{3}} \cdot I_{scd}$

From Eq. (3.39), $$\frac{T_{e\cdot st}}{T_{e\cdot fl}} = \frac{1}{3}\left[\frac{I_{sc\cdot d}}{I_{fl\cdot d}}\right]^2 \times s_{fl} \qquad \text{...(3.40)}$$

Here I_{scd} is the per-phase starting current with stator winding in delta.

Star-delta starter is cheap, it is therefore used extensively. This method is most suitable for drives where starting torque is not required to exceed 50% of full-load torque. Star-delta starting is, therefore, used for pumps, fans, propellers, machine tool drives, motor-generator sets etc.

For line voltage exceeding 3.3 kV, star-delta starting is not employed. It is because for such applications, stator winding in delta becomes quite expensive.

3.12.2. Starting of Slip-ring Induction Motors

Fig. 3.3 shows the connection scheme of a 3-phase slip-ring induction motor along with its starter. At the time of start, entire starting resistance is added to the rotor circuit. Now full supply voltage is applied to the stator terminals. Added starting resistance reduces the starting current. The rotor begins to rotate. Now external starting resistance is gradually decreased as the motor speeds up. Finally, under normal operation, starting resistance is cut out completely and the slip rings are short-circuited. The slip-ring induction motor now runs under normal operating conditions.

Example 3.11. *Calculate the percentage reduction in starting current and starting torque if the supply voltage to a 3-phase cage motor is 85% instead of rated voltage.*

Solution. Let V_L = rated motor voltage and

Z_{sc} = total leakage impedance referred to stator.

$\therefore$ Starting current with rated voltage $= \dfrac{V_L}{Z_{sc}} = I_{sc}$

Starting current with 85% of rated voltage $= \dfrac{0.85\,V_L}{Z_{sc}} = 0.85\,I_{sc}$

$\therefore$ Percentage reduction in starting current $= \dfrac{I_{sc} - 0.85\,I_{sc}}{I_{sc}} \times 100 =$ **15%**

As per Eq. (3.25), starting torque is proportional to supply voltage squared.

$\therefore$ Starting torque with rated voltage $= KV_L^2$ where K is any constant.

Starting torque with 85% of rated voltage $= K(0.85\,V_L)^2 = 0.7225\,KV_L^2$

$\therefore$ Percentage reduction in starting torque $= \dfrac{KV_L^2[1 - 0.7225]}{KV_L^2} \times 100 =$ **27.75%**

Example 3.12. *A 3-phase delta-connected squirrel cage induction motor takes a starting current of 60 A per phase when fed from rated voltage. Calculate, (a) line current with D.O.L. starting (b) phase and line starting currents with star-delta starter, (c) supply line and motor line starting currents with 80% tapping on the auto-transformer.*

Solution. *(a)* With delta connection, per-phase starting current = 60 A

Starting line current with delta connection, *i.e.* with direct switching = $\sqrt{3}$ × per-phase starting current = $\sqrt{3} \times 60 = 103.92$ A

$\therefore$ Starting line current with D.O.L. starting = **103.92 A**

(b) For star-delta starting, starting line current

$= \dfrac{1}{3}$ (starting line current with D.O.L. starting)

$= \dfrac{1}{3} \times 103.92 =$ **34.64 A**

Starting phase current and starting line current with star-delta starting are equal. Therefore, starting phase current with star-delta starting = **34.64 A**

(c) Per-phase starting current with rated voltage = 60 A = I_{sc}

For auto-transformer tapping at 80%, the transformation ratio $x = 0.80$.

∴ Per-phase motor starting current, from Eq. (3.31), is

$$= x \cdot I_{sc} = 0.8 \times 60 = \mathbf{48\ A}$$

∴ Motor line starting current with stator in delta = $\sqrt{3} \times 48 = \mathbf{83.136\ A}$

Per-phase starting current from supply mains, from Eq. (3.32), is

$$I_{st} = x^2 \cdot I_{sc} = (0.8)^2 \times 60 = 38.4 \text{ A}$$

∴ Starting line current from supply mains = $\sqrt{3} \times 38.4 = \mathbf{66.51\ A}$

3.13. SPEED CONTROL OF INDUCTION MOTORS

The operating speed of a 3-phase induction motor is given by

$$N_r = \frac{120 f_1}{P} (1 - s) \text{ rpm}$$

This expression shows that motor speed can be controlled by a change in the supply frequency f_1, number of poles P or the slip s.

The chief methods of speed control for a 3-phase induction motor are :

(a) pole changing control *(b)* stator voltage control

(c) stator frequency control *(d)* rotor resistance control and

(e) rotor slip-power control

These methods are now described one after other.

3.13.1. Pole Changing Techniques

A change in the number of poles changes the synchronous speed N_s and therefore the induction motor speed. The number of stator can be altered by the use of *(i)* multiple stator winding *(ii)* consequent pole technique and *(iii)* pole-amplitude modulation.

The method of speed control by pole-changing is usually restricted to squirrel-cage induction motors (SCIMs). It is due to the fact that the number of rotor poles in SCIMs automatically adjusts to the number of stator poles.

Multiple Stator Winding : In this method, stator has two separate windings. Each winding is wound for different number of poles. For example, a motor may have one 3-phase winding for 4 pole and the second 3-phase winding for 6 poles. For 50 Hz supply and a slip of 3%, 4-pole winding motor would operate at a speed of $\frac{120 \times 50}{4}(1 - 0.03) = 1455$ rpm. However, 6-pole winding would result in an operating speed of $\frac{120 \times 50}{6}(1 - 0.03) = 970$ rpm. In this manner, two different operating speeds can be obtained.

Only one winding is energised at a time. The idle winding is kept open-circuited so as to avoid the flow of circulating current and its heating.

Consequent Pole Technique : In this method, only one stator winding is used to give stator poles in the ratio 2 : 1.

Fig. 3.21 *(a)* shows a single-layer winding for one phase of a 3-phase stator winding. It consists of two coils I and II. Coil I has two terminals marked *a*, *b* and coil II terminals are *c*, *d*. If terminals *b*, *d* are connected together, Fig. 3.21 (*b*), two coils become in series and two poles, Fig. 3.21 (*a*), are produced giving a synchronous speed of 3000 rpm for a 50 Hz system. Figure on the right side of Fig.

3.21 (*a*) indicates current directions by crosses and dots in coils I and II. These two coils create two poles as shown in Fig. 3.21 (*a*). If terminal *a* is connected to *d* and *b* to *c*, coils I and II get connected in parallel as shown in Fig. 3.21 (*c*) and again two poles are created as shown in Fig. 3.21 (*a*).

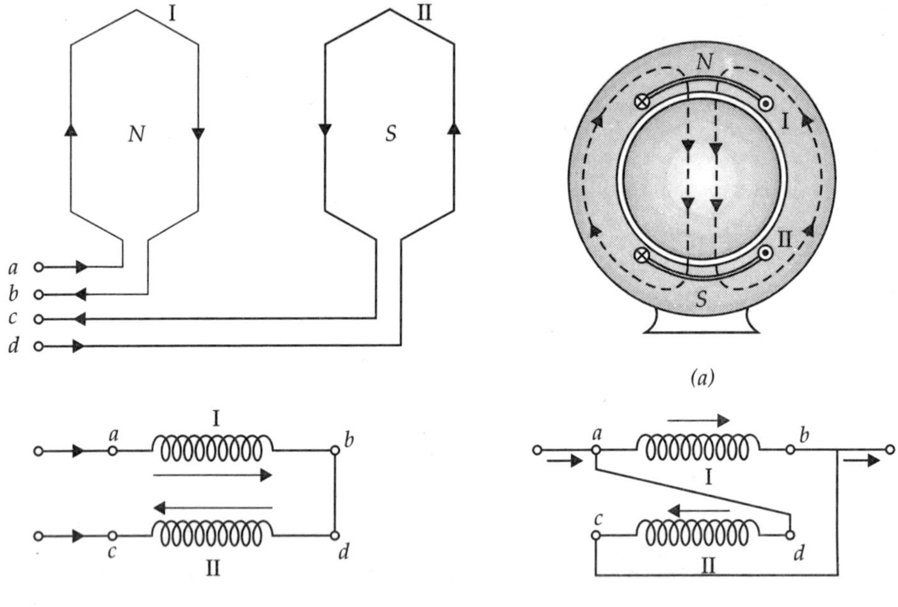

(*b*) Series : 2 poles (*c*) Parallel : 2 poles

Fig 3.21: High speed, production of two poles.

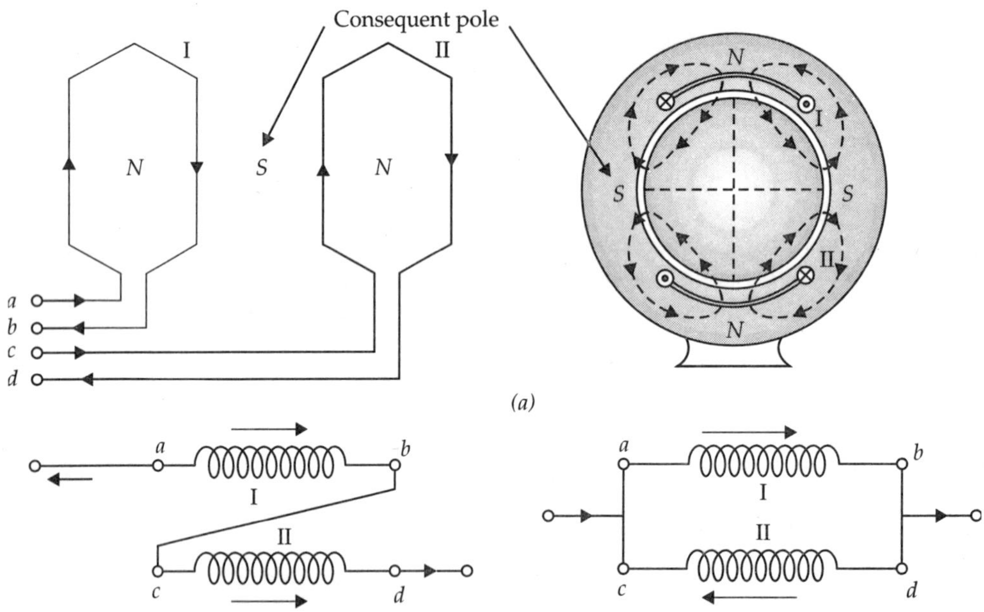

(*b*) Series: 4 poles (*c*) Parallel: 4 poles

Fig 3.22: Low speed, production of four poles.

If the direction of current in coil II is reversed as shown in Fig. 3.22 (*a*), two north poles are produced on stator. Magnetic flux from these two north poles must complete their magnetic circuit. In doing so, two south poles are automatically created in the interpolar space shown in the right side of Fig. 3.22 (*a*). These two induced poles are called **consequent poles**. This four pole connection of Fig. 3.22 *(a)* gives low speed operation at 1500 rpm.

As before, terminals *b, c* can be connected together, Fig. 3.22 *(b)*, giving series connection of coils I and II. Also, terminals *a* to *c* and *b* to *d* can be connected giving parallel connection of coils I and II as shown in Fig. 3.22 *(c)*.

The above basic principle can be extended to all the three phases of an induction motor. The connections amongst the three phases may be in delta or in star. Further, the coils may be connected in series or in parallel. With star or delta connections and series or parallel combination of coils, speed changes with constant torque, constant power or variable torque can be obtained.

Pole Amplitude Modulation (PMI) Technique : Pole amplitude modulation technique is a flexible method of pole changing. It can be used in applications where speed ratios other than 2 : 1 are required.

In its simplest form, pole amplitude modulation technique can be explained as follows.

In a 3-phase induction motor, when 3-phase balanced currents are applied to 3-phase winding, three-phase mmfs sinusoidally distributed along air-gap periphery are produced. These three mmfs can be written as

$$\left.\begin{aligned} \text{for phase } A: F_a &= F_{ma} \sin \frac{P}{2}\theta \\ \text{for phase } B: F_b &= F_{mb} \sin\left[\frac{P}{2}\theta - \frac{2\pi}{3}\right] \\ \text{for phase } C: F_c &= F_{mc} \sin\left[\frac{P}{2}\theta - \frac{4\pi}{3}\right] \end{aligned}\right\} \quad \text{...(3.41)}$$

where P is the number of poles and θ is the mechanical angle in radians. Note that for a balanced 3-phase system, $F_{ma} = F_{mb} = F_{mc}$.

Now three modulating mmf waves of amplitude F are applied to modulate the amplitudes F_{ma}, F_{mb}, F_{mc}. Three modulating mmf waves for phases A, B, C can be written as

$$\left.\begin{aligned} F_{ma} &= F \sin k\theta \\ F_{mb} &= F \sin(k\theta - \alpha) \\ F_{mc} &= F \sin(k\theta - 2\alpha) \end{aligned}\right\} \quad \text{...(3.42)}$$

where F is constant, k is any integer and $\alpha = \pm \dfrac{2\pi}{3}$

Substitution of Eq. (3.42) in Eq. (3.41) gives

$$\left.\begin{aligned} F_a &= F \sin\frac{P}{2}\theta \cdot \sin k\theta \\ F_b &= F \sin\left[\frac{P}{2}\theta - \frac{2\pi}{3}\right] \cdot \sin(k\theta - \alpha) \\ F_c &= F \sin\left[\frac{P}{2}\theta - \frac{4\pi}{3}\right] \cdot \sin(k\theta - 2\alpha) \end{aligned}\right\} \quad \text{...(3.43)}$$

But $\sin A \sin B = \dfrac{1}{2}[\cos(A - B) - \cos(A + B)]$. With its help, Eq. (3.43) can be written as

$$\left.\begin{aligned} F_a &= \frac{F}{2}\left[\cos\left(\frac{P}{2} - k\right)\theta - \cos\left(\frac{P}{2} + k\right)\theta\right] \\ F_b &= \frac{F}{2}\left[\cos\left\{\left(\frac{P}{2} - k\right)\theta - \frac{2\pi}{3} + \alpha\right\} - \cos\left\{\left(\frac{P}{2} + k\right)\theta - \frac{2\pi}{3} - \alpha\right\}\right] \\ F_c &= \frac{F}{2}\left[\cos\left\{\left(\frac{P}{2} - k\right)\theta - \frac{4\pi}{3} + 2\alpha\right\} - \cos\left\{\left(\frac{P}{2} + k\right)\theta - \frac{4\pi}{3} - 2\alpha\right\}\right] \end{aligned}\right\} \quad \text{...(3.44)}$$

Modulated mmf waves given by Eq. (3.44) shows that two sets of 3-phase mmfs producing $\left(\frac{P}{2}-k\right)$ and $\left(\frac{P}{2}+k\right)$ poles are produced. These two sets of poles develop torque in opposite directions. In order to obtain steady torque in one direction, it is necessary to suppress one of these pole numbers and retain the other pole number. There are two methods of connections to obtain the desired modulation.

First method : In first method, called **coil inversion method**, the second of each phase winding is reversed with respect to the first half. Fig. 3.23 shows the basic principle of this method. Mmf wave of stator wound for eight poles is shown in Fig. 3.23 *(a)*. For the sake of simplicity, the ideal sine wave is shown in the form of rectangles. The modulating wave having two poles is shown in Fig. 3.23 *(b)*. Multiplication of waveforms of Figs. 3.23 *(a)* and *(b)* gives the required modulated wave of Fig. 3.23 *(c)*. It is seen that negative half, marked-1, of modulating wave reverses the polarities of main poles 5, 6, 7 and 8 of Fig. 3.23 *(a)*. The reversed poles are shown dotted in Fig. 3.23 *(c)*. The extreme right *N* pole combines with extreme left *N* pole numbered 1 to produce resultant one *N* pole. The resultant modulated wave, therefore, has six poles, with encircled numbers 1 to 6 as illustrated in Fig. 3.23 *(c)*.

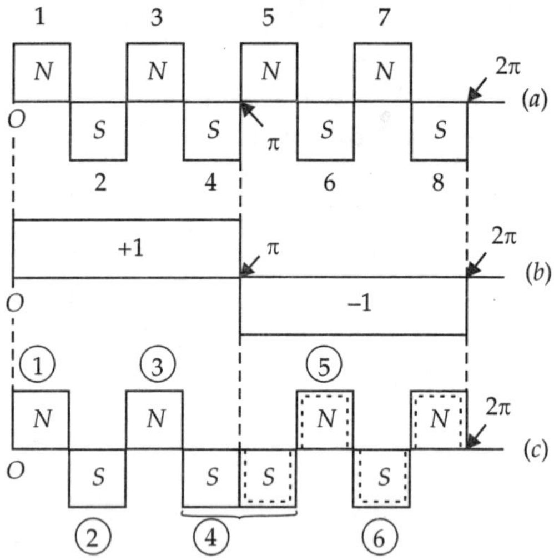

Fig 3.23: Coil inversion method *(a)* stator mmf main wave *(b)* modulating wave and *(c)* six-pole modulated wave.

Second method : In this method, called **coil inversion and omission method**, a section from each half of main winding is omitted. The second half of the winding is then reversed with respect to the first half. In Fig. 3.24 *(a)*, stator mmf wave for 8 poles is shown. In the modulating wave of Fig. 3.24 *(b)*, fourth and eighth coils are omitted. Multiplication of the waveforms of Figs. 3.24 *(a)* and *(b)* gives the required modulated wave of Fig. 3.24 *(c)*. In this figure, fifth, sixth and seventh coils are reversed with respect to first three coils one, two and three. There are thus six poles in the modulated wave of Fig. 3.24 *(c)*.

It is seen from above that a three-phase induction motor described here can run with original unmodulated 8 poles or with modulated six poles.

Motor performance with pole amplitude modulation is found to be much superior to double-winding motor. Pole amplitude modulation technique is used for fans, pumps and blowers.

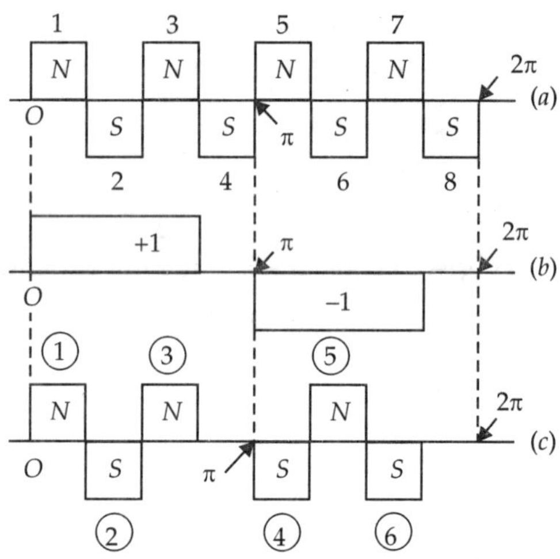

Fig 3.24: Coil inversion and omission method *(a)* stator mmf main wave *(b)* modulating wave and *(c)* six-pole modulated wave.

3.13.2. Stator Voltage Control

The speed of a 3-phase induction motor can be controlled by varying its supply voltage. Eq. (3.21) shows that torque developed in a 3-phase induction motor is proportional to square of the supply voltage. Eq. (3.23) shows that the slip at which maximum torque occurs does not depend on supply voltage. Also, note that variation of the supply voltage does not alter the motor synchronous speed. Based on these facts, the torque-speed characteristics of a 3-phase induction motor are drawn in Fig. 3.25 *(a)* for rated voltage V_1 and $V_1/2$. In this figure, torque-speed characteristic T_L for a fan-type load is also drawn. The intersection of motor and load torque curves gives the two operating speeds n_1 for voltage V_1 and n_2 for voltage $V_1/2$. This method of speed control is not so important because of the following disadvantages :

(i) Magnetic saturation does not allow speed control above rated speed,

(ii) Range of speed control is limited,

(iii) Low operating efficiency and

(iv) Poor speed regulation with change in load.

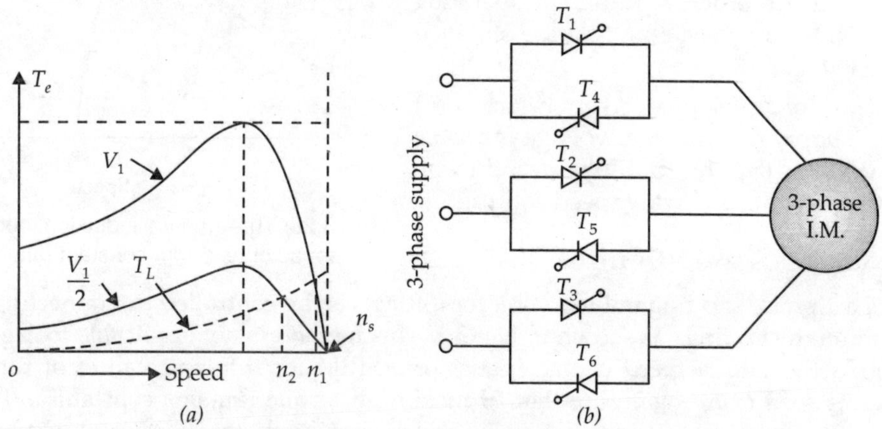

Fig 3.25: *(a)* Torque-speed characteristics under stator voltage control and *(b)* 3-phase ac voltage controller feeding a 3-phase induction motor.

For stator voltage control, a 3-phase ac voltage controller is usually employed. Fig. 3.25 *(b)* shows this controller feeding a 3-phase induction motor. By controlling the firing angle of thyristors connected in antiparallel in each phase, the rms value of stator voltage is regulated. As a consequence, the motor torque and speed are controlled.

3.13.3. Stator Frequency Control

In a 3-phase induction motor synchronous speed is given by $n_s = \frac{2f_1}{P}$ rps. Thus, synchronous speed and therefore motor speed can be controlled by varying the supply frequency f_1.

In a 3-phase induction motor, if stator leakage impedance drop is neglected, then from Eq. (3.7), $V_1 = E_1 = \sqrt{2} \cdot \pi f_1 \cdot \phi\, k_{w1} \cdot N_1$.

In case supply frequency f_1 is decreased by keeping V_1 constant, the speed is controlled, but air-gap flux ϕ increases, this causes magnetic saturation. This saturation further results in more losses, more motor heating and therefore poor motor efficiency. In view of this, air-gap flux should be kept constant by varying together both stator voltage V_1 and stator frequency f_1 so as to maintain ratio (V_1/f_1) constant. This type of motor control is known as **volts/hertz control**. From Eq. (3.24), maximum torque is

$$T_{em} = \frac{3}{\omega_s} \times \frac{V_1^2}{2\left[r_1^2 + \sqrt{r_1^2 + X^2}\right]} \text{ Nm} \qquad ...(3.24)$$

where $X = x_1 + x_2$

If stator resistance r_1 is neglected, then

$$T_{em} = \frac{3}{\omega_s} \cdot \frac{V_1^2}{2(x_1 + x_2)} \text{ Nm} \quad ...(3.45)$$

Since $\omega_s \propto f_1$ and $(x_1 + x_2) \propto f_1$, Eq. (3.45) can be written as

$$T_{em} \propto \left[\frac{V_1}{f_1}\right]^2$$

This shows that if ratio (V_1/F_1) is kept constant during the speed control of a 3-phase induction motor, maximum torque remains constant as shown in Fig. 3.26. For load torque T_L, different operating speeds n_1, n_2, n_3 for frequencies f_1, f_2, f_3 are obtained as illustrated in Fig. 3.26.

At present, voltage source inverters are most popular for supplying variable voltage variable frequency (*VVVF*) supply to 3-phase induction motors for their smooth and wide speed control.

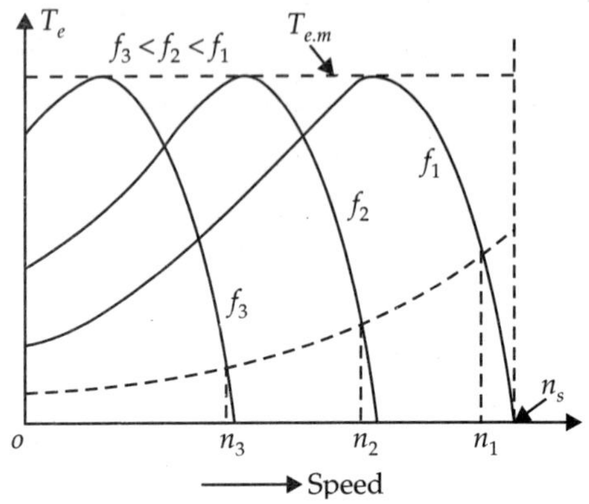

Fig 3.26: Three-phase induction motor torque-speed curves with constant ratio (V_1/f_1).

3.13.4. Rotor Resistance Control

The speed of a 3-phase slip ring induction motor (SRIM) can be controlled by connecting external resistances through slip rings as shown in Fig. 3.3. This method is not applicable to cage motors. Fig. 3.13 shows the torque-speed characteristics of a SRIM for different values of rotor circuit resistances. It is seen from this figure that *(i)* maximum torque remains constant and does not depend on rotor circuit resistance *(ii)* slip at which maximum torque occurs, increases with rotor circuit resistance *(iii)* starting torque increases with an increase in rotor circuit resistance *(iv)* synchronous speed remains the same and *(v)* speeds below rated can only be obtained.

The disadvantages of this method are *(i)* speeds below synchronous speed can only be obtained *(ii)* reduced efficiency at low operating speeds due to rotor circuit resistance and *(iii)* speed regulating is very poor.

This method of speed control is used when drop in speed is required for a short time. Examples of this type of load are overhead cranes, load equalization etc.

3.13.5. Rotor Slip Power Control

It is described that speed of a 3-phase SRIM can be controlled below synchronous speed by inserting external resistances is the rotor circuit. In this type of speed control, the slip power in the rotor circuit is wasted I^2R (= sPg) loss, thus reducing the efficiency of the drive. Instead of wasting this slip power in the rotor circuit, it can be recovered and fed back to the ac source for the motor speed control.

For the speed control of SRIM, slip power can be utilized in the cascade connection of two induction motors or by the rotor voltage injection technique. The most useful method of recovering the slip power is the rotor voltage injection technique and it is briefly discussed here.

Voltage Injection in Rotor Circuit : The voltage injection in the rotor circuit must be at slip frequency at all the rotor speeds.

If the injected emf in the rotor circuit is against the direction of rotor induced emf, net voltage in the rotor circuit gets reduced. As a consequence, rotor current decreases, motor torque ($\propto$ constant flux $\times$ rotor current I_2) decreases and therefore motor speed decreases. The motor now runs at subsynchronous speed below the rated speed. When the injected emf is additive to the rotor induced emf, the net voltage in the rotor circuit rises, rotor current increases, motor torque rises and therefore motor speed increases. Now the motor runs at more than the rated speed. If additive voltage is more, the motor may run at supersynchronous speed.

There are many techniques of injecting the control voltage at slip frequency into the rotor circuit. But here only one popular scheme will be described.

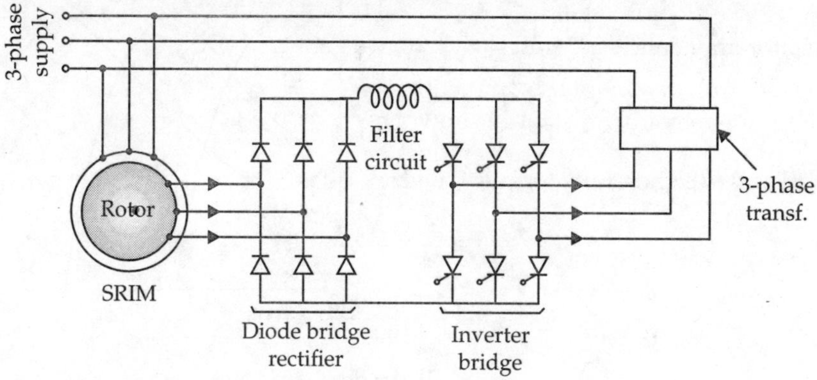

Fig 3.27: Static Kramer drive for the speed control of a 3-phase SRIM.

Static Kramer Drive : Fig 3.27 shows a static Kramer drive. It consists of a 3-phase SRIM, a rectifier diode bridge, a filter, an inverter bridge and a 3-phase transformer.

In this scheme of speed control, slip power is recovered from the rotor circuit of SRIM and fed to diode bridge rectifier. It converts slip frequency emf to dc. This dc is smoothed by a filter circuit and fed to dc terminals of the inverter bridge. This inverter converts dc power into ac power at line frequency. Inverter ac output power is fed back to ac source through a 3-phase transformer. Since the power flow through the rectifier is unidirectional, this scheme of Fig. 3.27 offers speed control of SRIM below synchronous speed only.

Example 3.13. *A 3-phase, 400 V, 6-pole, 50 Hz squirrel cage induction motor develops full load torque at 970 rpm. Neglect no-load current and rotational losses. In case supply voltage is reduced to 350 V with load torque remaining constant, calculate the motor speed.*

Solution. Synchronous speed, $N_s = \dfrac{120 \times 50}{6} = 1000$ rpm

Full load slip, $s_1 = \dfrac{1000 - 970}{6} = 0.03.$

From Eq. (3.22), the motor torque is $T_e \propto k\, V_1^2 s_1$

$\therefore$ $T_{e1} = T_L \propto k\,(400)^2 \times 0.03$

and $T_{e2} = T_L \propto k\,(350)^2 \times s_2$

From above, $\dfrac{T_{e1}}{T_{e2}} = 1 = \dfrac{(400)^2 \times 0.03}{(350)^2 \times s_2}$

$\therefore$ New slip, $s_2 = \left(\dfrac{400}{350}\right)^2 \times 0.03 = 0.0392$

$\therefore$ Motor speed at reduced voltage of 350 V is given by

$$\frac{120 f_1}{P}(1 - s_2) = \frac{120 \times 50}{6}[1 - 0.0392] = 960.8 \text{ rpm.}$$

Example 3.14 *A 6-pole, 50 Hz, slip ring induction motor has full load speed of 960 rpm. Its rotor impedance is 0.25 + j 0.00 Ω per phase. If the speed is to be reduced to 800 rpm at full load torque, calculate the additional resistance per phase to be inserted in the rotor circuit. Neglect stator impedance.*

Solution. For a 3-phase induction motor, developed torque, from Eq. (3.21), is

$$T_e = \frac{3}{\omega_s} \cdot \frac{V_1^2}{\left(r_1 + \frac{r_2}{s}\right)^2 + (x_1 + x_2)^2} \cdot \frac{r_2}{s}$$

Neglecting stator impedance, *i.e.* with $r_1 = x_1 = 0$, we get

$$T_e = \frac{3}{\omega_s} \frac{V_1^2}{\left(\frac{r_2}{s}\right)^2 + x_2^2} \times \frac{r_2}{s}$$

In this example, $x_2 = 0$. Therefore, torque T_e with $x_2 = 0$ is

$$T_e = \frac{3}{\omega_s} \cdot \frac{V_1^2 s}{r_2}$$

Here slip, $$s_1 = \frac{1000 - 960}{1000} = 0.04$$

For speed 800 rpm, $$\text{slip } s_2 = \frac{1000 - 800}{1000} = 0.2$$

For constant full load torque,

$$T_{e1} = T_L = \frac{3}{\omega_s} \cdot \frac{V_1^2 \times 0.04}{0.25}$$

Also $$T_{e2} = T_L = \frac{3}{\omega_s} \times \frac{V_1^2 \times 0.2}{R_2}$$

From above, $$1 = \frac{V_1^2 \times 0.04}{0.25} \times \frac{R_2}{V_1^2 \times 0.2} = \frac{R_2 \times 0.04}{0.25 \times 0.2}$$

∴ $$R_2 = \frac{0.25 \times 0.2}{0.04} = 1.25\ \Omega$$

∴ External or additional resistance to be inserted in the rotor circuit

$$= R_2 - r_2 = 1.25 - 0.25 = \mathbf{1.00\ \Omega}$$

3.14. ELECTRIC BRAKING OF INDUCTION MOTORS

In modern electric drives, sometimes it becomes necessary to stop an induction motor and its coupled load quickly. At times, quick reversal of direction of rotation is also needed in industry. Quick braking and rapid reversal of induction motors often lead to *(i)* better quality product and *(ii)* enhanced output of industry. An induction motor is said to be operating in electric braking mode if the direction of rotation and direction of developed torque are opposing each other.

A motor, during electric braking conditions, operates under severe duty cycle. Therefore, electric braking is employed only when it is highly desirable to control braking time, deceleration etc. There are three methods of electric braking. These are *(i)* regenerative braking *(ii)* plugging or counter-current braking and *(iii)* dynamic braking. During electric braking, operating characteristics of motor depend upon the method of braking employed.

3.14.1. Regenerative Braking

Regenerative braking takes place when the load forces the motor to run above synchronous speed.

When the rotor speed, as when lowering of load in a crane or a hoist, becomes more than rotating field speed, the slip becomes negative. A negative slip means that the induction machine now operates as an induction generator in the second quadrant as shown in Fig. 3.28 and returns power to the supply line. The power delivered to the supply is given by the product of regenerative braking torque and the corresponding rotor speed. When rotor speed falls to synchronous speed, the regenerative braking comes to an end.

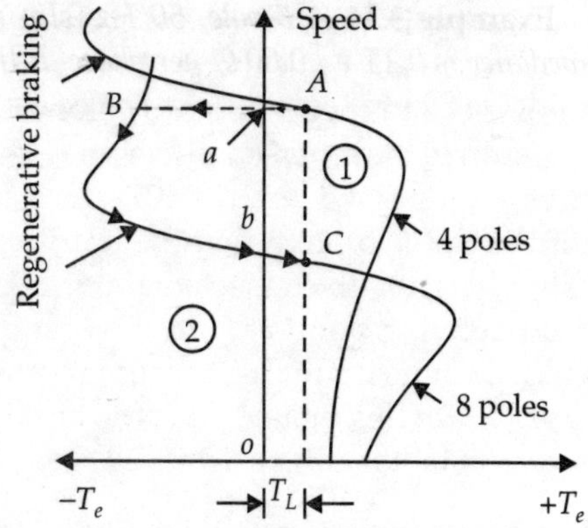

Fig 3.28: Regenerative braking of 3-phase induction motor.

Regenerative braking range can be increased if the motor has pole-changing winding. For example, in Fig. 3.28, A is the operating point for 4 pole operation for a load torque T_L. When the number of poles is suddenly increased to 8 poles, the operating point shifts from *A* to *B* and regenerative braking occurs, because now slip = $\frac{ob - oa}{ob}$ becomes negative. The operating point *B* travels to the new operating *C* along the arrows as indicated in Fig. 3.28. The regenerative braking ceases when the new synchronous speed *ob*, corresponding to 8 poles, is reached. This technique is useful only in squirrel cage motors, because in wound-rotor induction motors, the poles on stator and rotor must be changed simultaneously.

3.14.2. Plugging

Plugging, or counter-current braking, involves interchanging supply leads of any two stator terminals. At the time of interchanging, direction of rotating magnetic field gets reversed with rotor still rotating in the initial direction. Thus, electromagnetic torque is developed opposite to the direction of rotation. This braking torque brings the rotor to stop quickly. The supply terminals should be disconnected when the motor speed becomes near to zero. Otherwise, the motor would start to rotate in the opposite direction.

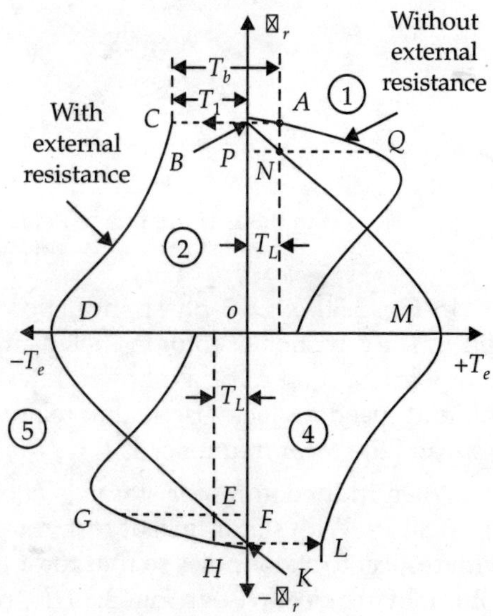

Fig 3.29: Speed-torque characteristics during plugging of SRIM.

During plugging period, the rotor induced emf becomes very high because now the slip is high $(2 - s)$. This results in very high currents in the rotor. Consequently, current drawn from the supply mains is quite large. In SRIM, in order to limit such high currents, external resistances are inserted in the rotor circuit during plugging.

The operation of a slip ring induction motor during plugging, with external resistance inserted in the rotor circuit for limiting the line current is illustrated in Fig. 3.29. Initially, for load torque T_L, operating point is A with rotor speed equal to *oB*, with no external resistance in the rotor circuit. When two supply leads are interchanged and at the same time an external resistance is inserted in the rotor circuit, the operating point *A* shifts to point C in the second quadrant so that now initial braking torque is T_b = load torque T_L + backward torque T_1. Braking action now takes place along the curve *CD*. Just before point *D*, supply should be disconnected to stop the motor at *D*. In case the supply is not switched off, the motor starts accelerating in the reversed direction along the curve *DE*. Here *E* is the final operating point in the third quadrant. If the external rotor circuit resistance is now removed, point *E* shifts at once to point *G* and then to point *H* along the curve *GH*. Point *H* corresponds to the induction motor operation in the reversed direction with rotor speed $OK = OB$ and load torque T_L. If any two supply wires are reversed again with simultaneous insertion of external resistance in the rotor circuit, point *H* shifts to point *L* in the fourth quadrant and then the motor operates along the curve *LM*. If supply is not disconnected at point *M*, the motor operation continues along the curve *MN*, with final operating point at *N* in the first quadrant. The motor speed is now equal to *OP*. If now the external rotor circuit resistance is removed, point *N* shifts to point *Q* and then to point *A* along the curve *QA*. In this manner, electric braking by plugging and the four-quadrant operation of 3-phase induction motor can be achieved.

3.14.3. Dynamic Braking

Dynamic braking of a 3-phase induction motor is achieved if its stator winding, after being disconnected from three-phase supply, is switched on to a dc source. Under normal operating conditions, the stator field moves faster than the rotor conductors by slip speed sn_s.

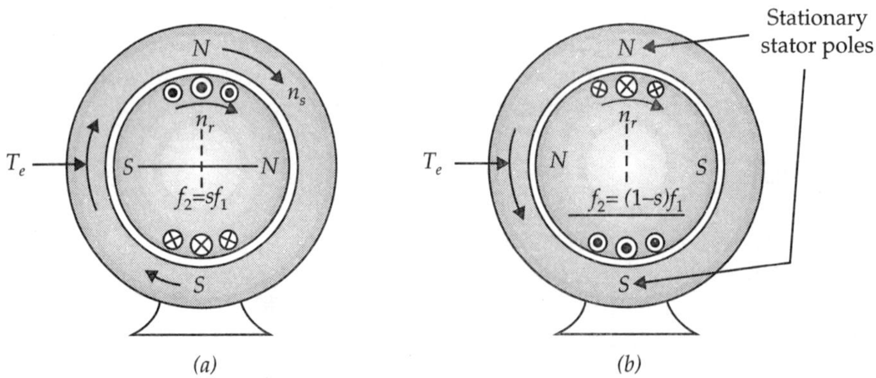

Fig 3.30: Three-phase induction motor under *(a)* normal motor operation and *(b)* dynamic braking condition.

In Fig. 3.30 *(a)*, a 3-phase induction motor is shown running under normal conditions with slip *s*. The direction of rotor inducted emf is indicated by dots and crosses. Roots current produces two poles N, S on rotor as shown. Interaction between stator and rotor poles causes the rotor to rotate at speed n_r clockwise so that relative speed between stator field and rotor structure is $(n_s - n_r) = sn_s$ and the rotor frequency is $f_2 = s\,f_1$.

When induction motor stator is energised with dc, stator field becomes stationary in space, Fig. 3.30 *(b)*. With stator field at rest, rotor now moves clockwise at a relative speed of $n_r = n_s\,(1 - s)$ with respect to stator poles so that rotor frequency is $f_2 = (1 - s)\,f_1 = s\,f_1$. With stator poles at rest and rotor moving clockwise in Fig. 3.30 *(b)*, right hand rule gives the direction of emf induced in rotor conductors. This induced emf and current is indicated by crosses under *N* pole and dots under *S* pole. Rotor induced current creates two poles *N*, *S* on the rotor. Interaction between stator and rotor poles produce anticlockwise torque which is called **dynamic braking torque**.

The direct current supply, for applying to the stator for dynamic braking, can be obtained from a separate dc source as shown in Fig. 3.31 *(a)*. DC supply can also be obtained from the same ac source through a transformer rectifier unit as illustrated in Fig. 3.31 *(b)*. A series resistor R_1 helps to limit the stator current. For a slip ring induction motor, additional resistance is inserted in the rotor circuit so as to obtain higher dynamic braking torque.

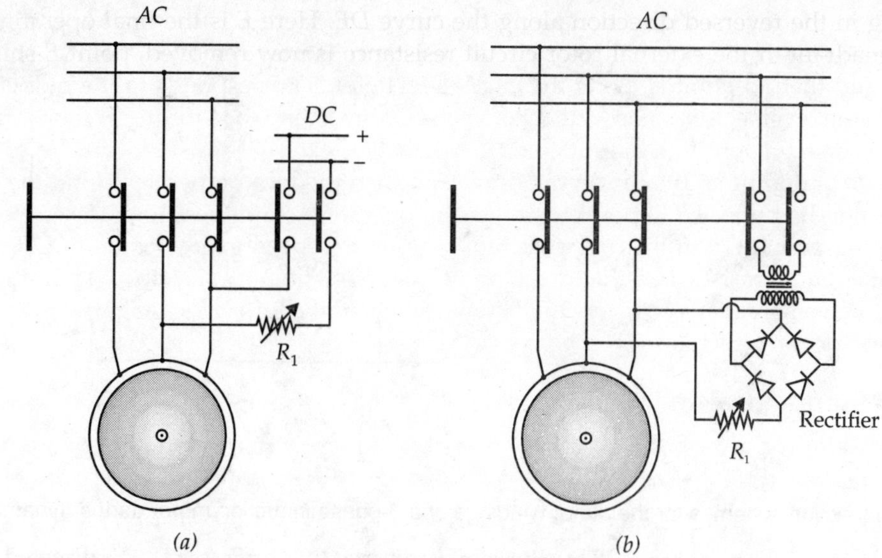

Fig 3.31: D.C. dynamic braking of 3-phase induction motors.

It is already stated above that under normal running, rotor frequency is $s\,f_1$ and at the instant dynamic braking is applied, the rotor frequency becomes $(1-s)\,f_1 = Sf_1$. This shows that induction motor performance during dynamic braking can be obtained by using the induction motor equivalent circuit merely by replacing s by $(1-s) = S$. Further, since dc is given to stator, its leakage reactance x_1 is of no interest except during transients. The stator resistance is required only to know the dc excitation voltage for a given value of stator current. There is no stator iron loss and the rotor iron loss merely increases the rotor circuit resistance. Keeping these facts in mind, the equivalent circuit of Fig. 3.10 *(a)* for a polyphase induction motor can be drawn as shown in Fig. 3.32 *(a)* for the dynamic braking analysis of a 3-phase induction motor. This equivalent circuit, modified by dividing throughout by $S\ (= 1 - s)$ is as shown in Fig. 3.32 *(b)*.

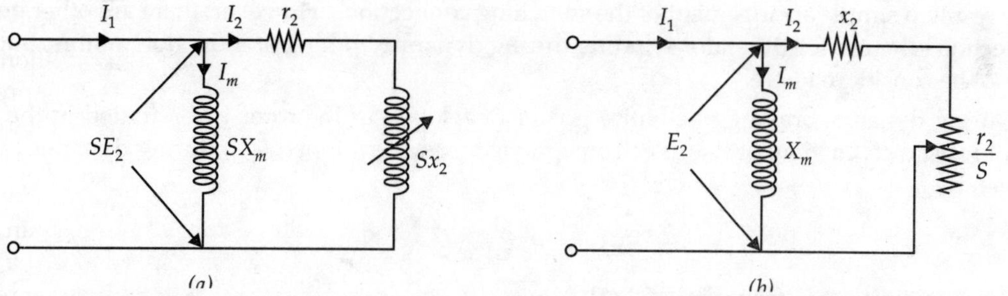

Fig 3.32: Equivalent circuits during dynamic braking of a polyphase induction motor.

Stator winding under dynamic braking conditions carries dc. But for analysis purposes, it may be assumed that stator carries alternating current I_1 which produces the same magnitude of mmf as produced by direct current I_{dc}. The relation between I_1 and I_{dc} depends upon the stator-winding connections during the dynamic braking. The mmf produced by a 3-phase stator winding, carrying an alternating current I_1 rms is given by $\frac{3}{2}(\sqrt{2}\ I_1)\ N_1$. Here N_1 is the effective stator series turns per phase.

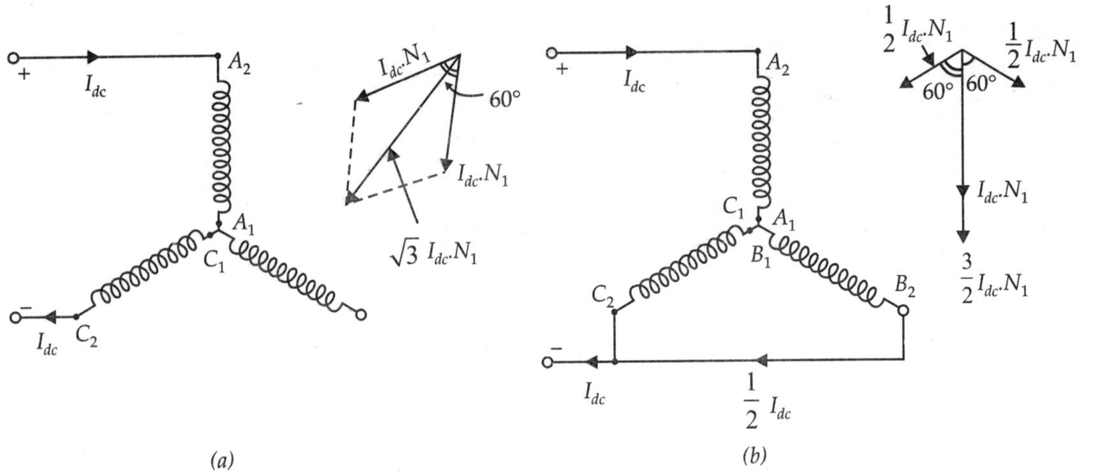

Fig 3.33: Connection schemes for the stator windings of a 3-phase induction motor during dynamic braking.

For stator connections of Fig. 3.33 *(a)*, the mmf produced by phase A is $I_{dc} \cdot N_1$ directed vertically downward as shown in the figure. Mmf produced by phase *C* is $I_{dc} \cdot N_1$ but it is displaced by 60° from phase *A* mmf as depicted in Fig. 3.33 *(a)*. Resultant mmf due to phases A and C is seen to be $\sqrt{3}\ I_{dc} \cdot N_1$. Therefore, for stator winding connections of Fig. 3.33 *(a)*, the equivalent stator current I_1, producing the same mmf as developed by I_{dc} is given by the relation,

$$\frac{3}{2}\ (\sqrt{2}\ I_1)\ N_1 = \sqrt{3}\ I_{dc} \cdot N_1 \text{ or } I_1 = \sqrt{\frac{2}{3}} \cdot I_{dc} \qquad \text{...(3.46)}$$

An examination of Fig. 3.33 *(b)* shows that $\frac{3}{2}(\sqrt{2}\ I_1)\ N_1 = \frac{3}{2}\ I_{dc} \cdot N_1$

or

$$I_1 = \frac{1}{\sqrt{2}} \cdot I_{dc} \qquad \text{...(3.47)}$$

Two connection schemes shown in Fig. 3.33 are more common in drive systems, mainly because these result in simple arrangement of the switching connections. However, there are other possible connection schemes for the stator winding during dynamic braking of induction motors, but these will not be considered here.

During dynamic braking, the entire power developed in the rotor is dissipated in the rotor-circuit resistance. In view of this, electromagnetic torque developed (T_{ed}) during dynamic braking is given by

$$T_{ed} = \frac{3}{\omega_s} \cdot I_2^2\ \frac{r_2}{S} \text{ Nm}$$

But I_2 in terms of I_1, from Fig. 3.32 *(b)*, is

$$\bar{I}_2 = \bar{I}_1\ \frac{jX_m}{\frac{r_2}{S} + j(X_m + x_2)^2} \qquad \text{...(3.48)}$$

$$\therefore \quad T_{ed} = \frac{3}{\omega_s} \cdot \frac{I_1^2 \cdot X_m^2}{\left(\frac{r_2}{S}\right)^2 + (X_m + x_2)^2} \cdot \frac{r_2}{S} \qquad \text{...(3.49)}$$

As in a polyphase induction motor, the dynamic braking torque is maximum when power delivered to $\frac{r_2}{S}$ is maximum in Fig. 3.32 *(b)*.

$$\therefore \qquad \frac{r_2}{S_{mT}} = (x_2 + X_m)$$

Thus, the slip at which maximum dynamic braking torque occurs is given by

$$S_{mT} = \frac{r_2}{(x_2 + X_m)} \qquad ...(3.50)$$

Note here that $S = 1 - s$ and likewise $S_{mT} = 1 - s_{mT}$.

In order to obtain the magnitude of maximum braking torque, substitute the value of $\frac{r_2}{S_{mT}}$ in Eq. (3.49)

$$\therefore \qquad T_{ed \cdot m} = \frac{3}{\omega_s} \cdot \frac{I_1^2 X_m^2}{(X_m + x_2)^2 + (X_m + x_2)^2} \times (X_m + x_2)$$

$$= \frac{3}{\omega_s} \cdot \frac{I_1^2 X_m^2}{2(X_m + x_2)} \qquad ...(3.51)$$

Dynamic braking of induction motors gives smooth stop, results in less rotor-circuit loss and has no tendency to reverse. This method is, however, less quick than plugging.

Example 3.15. *A 3-phase, 400 V, 50 Hz, 6-pole, star-connected induction motor has the following parameters:*

$r_1 + jx_1 = 0.2 + j\,0.6\ \Omega$, $r_2 + jx_2 = 0.3 + j\,1.0\ \Omega$ (referred to stator), full load slip = 0.04. No-load current is assumed negligible.

(a) Determine the initial braking torque soon after plugging.

(b) Determine the initial braking torque if dc is fed to one stator phase in series with the other two in parallel. Find the magnitude of dc excitation also.

Solution. Per-phase voltage $= \frac{400}{\sqrt{3}} = 230.95$ V

Synchronous speed, $\omega_s = \frac{4\pi f_1}{P} = \frac{4\pi \times 50}{6} = \frac{100\pi}{3}$ rad/sec.

Here no-load current is neglected. Therefore, rotor current from Fig. 3.10 *(a)* is

$$I_2 = \frac{V_1}{\sqrt{\left(r_1 + \frac{r_2}{s}\right)^2 + (x_1 + x_2)^2}}$$

$\therefore$ Full-load torque, with $s_{fl} = 0.04$ is

$$T_{efl} = \frac{3}{\omega_s} \cdot I_2^2 \frac{r_2}{s_{fl}} = \frac{3}{\omega_s} \cdot \frac{V_1^2}{\left(r_1 + \frac{r_2}{s_{fl}}\right)^2 + (x_1 + x_2)^2} \cdot \frac{r_2}{s_{fl}}$$

$$= \frac{3 \times 3}{100\pi} \times \frac{230.95^2}{\left[0.2 + \frac{0.3}{0.04}\right]^2 + 1.6^2} \times \frac{0.3}{0.04} = 185.29 \text{ Nm}$$

(a) When plugging is carried out, slip becomes $2 - s = 2 - 0.04 = 1.96$.

$\therefore$ Plugging torque is

$$T_1 = \frac{3 \times 3}{100\pi} \times \frac{230.95^2}{\left[0.2 + \frac{0.3}{1.96}\right]^2 + 1.6^2} \times \frac{0.3}{1.96} = 87.12 \text{ Nm}$$

$\therefore$ Total initial plugging torque $= T_1 + T_{efl} = 87.12 + 185.29 =$ **272.41** Nm

(b) The induction motor equivalent circuit corresponding to full-load slip 0.04 and that during dynamic braking at rated speed with slip 1.96 are given in Figs. 3.34 *(a)* and *(b)* respectively.

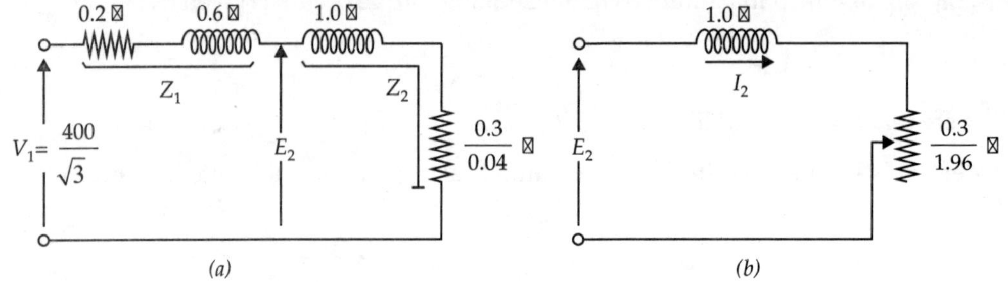

Fig 3.34: Induction motor equivalent circuit under *(a)* normal running with slip 0.04 and *(b)* dynamic braking with slip 1.96.

From Fig. 3.34 *(a)*, $$E_2 = \frac{V_1}{z_1 + z_2} \times z_2$$

Here $z_1 + z_2 = 0.2 + j\,0.6 + \frac{0.3}{0.04} + j\,1.0 = (7.7 + j\,1.6)\ \Omega$

$$\therefore \quad E_2 = \frac{7.5 + j1}{7.7 + j1.6} \times \frac{400}{\sqrt{3}} = \sqrt{\frac{7.5^2 + 1^2}{7.7^2 + 1.6^2}} \times 230.95 = 222.2 \text{ V}$$

From Fig. 3.34 *(b)*, rotor current is

$$I_2 = \frac{E_2}{\sqrt{\left[\frac{r_2}{S}\right]^2 + x_2^2}} = \frac{222.2}{\sqrt{\left[\frac{0.3}{0.96}\right]^2 + 1^2}} = 212.085 \text{ A}$$

$\therefore$ Dynamic braking torque, $$T_{ed} = \frac{3}{\omega_s} \times I_2^2 \cdot \frac{r_2}{S}$$

$$= \frac{3 \times 3}{100\pi}(212.085)^2 \times \frac{0.3}{0.96} = 402.68 \text{ Nm}$$

$\therefore$ Total initial dynamic braking torque = $T_{ed} + T_{e \cdot fl} = 402.68 + 185.29 =$ **587.97** Nm

With one stator phase in series with other two in parallel, the dc excitation current, from Eq. (3.47), is given by $I_{dc} = \sqrt{2}\ I_1$. Here $I_1 = I_2$, because no-load current is neglected.

$\therefore$ DC excitation current, $$I_{dc} = \sqrt{2} \times I_2 = \sqrt{2} \times 212.085 = \mathbf{299.89\ A}$$

3.15. GENERATOR OPERATION

Here generator operation of a three-phase induction motor is described.

Fig. 3.35 shows the complete torque-speed characteristics of a 3-phase induction motor over its entire speed range. An induction motor, when connected to a three-phase supply, runs at a speed less than synchronous speed n_s. During motoring mode, it draws magnetizing current from the supply mains to set up the rotating magnetic field. If the rotor speed is raised above synchronous speed n_s by means of a prime-mover, then as per Eq. (3.2), slip becomes negative. Eq. (3.10) shows that now the air-gap power is negative. In other words, now the air-gap power flows from rotor to stator. Also, from Eq. (3.21), the torque becomes negative for negative slip, indicating that electrical torque opposes the prime-mover torque. This means that at supersynchronous speed, the power flows from rotor to stator, thus rotor absorbs power from the shaft or the prime-mover.

Consequently, the induction machine now works as an induction generator at supersynchronous speed and delivers energy to the supply mains. The output of induction generator depends on the magnitude of negative slip. In Fig. 3.35, point *B* indicates the maximum torque that a prime-mover can apply to induction generator. If prime-mover torque exceeds this maximum torque given by point *B*, induction generator would overspeed and at some value of negative slip, power generation would come to an end.

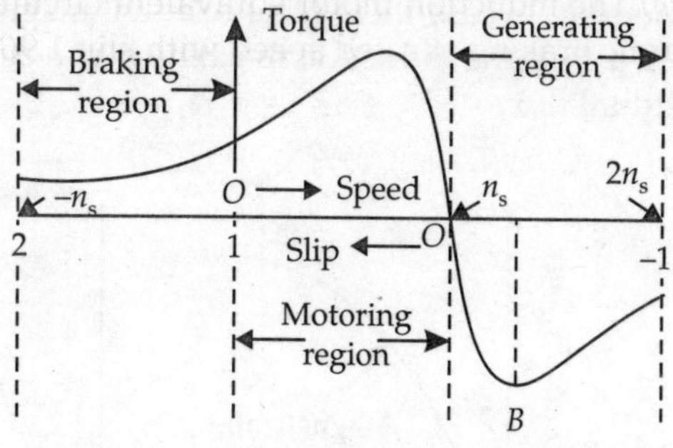

Fig 3.35: Torque-speed characteristics of a 3-phase induction motor showing braking, motoring and generating regions.

Rotating magnetic field in a 3-phase induction motor is set up by the magnetizing current drawn from the supply mains. This magnetizing current must be available even when the speed is made above synchronous speed. This shows that induction generator is not self-excited generator. Thus, induction generator cannot work in isolation, it must be operated in parallel with bus bar or synchronous generator which can supply its magnetizing current. Therefore, the supply system determines the voltage and frequency of the induction generator. Since the induction generator runs at supersynchronous speed, it is also called asynchronous generator.

The induction generator described above can be termed as **externally-excited induction generator**. It is because magnetizing reactive power needed to set up rotating field is taken from an external power supply network.

3.15.1. Self-excited Induction Generator

This type of generator does not require any external supply network. In the self-excited induction generator, a capacitor bank is connected across its stator terminals as shown in Fig. 3.36. The three-phase capacitor bank supplies the total lagging reactive power needed by both the induction generator and the load. In Fig. 3.36, reactive power output from capacitor bank $Q = Q_1$, reactive power needed by induction generator + Q_2, reactive power needed by the load.

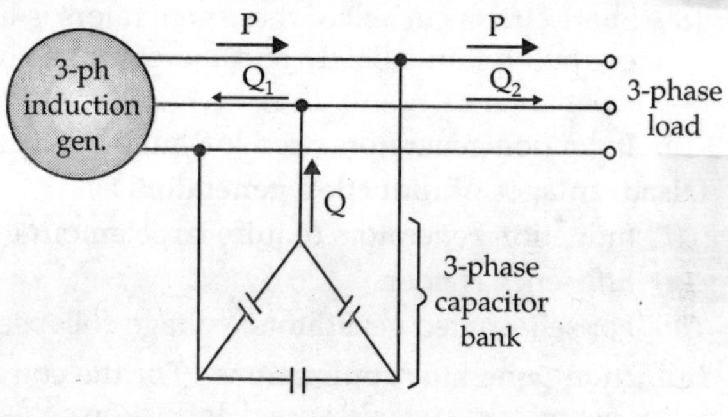

Fig 3.36: Three-phase capacitor bank connected across 3-phase induction motor.

Stator terminal voltage of induction generator depends upon its magnetization curve as shown in Fig. 3.37 *(a)*. The reactive current of a capacitor depends on the voltage across its terminals as shown in Fig. 3.37 *(b)*. This figure also shows two load lines of capacitor bank where $C_1 > C_2$. When 3-phase capacitor bank is connected across induction generator terminals, the no-load terminal voltage of generator is given by the point of intersection of generator magnetization curve and capacitor load lines as shown in Fig. 3.37 *(c)*. Here, for C_1 and C_2, the respective no-load voltages are V_1 and V_2 as indicated in the figure.

When the induction generator is driven, its residual magnetization generates a small terminal voltage which sends a current through capacitor. This capacitor current increases the generated voltage, which in turn increases the capacitor current. This cumulative process continues till the generated voltage builds up to the point of intersection of capacitor load line and the generator magnetization curve, see Fig. 3.37 *(c)*. This voltage build up is similar to that in a self-excited dc generator. In case there is no residual magnetism, the induction generator would not build up. In such a case, the induction machine is run as a 3-phase induction motor for some time to create the residual flux.

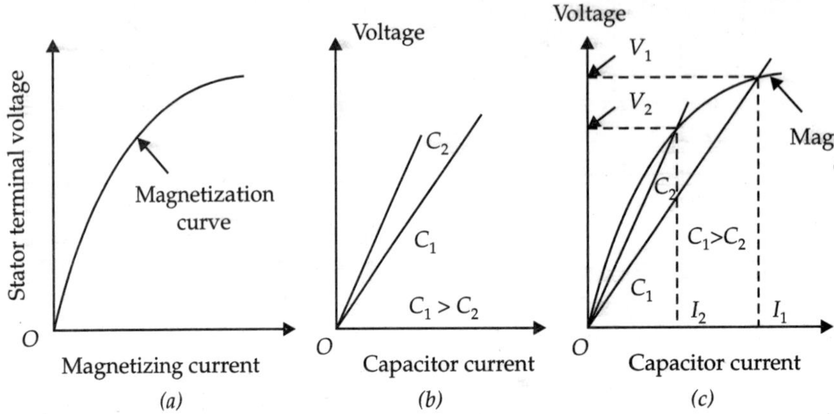

Fig 3.37: Characteristics of *(a)* induction generator alone *(b)* capacitor bank alone and *(c)* no-load voltages V_1, V_2 for C_1, C_2.

Advantages of induction generators :

(i) An ordinary cage induction motor, which is rugged and robust, can be made to run as induction generator.

(ii) These generators do not hunt.

(iii) It is small size per kW output.

(iv) Short-circuit current of these generators is limited. It is because a short circuit reduces the excitation immediately and therefore its short circuit current also gets reduced without delay.

(v) Induction generators need low maintenance.

Disadvantages of induction generators :

(i) Induction generators require large amount of reactive power.

(ii) Efficiency is poor.

(iii) For self-excited generators, voltage collapses very rapidly for power factor loads.

Induction generator applications : For the conversion of wind energy into electrical energy, induction generators are most suited. Induction generators are also used in unattended hydroplants and feed power to a large power distribution network.

3.16. DOUBLY-FED INDUCTION MACHINES

A doubly-fed induction machine (DFIM) is a slip-ring induction machine (SRIM) with its stator and rotor winding connected to separate ac sources at different voltages and frequencies. DFIM can be used as a motor for the speed control of large pumps. The object of this article is to discuss the basic principles of operation as a DFI motor and also as a DFI generator.

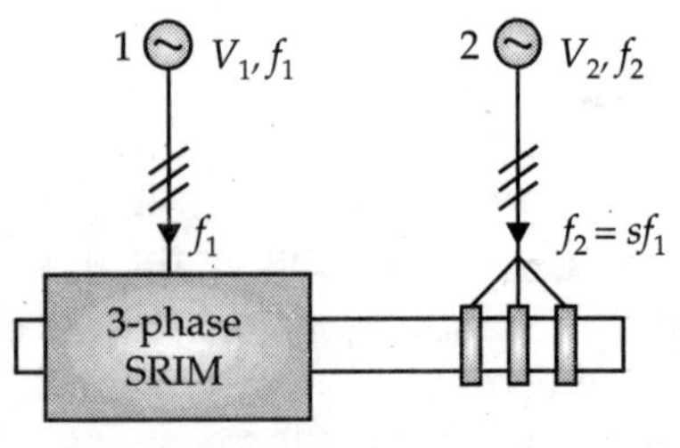

Fig 3.38: Doubly-fed induction motor fed from two separate ac sources.

3.16.1. Doubly-fed Induction Motor

A 3-phase SRIM fed from two separate voltage sources is shown in Fig. 3.38. Stator is connected to voltage source V_1, f_1 and rotor to another voltage source V_2, f_2. Power to stator at V_1, f_1 will create stator rotating flux and power to rotor at V_2, f_2 will create rotor rotating flux.

$$\text{Speed of stator produced flux} = \frac{120\, f_1}{P} \text{ rpm (say, clockwise)}$$

$$\text{Speed of rotor produced flux} = \frac{120\, f_2}{P} \text{ rpm}$$

A steady electromagnetic torque would develop only when relative speed between stator field and rotor field is zero. In case rotor produced flux rotates in the direction of stator flux, *i.e.* clockwise, then rotor speed (clockwise) + speed of rotor flux (clockwise) = speed of stator flux (clockwise).

or
$$N_r + \frac{120\, f_2}{P} = \frac{120\, f_1}{P}$$

∴ Rotor speed,
$$N_r = \frac{120}{P}[f_1 - f_2] = \frac{120\, f_1}{P}\left[1 - \frac{f_2}{f_1}\right]$$

$$= \frac{120\, f_1}{P}(1 - s) = N_s(1 - s) \qquad \text{...(3.52)}$$

Under the conditions stated above, the rotor runs at subsynchronous speed given by Eq. (3.52).

Let us now interchange any two supply leads feeding power to rotor. With this change, rotor produced flux would start rotating anticlockwise at speed $\frac{120\, f_2}{P}$ rpm. Now steady torque can develop only when rotor speed (clockwise) – speed of rotor flux (anticlockwise) = speed of stator flux (clockwise)

or
$$N_r - \frac{120\, f_2}{P} = \frac{120\, f_1}{P}$$

∴ Rotor speed,
$$N_r = \frac{120}{P}[f_1 + f_2] = \frac{120\, f_1}{P}\left[1 + \frac{f_2}{f_1}\right]$$

$$= \frac{120\, f_1}{P}[1 + s] = N_s(1 + s) \qquad \text{...(3.53)}$$

Under the conditions stated above, the rotor must run at supersynchronous speed given by Eq. (3.53).

From above, it can be stated, in general, that rotor of DFI motor runs at:

(i) subsynchronous speed for positive sequence rotor currents and

(ii) supersynchronous speed for negative sequence rotor currents.

3.16.1.1. Power flow in DFI motor

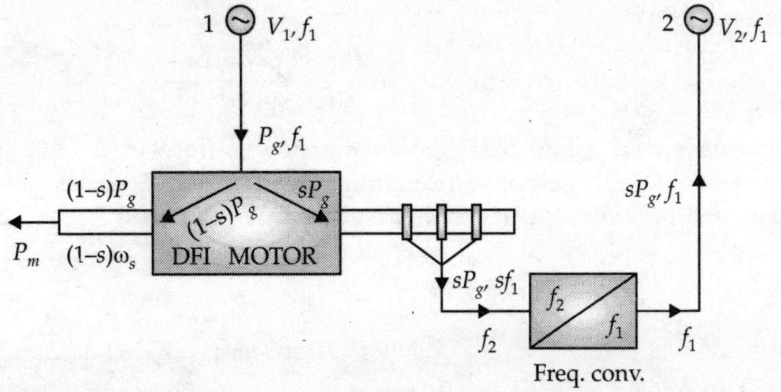

Fig 3.39: Power flow during subsynchronous operation of DFI motor.

Here the power flow in a DFI motor is examined when it runs at subsynchronous as well as supersynchronous speeds.

Subsynchronous speed : Fig. 3.39 shows the power flow in a DFI motor when running at subsynchronous speed. With f_1 = stator frequency and f_2 = rotor frequency, the slip $s = \frac{f_2}{f_1}$ is fixed. Therefore, rotor speed $= \frac{120\, f_1}{P}\left[1 - \frac{f_2}{f_1}\right] = \frac{120\, f_1}{P}(1 - s)$ is also fixed. In a way, DFI motor now operates as a special type of synchronous motor at constant speed given by Eq. (3.52).

In Fig. 3.39, P_g = air-gap power = power input to rotor. Here all losses are neglected. Therefore, as in a SRIM, we have, shaft power, $P_m = (1 - s)\, P_g$

power at slip rings $= P_g - P_m = s\, P_g$

This slip power $s\, P_g$ at frequency $f_2 = s f_1$ is converted to power sP_g at frequency f_1 by frequency converter and is then fed to source 2 as shown in Fig. 3.39.

Net power input to DFI motor from both sources $= P_g - sP_g = (1 - s)\, P_g$

Also, shaft power output $= (1 - s)\, P_g$

As all losses are ignored, net power input = shaft power output, and therefore, efficiency of the drive scheme is 100%.

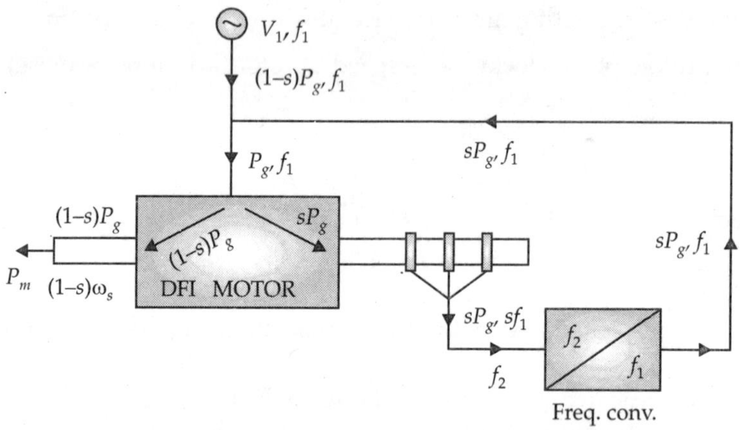

Fig 3.40: Power flow in DFI motor running at subsynchronous speed.

The scheme of DFI motor connections as shown in Fig. 3.39 can also be re-arranged as shown in Fig. 3.40. As before, power input from source $V_1, f_1 = (1 - s)\, P_g$ = shaft power output. In Fig. 3.39 or 3.40, shaft speed $= (1 - s)\, \omega_s$.

$$\therefore \quad \text{Torque} = \frac{\text{shaft power output}}{\text{shaft speed}} = \frac{(1-s)P_g}{(1-s)\cdot\omega_s} = \frac{P_g}{\omega_s}$$

Supersynchronous speed : Fig. 3.41 shows the power flow in a DFI motor running at supersynchronous speed. In a three-phase induction motor, the slip at supersynchronous speed is negative. As a result shaft power output would be given by $P_m = (1 + s)\, P_g$.

Shaft speed, $\omega_r = (1 + s)\cdot\omega_s$

$$\text{Torque} = \frac{P_m}{\omega_r} = \frac{(1+s)P_g}{(1+s)\omega_s} = \frac{P_g}{\omega_s}$$

Power fed **into** slip rings $= s\, P_g$

Net power taken from source $V_1, f_1 = P_g + s\,P_g = (1 + s)\,P_g$ = shaft power output.

It is seen from above that motor torque at both subsynchronous and supersynchronous speeds remain the same.

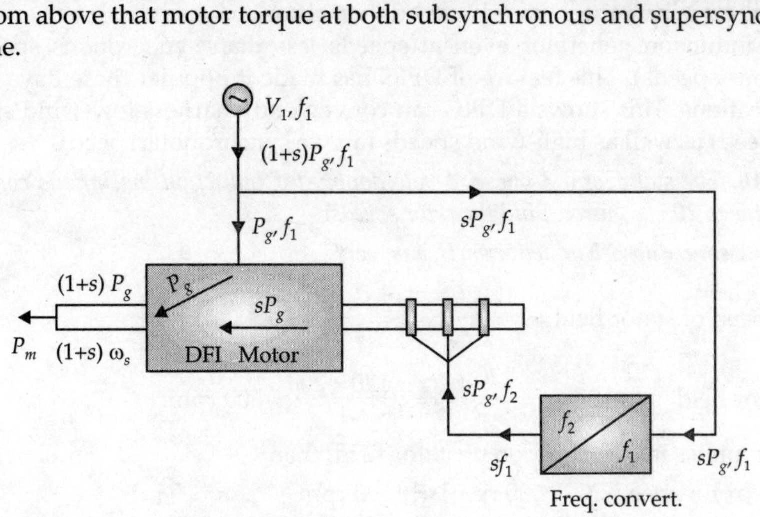

Fig 3.41: Power flow in DFI motor running at supersynchronous speed.

3.16.1.2. Power flow in DFI generator

Power flow in a DFI motor has been discussed at both subsynchronous and supersynchronous speeds. We will now discuss power flow in a DFI generator at speeds below and above synchronous speed.

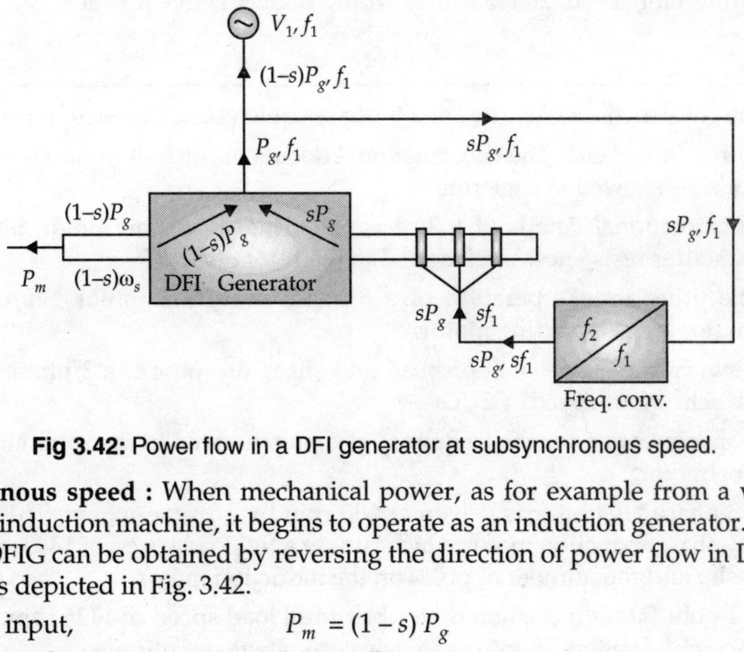

Fig 3.42: Power flow in a DFI generator at subsynchronous speed.

Subsynchronous speed : When mechanical power, as for example from a wind mill, flows into the shaft of induction machine, it begins to operate as an induction generator. The direction of power flow in DFIG can be obtained by reversing the direction of power flow in DFI motor of Fig. 3.40 ; it is now as depicted in Fig. 3.42.

Shaft power input, $P_m = (1 - s)\,P_g$

Power input at slip rings $= s\,P_g$

Stator power output $= (1 - s)\,P_g + s\,P_g = P_g$

Power input to source $V_1, f_1 = (P_g - s\,P_g) = (1 - s)\,P_g$ = shaft power input

$$\text{Torque} = \frac{P_g}{\omega_s}$$

Supersynchronous speed : It is left as an exercise for the reader. A SCIM can operate as an induction generator when rotor speed exceeds synchronous speed. However, a DFI machine can operate as induction generator even at speeds less than synchronous speed (and also at supersynchronous speeds). This feature of DFIG has made it popular these days for wind-power generator applications. This shows a DFIG can conveniently harness low-wind speeds (less than synchronous speed) as well as high-wind speeds (above synchronous speed).

Example 3.16. *The stator of a 3-phase, 4-pole doubly-fed induction machine is connected to 50 Hz source and the rotor to 20 Hz source. Find the rotor speeds.*

Does the 20 Hz source absorb or deliver active power?

Solution. Speed of stator field $= \dfrac{120\, f_1}{P} = \dfrac{120 \times 50}{4} = 1500$ rpm.

Speed of rotor field $\dfrac{120\, f_2}{P} = \dfrac{120 \times 20}{4} = 600$ rpm.

If rotor field rotates in the direction of stator field, then

$$[\text{rotor speed, } N_r + 600 \text{ rpm}] = 1500 \text{ rpm}$$

$\therefore$ Rotor speed, $N_r = 1500 - 600 = 900$ rpm.

In case rotor field rotates opposite to the dirction of stator field, then

$$[N_r - 600] = 1500 \text{ rpm.}$$

$\therefore$ Rotor speed, $N_r = 1500 + 600 = 2100$ rpm.

At rotor speed 900 rpm, 20 Hz source would absorb active power.

But at 2100 rpm rotor speed, 20 Hz source would deliver active power.

PROBLEMS

3.1. Describe the constructional features of a 3-phase squirrel-cage induction motor.

Discuss, with a neat sketch, the constructional details of rotor of a squirrel-cage motor. Why are the rotor slots skewed in cage rotor?

3.2. Give the constructional details of a 3-phase slip-ring induction motor. Show, with a neat sketch, how starter resistances are inserted in the rotor circuit.

3.3. Describe the principle of operation of a 3-phase induction motor. Show that a 3-phase induction motor is a self starting motor.

3.4. *(a)* Define synchronous speed, slip speed and slip. Can rotor of a 3-phase induction motor run at synchronous speed? Discuss.

(b) Derive an expression for the frequency of emf generated in the rotor circuit of a 3-phase induction motor.

3.5. A 10 pole, 3-phase alternator is driven at 600 rpm by a prime-mover. This alternator feeds power to a 3-phase induction motor which runs at a full load speed of 1440 rpm. Calculate the percentage slip and the number of poles on the induction motor. [**Ans.** 4%, 4 poles]

3.6. A 3-phase, 4-pole, 50 Hz induction motor has a full load speed of 1425 rpm. Calculate *(a)* the slip and *(b)* complete alternations made by rotor voltage per minute.

[**Hint.** One complete alternation = one cycle of rotor frequency.] [**Ans.** *(a)* 0.05, *(b)* 150]

3.7. Write expression for the emf induced in the rotor circuit at standstill. What are the various terms involved in this expression? Hence, derive expressions for *(a)* emf induced in rotor at any slip *s* *(b)* rotor current and power factor at standstill and also at any slip *s*.

3.8. A 3-phase, 420 V, 6 pole, 50 Hz induction motor has rotor leakage impedance of $0.1 + j\,0.6\ \Omega$ per phase. Per-phase ratio of stator to rotor turns is 2 : 1. The stator is in delta but rotor is star connected. Calculate *(a)* voltage between two slip rings at standstill and *(b)* rotor current and power factor at standstill and at a slip of 0.04.

[**Ans.** *(a)* 363.72 V *(b)* At standstill : 86.31 A, 0.1644 lag ; at slip 0.04 : 20.42 A, 0.9724 lag]

3.9. Draw the power flow diagram of a 3-phase induction motor. Explain the various losses and powers involved in this diagram.

3.10. A 400 V, 3-phase, 6-pole, 50 Hz induction motor develops a mechanical power of 10 kW at a speed of 970 rpm and at a power factor of 0.86. Calculate

(a) slip

(b) rotor ohmic loss

(c) total input if stator losses are 1000 W and

(d) line current. [**Ans.** *(a)* 0.03 *(b)* 309.28 W *(c)* 11309.28 W *(d)* 18.981 A]

3.11. For a 3-phase induction motor, draw the stator circuit model, rotor circuit model and hence derive the exact equivalent circuit of a 3-phase induction motor.

3.12. Draw the exact equivalent circuit of a 3-phase induction motor and mention clearly what the various parameters involved in this circuit represent.

3.13. Draw the approximate equivalent circuit of a 3-phase induction motor from its exact equivalent circuit. Hence derive an expression for torque and draw therefrom torque-speed characteristics of a 3-phase induction motor.

3.14. From the approximate equivalent circuit of a 3-phase induction motor, derive an expression for maximum developed torque. What observations can be made from this torque expression?

3.15. A 6-pole, 50 Hz, 950 rpm, three-phase induction motor develops a maximum torque of 200 Nm at 850 rpm. Determine its starting and full-load torques. [**Ans.** 58.677 Nm, 120 Nm]

3.16. A 3-phase, 10 pole, 50 Hz, 570 rpm induction motor has per phase standstill rotor leakage impedance of $0.3 + j\,2.4\ \Omega$. Calculate *(a)* the speed at which maximum torque occurs *(b)* the ratio of full load torque to maximum torque and *(c)* the ratio of starting torque to maximum torque. [**Ans.** *(a)* 525 rpm *(b)* 0.6897 *(c)* 0.2462]

3.17. A 6-pole, 50 Hz, 3-phase induction motor develops a maximum torque of 100 Nm at 900 rpm. The star-connected rotor has per-phase resistance of 0.2 Ω per phase. Find the resistance to be inserted in each rotor phase for developing a starting torque equal to half the maximum torque. [**Ans.** 0.335 Ω]

3.18. For a 3-phase induction motor, show that

$$\frac{T_e}{T_{e \cdot m}} = \frac{2}{\dfrac{s}{s_{mT}} + \dfrac{s_{mT}}{s}}$$

where T_{em} = maximum torque, s_{mT} = slip at maximum torque

and T_e = torque at any slip s.

State the assumptions made if any.

3.19. Draw the phasor diagram of a 3-phase induction motor and indicate the various terms used. Show, from the phasor diagram, that motor power factor is quite poor at starting.

3.20. Discuss the effect of variation of the following parameters on the torque-speed characteristics of a 3-phase induction motor :

(a) stator resistance variation *(b)* rotor resistance variation

(*c*) stator voltage variation (*c*) stator frequency variation.

3.21. (*a*) Describe the direct-on-line method of starting a 3-phase cage induction motor with a suitable diagram.

(*b*) A 4-pole, 50 Hz, 1440 rpm cage induction motor has short circuit current equal to 5 times the full load current. Calculate the starting torque in terms of full load torque with direct-on-line starting. **[Ans.** (*b*) 1.0]

3.22. When a 3-phase induction motor is started from the mains, the starting torque is found to be equal to 1.44 times the full load torque. Find the starting current in terms of full load current for a full-load slip of 0.04. **[Ans.** Ist = 6 I_{fl}]

3.23. A 4-pole, 50 Hz, 3-phase induction motor has per phase rotor leakage impedance of 0.4 + *j*.2 Ω. Calculate (*a*) speed at maximum torque and (*b*) external resistance per phase to be inserted in rotor circuit to obtain 70% of maximum torque at starting. **[Ans.** (*a*) 1200 rpm (*b*) 0.4168 Ω]

3.24. (*a*) Describe auto-transformer starting of a cage induction motor with relevant diagrams.

(*b*) A cage induction motor has short circuit current equal to 5 times the full load current and full load slip is 0.04. Calculate the auto-transformer ratio so that supply current does not exceed 2 times the full load current. Find also the starting torque in terms of full-load torque. **[Ans.** (*b*) 0.6325, 0.4 T_{efl}]

3.25. Describe star-delta starting of a 3-phase induction motor. Illustrate your answer with a relevant diagram. Show that with star-delta starting, a motor behaves as if it is started by an auto-transformer with 58% tapping.

3.26. (*a*) Enumerate the main methods for the speed control of 3-phase induction motors.

(*b*) Describe multipolar stator winding technique for the speed control of a 3-phase induction motor.

3.27. Explain, with relevant diagrams, the consequent pole technique for the speed control of 3-phase induction motors. Discuss how consequent-poles are induced leading to low-speed motor operation.

3.28. Describe the pole amplitude modulation technique for the speed control of 3-phase induction motors.

3.29. Explain how the speed of a 3-phase induction motor can be controlled by stator voltage control. What are its disadvantages?

3.30. Explain the stator frequency control method for the speed control of a 3-phase induction motor. Discuss why the ratio voltage to frequency should be kept constant in this method.

3.31. Describe the rotor resistance control technique for the speed control of a 3-phase induction motor. Illustrate your answer with torque-speed characteristics. What are the disadvantages of this method?

3.32. (*a*) What are the advantages of rotor slip-power control over rotor resistance control used for the speed control of 3-phase induction motors?

(*b*) Discuss briefly how voltage injection in the rotor circuit of a slip ring induction motor can control its speed.

3.33. Describe, with a suitable diagram, the static Kramer drive for the speed control of a 3-phase slip-ring induction motor.

3.34. (*a*) Explain the need for electric braking of polyphase induction motors.

(*b*) Explain regenerative braking of three-phase induction motors. Discuss how regenerative braking range can be increased for a pole-changing induction motor.

3.35. Discuss how electric braking by plugging can be achieved in three-phase induction motors? Explain four quadrant operation of both squirrel cage and wound-rotor 3-phase induction motors.

3.36. *(a)* During dynamic braking, the direction of rotor currents becomes opposite to its direction during normal motor operation. Explain.

(b) Draw the equivalent circuit during the dynamic braking of a three-phase induction motor and explain how it can be derived from the three-phase induction-motor equivalent circuit.

3.37. *(a)* Give two important connection schemes for the stator windings of a three-phase induction motor during dynamic braking. For these two schemes, derive the relation between alternating and direct currents in the stator.

(b) Show that the maximum torque $T_{ed \cdot m}$, developed during dynamic braking, is given by

$$T_{ed \cdot m} = \frac{3}{\omega_s} \cdot \frac{I_1^2 \cdot X_m^2}{2(x_2 + X_m)}$$

3.38. *(a)* Draw torque-speed characteristics of a 3-phase induction motor for all possible operating modes. Give the induction machine operation in these operating modes.

(b) Explain how a 3-phase induction motor can be made to operate as an induction generator. Can this generator work in isolation? Give its limitations.

3.39. Explain self-excited 3-phase induction generator with suitable diagrams. Explain the voltage build up process in this generator.

Give the advantages and disadvantages of self-excited 3-phase induction generator.

3.40. A doubly-fed induction machine has its stator connected to source V_1, f_1 and rotor to source V_2, f_2. Show, on a relevant diagram, the power flow when the machine runs as a motor at subsynchronous speed. Is it possible to connect this scheme to one source V_1, f_1? Discuss.

3.41. A doubly-fed induction machine is running at subsynchronous speed. Is the rotor delivering power to, or absorbing power from, the frequency converter if it acts as *(a)* motor and *(b)* generator.

Objective Type Questions

1. In a 3-phase induction motor, the function of stator frame is to

(a) provide path for the flux

(b) protect the whole machine

(c) provide mechanical support to stator frame

(d) help the cooling of machine.

2. Read the following statements for a 3-phase induction motor :

1. stator frame is made from cast iron
2. stator core is made from cast iron
3. two end covers are made from silcon steel
4. stator core is made from steel laminations.

From above, the correct statements are

(a) 1, 2, 3 *(b)* 1, 4 *(c)* 1, 2, 4 *(d)* 1, 3, 4

3. In a 3-phase squirrel cage induction motor,

1. rotor slots are skewed

2. rotor slots contain insulated bars
3. rotor is made from cast steel
4. rotor is made from circular laminations.

From above, the correct statements are

(a) 1, 2, 4 (b) 1, 2, 3 (c) 1, 4 (d) 1, 3, 4

4. In a 3-phase induction motor, the relative speed between stator flux and rotor flux is equal to

(a) zero (b) synchronous speed N_s
(c) rotor speed N_r (d) $N_s - N_r$.

5. In a 3-phase induction motor, rotor speed with respect to stator field is

(a) zero (b) synchronous speed N_s
(c) rotor speed N_r (d) $N_s - N_r$.

6. The effect of increasing the air-gap length in a 3-phase induction motor is to

1. reduce the air gap flux
2. reduce the magnetizing current
3. worsen the power factor
4. improve the power factor
5. reduce the torque

From above, the correct answer is

(a) 1, 3, 5 (b) 2, 4, 5 (c) 3, 5 (d) 2, 3, 5

7. In a 3-phase induction motor, the speed of rotor field in air gap is equal to

(a) zero (b) synchronous speed
(c) rotor speed N_r (d) $N_s - N_r$.

8. The absolute speed of the magnetic field in space of a 3-phase rotor-fed induction motor is

(a) synchronous speed N_s (b) rotor speed N_r
(c) $(N_s - N_r)$ (d) $N_s + N_r$

9. The variable resistance representing the mechanical load in the equivalent circuit of a 3-phase induction motor is given by

(a) $r_2(s-1)$ (b) $r_2\left[\frac{1}{s}-1\right]$ (c) $r_2\left[1-\frac{1}{s}\right]$ (d) $r_2(1-s)$

10. If ω_s = synchronous speed in mechanical rad/sec, then torque in a 3-phase induction motor is given by

(a) $\dfrac{3I_2^2 r_2}{s \cdot \frac{P}{2} \cdot \omega_s}$ (b) $\dfrac{3I_2^2 r_2}{s \cdot \omega_s}$ (c) $\dfrac{3I_2^2 r_2}{\omega_s}$ (d) $\dfrac{3I_2^2 r_2}{s}$

11. If stator impedance of a 3-phase IM is neglected, then the maximum torque (V_1 = stator phase voltage) is given by

(a) $\dfrac{3}{\omega_s} \cdot \dfrac{V_1^2}{x_2}$ (b) $\dfrac{3}{\omega_s} \cdot \dfrac{V_1^2}{r_2}$ (c) $\dfrac{3}{\omega_s} \cdot \dfrac{V_1^2}{2r_2}$ (d) $\dfrac{3}{\omega_s} \cdot \dfrac{V_1^2}{2 \cdot x_2}$

12. In a three-phase induction motor, if stator resistance is increased, then

1. maximum torque reduces
2. maximum torque remains constant

3. starting torque is reduced
4. slip at which maximum torque occurs increases

From above, the correct statements are

(a) 1, 3 *(b)* 2, 3 *(c)* 3, 4 *(d)* 1, 3, 4

13. In a 3-phase I_m, if rotor circuit resistance is increased, then
1. maximum torque remains same
2. starting torque reduces
3. starting current reduces
4. slip at which maximum torque occurs increases.

From above, the correct answer is

(a) 1, 2, 3 *(b)* 2, 3, 4 *(c)* 3, 4 *(d)* 1, 3, 4

14. In a 3-phase induction motor, if stator voltage decreass
1. maximum torque decreases
2. slip at which maximum torque occurs decreases
3. starting torque decreases
4. speed decreases for constant load torque.

From above, the correct statements are

(a) 1, 2, 3 *(b)* 1, 3, 4 *(c)* 3, 4 *(d)* 1, 2, 4

15. In a 3-phase IM, if stator frequency is lowered, then
1. starting torque decreases
2. maximum torque increases
3. slip at which maximum torque occurs decreases
4. the motor running speed decreases

From above, the correct answer is

(a) 1, 2, 3 *(b)* 1, 3, 4 *(c)* 1, 4 *(d)* 2, 4

16. No load current of a 3-phase IM in terms of its rated current is

(a) 10 to 20% *(b)* 2 to 6% *(c)* 20 to 30% *(d)* 30 to 50%

17. In a 3-phase induction motor, electrical torque T_e at any slip s and maximum torque T_{em} at slip s_{mT} are related as under :

(a) $\frac{T_e}{T_{e \cdot m}} = \frac{2s \cdot s_{mT}}{s^2 + s_{mT}}$ *(b)* $\frac{T_e}{T_{e \cdot m}} = \frac{2\, s_{mT}}{s^2 + s_{mT}^2}$ *(c)* $\frac{T_e}{T_{e \cdot m}} = \frac{2s}{s^2 + s_{mT}^2}$ *(d)* $\frac{T_e}{T_{e \cdot m}} = \frac{2s \cdot s_{mT}}{s^2 + s_{mT}^2}$

18. As compared to D.O.L. starting, a cage IM with star-delta starting shall have

(a) more starting torque *(b)* more starting current

(c) reduced starting current *(d)* smooth acceleration.

19. A starting torque of 100 Nm is developed in a 3-phase cage motor by an auto-transformer starter with a tapping of 40%. If the tapping of auto-transformer starter is changed to 80%, then the starting torque would be

(a) 400 Nm *(b)* 200 Nm *(c)* 50 Nm *(d)* 25 Nm

20. During the no-load test, the power input to a 3-phase induction motor has to supply

(a) core loss, friction and windage (FW) loss

(b) small ohmic loss and FW loss

(c) small ohmic loss, core loss and FW loss

(d) small ohmic loss, FW loss and stray load loss.

21. The stator of a 2/4 pole changing cage motor is initially wound for 2-pole. The reconnection of the stator winding to 4 poles through a change-over switch, while the motor is running, would result in

(a) constant torque drive

(b) constant power drive

(c) plugging to standstill

(d) regenerative braking to half the original speed. *[I.E.S. 1992]*

22. Stator of a doubly-fed induction machine is fed from source V_1, f_1 and its rotor from source V_2, f_2. The two possible rotor speeds are

(a) $\frac{120f_1}{P}\left[1-\frac{f_1}{f_2}\right], \frac{120f_1}{P}\left[1+\frac{f_1}{f_2}\right]$

(b) $\frac{120f_1}{P}\left[1+\frac{f_1}{f_2}\right], \frac{120f_1}{P}\left[1+\frac{f_2}{f_1}\right]$

(c) $\frac{120f_1}{P}\left[1-\frac{f_2}{f_1}\right], \frac{120f_1}{P}\left[1+\frac{f_2}{f_1}\right]$

(d) $\frac{120f_1}{P}\left[1-\frac{f_2}{f_1}\right], \frac{120f_1}{P}\left[1+\frac{f_1}{f_2}\right]$

Answers

1. (c)	2. (b)	3. (c)	4. (a)	5. (d)
6. (c)	7. (b)	8. (c)	9. (d)	10. (b)
11. (d)	12. (a)	13. (d)	14. (b)	15. (d)
16. (d)	17. (d)	18. (c)	19. (a)	20. (c)
21. (d)	22. (c)			

Chapter 4

Single Phase Induction Motors

Single-phase induction motors in the range of fraction of a kW to about 5 kW are used extensively where 3-phase supply is not available. These motors find use in fans, washing machines, refrigerators, blowers, centrifugal pumps and the like. In very small sizes, these are used in hair-dryers, toys, vending machines etc. Single phase induction motors operate at low power factors and are less efficient as compared to 3-phase induction motors.

A single-phase induction motor has no inherent starting torque. Therefore, some special devices have to be used for the starting of these motors.

4.1. CONSTRUCTIONAL FEATURES

The rotor of a single phase induction motor is exactly similar to the squirrel cage rotor of a 3-phase induction motor shown in Fig. 3.2.

The stator of a single-phase induction motor carries two windings, namely, main (or running) winding and auxiliary (or starting) winding. Both windings are of the single layer concentric type. Fig. 4.1 illustrates both main and auxiliary windings for a 4-pole, single-phase induction motor with 24 stator slots. In this figure, only a part of both main and auxiliary windings is shown for the sake of clarity. An examination of this figure reveals that angle between the starting points S_M of main winding and S_A of auxiliary winding are space displaced by 90°. In other words magnetic axes of main auxiliary windings are in space quadrature.

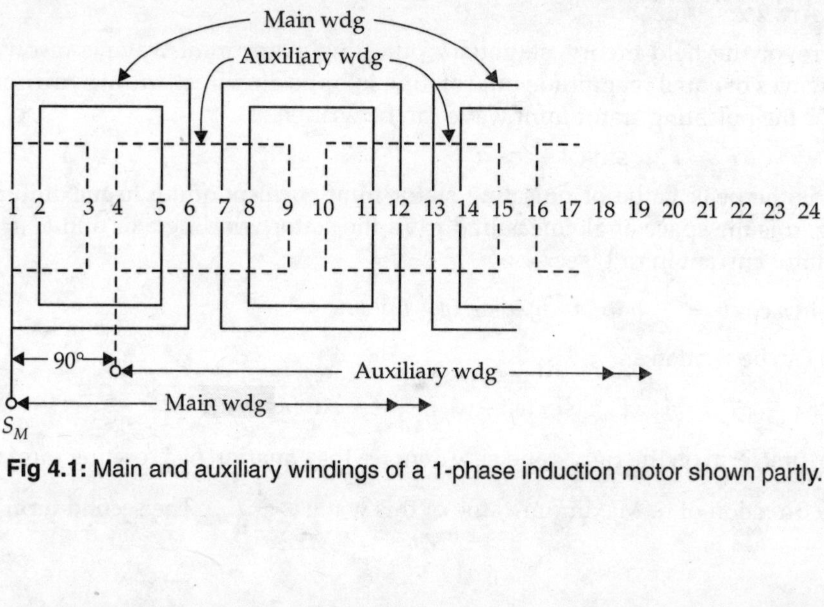

Fig 4.1: Main and auxiliary windings of a 1-phase induction motor shown partly.

The two windings in space quadrature are usually represented as shown in Fig. 4.2. Here, main winding is taken along the horizontal axis whereas auxiliary winding is shown along the vertical axis. The rotor is shown to have a few number of bars.

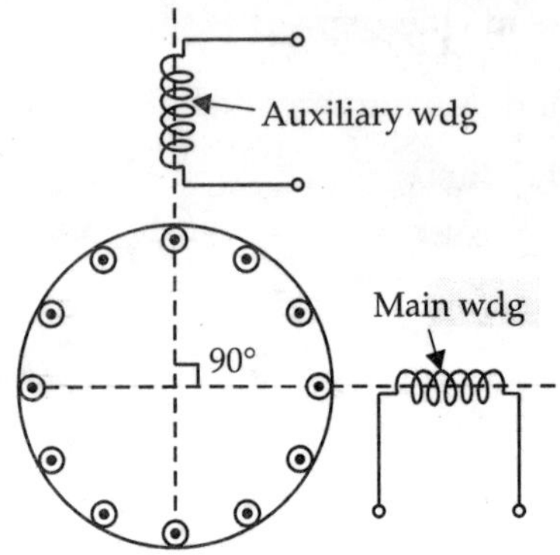

Fig 4.2: Main and auxiliary windings of a 1-phase induction motor.

4.2. SINGLE-PHASE INDUCTION MOTOR PRINCIPLE

A single-phase induction motor with its main winding is shown in Fig. 4.3. The rotor is at standstill. When single-phase supply is given to main winding, a pulsating field ϕ_s is produced along the axis of main winding. By transformer action, currents are induced in the rotor bars. These rotor bar currents set up rotor flux ϕ_r along the main winding axis. However, the rotor flux ϕ_r opposes the stator flux ϕ_s at all instants of time, Fig. 4.3. Since the stator flux ϕ_s and rotor flux ϕ_r are along the same axis, the torque angle between ϕ_s and ϕ_r is 180°. The starting torque, proportional to $\phi_s \cdot \phi_r \cdot \sin 180°$, is therefore zero.

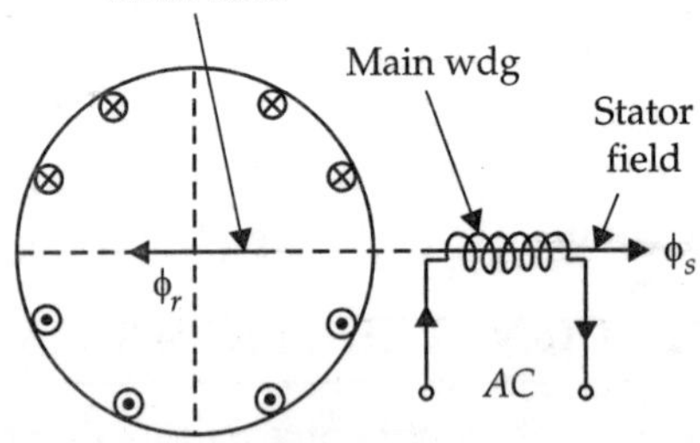

Fig 4.3: Single-phase induction motor at standstill.

It is seen from above that a single-phase induction motor has no inherent starting torque. But, once an initial starting torque is given to rotor in any direction, the rotor builds up speed in that direction and continues running at a speed less than synchronous speed.

The analysis of single-phase induction motor can be carried out either by double-revolving field theory or by cross-field theory. Here only double-revolving field theory would be described for analysis purposes.

4.3. DOUBLE REVOLVING FIELD THEORY

When single-phase supply is given to a stator coil, a stationary pulsating stator mmf wave is produced, see Art. 2.2.

In double revolving field theory, stationary pulsating stator mmf wave is resolved into two rotating mmf waves of equal magnitude but rotating in opposite directions at synchronous speed. An equation for the pulsating stator mmf wave can be written as

$$F_s = F_{sm} \cdot \sin \omega t - \cos \alpha \qquad ...(4.1)$$

where F_{sm} is the peak value of pulsating stator mmf corresponding to maximum current in stator winding, α is the space angle measured from the stator winding axis and ω (= $2 \pi f$) is the frequency of stator current in rad/sec.

But $$\sin a \cos b = \frac{1}{2} [\sin (a - b) + \sin (a + b)]$$

∴ Eq. (4.1) can be written as

$$F_s = \frac{1}{2} \cdot F_{sm} \cdot \sin (\omega t - \alpha) + \frac{1}{2} F_{sm} \sin (\omega t + \alpha) \qquad ...(4.2)$$

In Eq. (4.2), first term on the right hand side denotes the equation of a rotating mmf travelling in the forward (*f*) direction of α. Maximum value of this wave is $\frac{1}{2} F_{sm}$. The second term on the right hand side represents the equation of rotating mmf wave travelling in the backward *(b)* direction of α. Maximum value of this wave is also $\frac{1}{2}F_{sm}$. Note that forward rotating mmf wave travels in the direction of rotor rotation. Naturally, the backward rotating mmf wave travels in a direction opposite to rotor rotation. This shows that

$\frac{1}{2}F_{sm}\cdot\sin(\omega t-\alpha)$ is the forward rotating mmf wave

and $\frac{1}{2}F_{sm}\cdot\sin(\omega t+\alpha)$ is the backward rotating mmf wave.

It is seen from above that stationary pulsating stator mmf wave can be resolved into two rotating mmf waves of constant amplitude but rotating in opposite directions at synchronous speed.

Note that *(i)* forward and backward rotating mmf waves are of equal magnitude at all rotor speeds, *(ii)* forward and backward flux waves are equal only at standstill and *(iii)* at all other rotor speeds, forward flux wave is much higher than the backward flux wave (this is proved later in this chapter).

Each of these two rotating flux wave produce their own torque, similar to the production of torque in a 3-phase induction motor. Forward and backward fields produce induction motor torques T_f and T_b respectively, but these are in opposite directions as shown by dashed curves in Fig. 4.4. The resultant torque-speed curve is obtained by the algebraic sum of two torques T_f and T_b as illustrated in Fig. 4.4. This Figure shows that the resultant motor torque is zero *(i)* when rotor speed is zero and *(ii)* when rotor speed is a little less than synchronous speed n_s. This figure 4.4 also shows that single-phase induction motor, **with main winding alone**, can run in either direction if an initial torque, greater than friction and load torque is applied to its shaft. Also note that at synchronous speed, single-phase induction motor has negative torque.

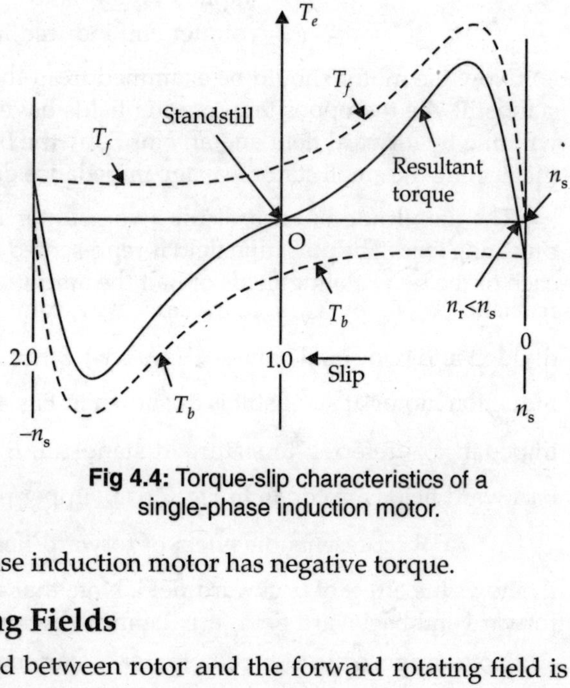

Fig 4.4: Torque-slip characteristics of a single-phase induction motor.

4.3.1. Slip with Respect to Two Rotating Fields

If the rotor runs at a speed n_r, the relative speed between rotor and the forward rotating field is $(n_s - n_r)$ rps, just as in a 3-phase induction motor.

∴ Slip speed with respect to forward rotating field = $n_s - n_r$ and the slip of the rotor emf is given by

$$s_f = \frac{n_s - n_r}{n_s} = s$$

The relative speed between rotor and the backward rotating field is $(n_s + n_r)$ rps. Therefore, slip of rotor emf due to backward rotating field is

$$s_b = \frac{n_s + n_r}{n_s} = \frac{n_s + n_s(1-s)}{n_s} = 2 - s$$

4.4. EQUIVALENT CIRCUIT

The equivalent circuit for a 1-phase induction motor is now developed with only main winding in circuit.

When the motor is at standstill and the main winding alone is excited as shown in Fig. 4.3, then single-phase induction motor behaves like a single-phase transformer with its secondary short circuited. Therefore, the equivalent circuit of a 1-phase induction motor with standstill rotor is as shown in Fig. 4.5. Here core-loss resistance is omitted. The core loss would, however, be taken into consideration along with friction and windage losses. In Fig. 4.5,

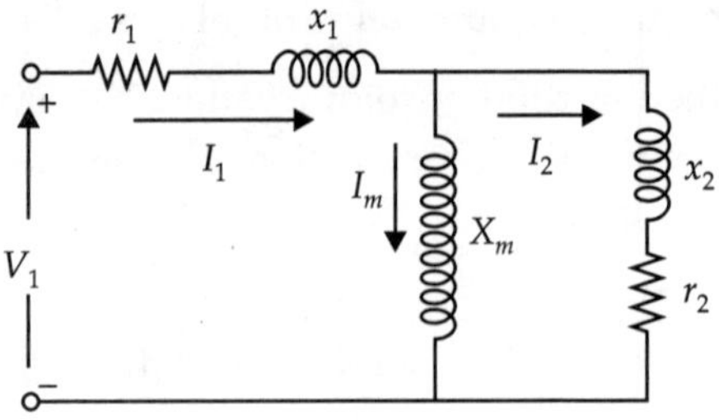

Fig 4.5: Single-phase induction motor equivalent circuit at standstill.

$r_1 + j\,x_1$ = stator leakage impedance of main winding,

$r_2 + j\,x_2$ = standstill rotor leakage impedance referred to stator,

X_m = magnetizing reactance,

V_1 = applied voltage and

E = counter emf induced in main stator winding by the pulsating field.

Now the motor should be examined from the viewpoint of double revolving field theory. At standstill, the too oppositely rotating fields have equal amplitude. An emf E_f is induced in stator winding by forward field and an emf E_b by the backward field. The phasor sum of E_f and E_b is V_1 (neglecting the small stator leakage impedance drop).

The amplitude of each of the two counter rotating fields is equal to half the amplitude of pulsating field. The pulsating field is represented by magnetizing reactance X_m in Fig. 4.5. Likewise, each of the two rotating fields of half the amplitude can be represented by half of the magnetizing reactance X_m, *i.e.* by $X_m/2$. In the same way, rotor leakage impedance, in parallel with $X_m/2$, can be divided into two equal halves $\frac{1}{2}(r_2 + j\,x_2)$. Since $\overline{V}_1 = \overline{E}_f + \overline{E}_b$, the equivalent circuit of a 1-phase induction motor at standstill is as shown in Fig. 4.6 *(a)*. It should be understood that rotor leakage impedance is referred to stator. At standstill, $E_f = E_b = \frac{E}{2}$, because amplitudes of forward and backward fields are equal. In Fig. 7.6 *(a)*, upper portion connected across E_f [$X_m/2$ in parallel with $\frac{1}{2}(r_2 + j\,x_2)$] represents the effect of forward field. Similarly, the lower portion connected across E_b shows the effect of backward field. Note that at standstill, the circuits representing the effect of forward and backward fields are identical, because $E_f = E_b = E/2$.

Now suppose the induction motor is started by auxiliary means and the rotor is running with only main winding in circuit. Under these conditions, rotor rotates with slip s with respect to forward field and with slip $(2 - s)$ relative to the backward field. Thus, effective rotor resistance in the circuit associated with forward rotating field is r_2/s. Similarly, the effective rotor resistance in the circuit associated with backward rotating field is $\frac{r_2}{2(2-s)}$. Therefore, for any rotor speed, equivalent circuit of Fig. 4.6 *(b)* is obtained with only main winding in circuit. In this figure, Z_f given by $\frac{1}{2}\left[\frac{r_2}{s} + jx_2\right]$ in parallel with $\frac{1}{2}X_m$, is called **forward field impedance.** Similarly, Z_b, equal to $\frac{1}{2}\left[\frac{r_2}{2(2-s)} + jx_2\right]$ in parallel with $\frac{1}{2}X_m$, is known as **backward field impedance**.

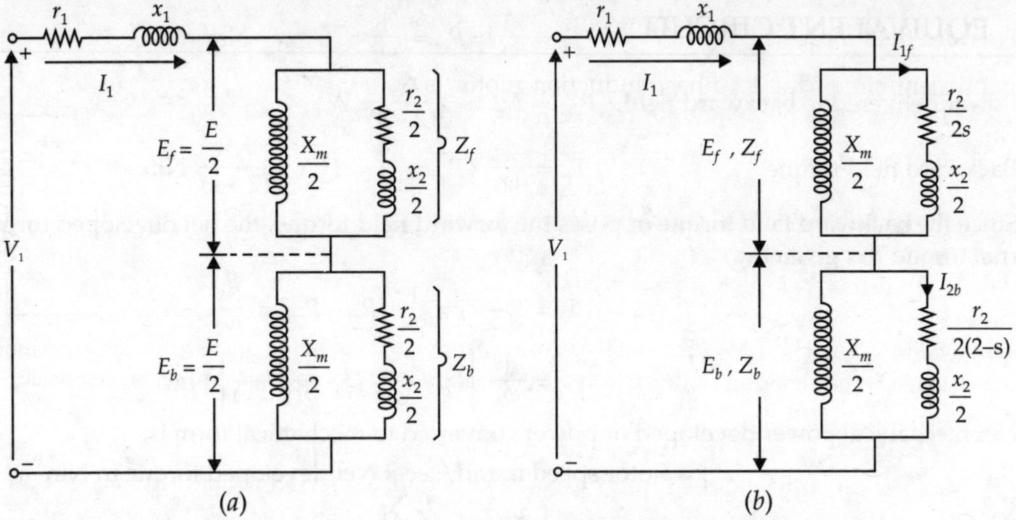

Fig 4.6: Equivalent circuit for a 1-phase induction motor *(a)* at standstill and *(b)* with the rotor running at slip *s*.

Now suppose the induction motor is started by auxiliary means and the rotor is running with only main winding in circuit. Under these conditions, rotor rotates with slip s with respect to forward field and with slip $(2 - s)$ relative to the backward field. Thus, effective rotor resistance in the circuit associated with forward rotating field is r_2/s. Similarly, the effective rotor resistance in the circuit associated with backward rotating field is $\frac{r_2}{2(2-s)}$. Therefore, for any rotor speed, equivalent circuit of Fig. 4.6 *(b)* is obtained with only main winding in circuit. In this figure, Z_f given by $\frac{1}{2}\left[\frac{r_2}{s} + jx_2\right]$ in parallel with $\frac{1}{2} X_m$, is called **forward field impedance.** Similarly, Z_b, equal to $\frac{1}{2}\left[\frac{r_2}{2(2-s)} + jx_2\right]$ in parallel with $\frac{1}{2} X_m$, is known as **backward field impedance**.

Under running conditions, slip s is small, therefore $\frac{r_2}{2s}$ is much larger than $\frac{r_2}{2(2-s)}$. In other words, at small value of slip s, Z_f is much larger than Z_b. This amounts to an increase in E_f and decrease of E_b at small slip s, though at standstill, $E_f = E_b$. Therefore, the forward flux ϕ_f, proportional to E_f, increases and backward flux ϕ_b, proportional to E_b, decreases as the rotor speed increases. It can, therefore, be concluded that

$$\frac{\phi_f}{\phi_b} = \frac{E_f}{E_b} = \frac{Z_f}{Z_b} \qquad ...(4.3)$$

4.5. PERFORMANCE CALCULATIONS

The performance calculations for a single-phase induction motor, running with main winding alone, can be obtained from the equivalent circuit of 4.6 *(b)*. These calculations are similar to those applied to the equivalent circuit of a 3-phase induction motor. Forward and backward components of current (referred to stator) I_{2f} and I_{2b} can be calculated from the equivalent circuit of Fig. 4.6 *(b)*.

Power delivered to forward field, $P_{gf} = I_{2f}^2 \times \frac{r_2}{2s}$ W

Forward field torque, $$T_f = \frac{1}{\omega_s} \cdot P_{gf} = \frac{1}{\omega_s} \cdot I_{2f}^2 \cdot \frac{r_2}{2s} \text{ Nm}$$

Power delivered to backward field, $$P_{gb} = I_{2b}^2 \times \frac{r_2}{2(2-s)} \text{ W}$$

Backward field torque, $$T_b = \frac{1}{\omega_s} \cdot P_{gb} = \frac{1}{\omega_s} \cdot I_{2b}^2 \cdot \frac{r_2}{2(2-s)} \text{ Nm}$$

Since the backward field torque opposes the forward field torque, the net developed torque or internal torque T is given by

$$T = T_f - T_b = \frac{1}{\omega_s} [P_{gf} - P_{gb}] = \frac{P_g}{\omega_s}$$

$$= \frac{1}{\omega_s} \left[I_{2f}^2 \cdot \frac{r_2}{2s} - I_{2b}^2 \cdot \frac{r_2}{2(2-s)} \right] \text{ Nm} \qquad ...(4.4)$$

Net mechanical power developed or power converted to mechanical form is,

$$P_m = \text{Rotor speed in rad/sec} \times \text{Net developed torque in Nm}$$

$$= (1-s)\,\omega_s \cdot \left[\frac{1}{\omega_s} (P_{gf} - P_{gb}) \right]$$

$$= (1-s)\,[P_{gf} - P_{gb}] \qquad ...(4.5)$$

Forward field rotor ohmic loss $= s \cdot P_{gf}$

Backward field rotor ohmic loss $= (2-s) \cdot P_{gb}$

Total rotor ohmic losses $= s \cdot P_{gf} + (2-s) \cdot P_{gb}$

Shaft power, or output, power, $P_{sh} = P_m -$ [F and W losses + core losses]

$$\text{Shaft, or output, torque} = \frac{P_m - \text{rotational losses}}{(1-s)\omega_s}$$

Note that rotational losses = F and W losses + core losses

Alternatively : Shaft torque can also be calculated as under :

From Fig. 4.6 (*b*),

Forward field impedance, $$Z_f = R_f + j\,X_f = \frac{j\frac{X_m}{2}\left[\frac{r_2}{2s} + j\frac{x_2}{2}\right]}{\frac{r_2}{2s} + j\left[\frac{x_2}{2} + \frac{X_m}{2}\right]} \qquad ...(4.6)$$

and backward field impedance, $$Z_b = R_b + j\,X_b = \frac{j\frac{X_m}{2}\left[\frac{r_2}{2(2-s)} + j\frac{x_2}{2}\right]}{\frac{r_2}{2(2-s)} + j\left[\frac{x_2}{2} + \frac{X_m}{2}\right]} \qquad ...(4.7)$$

Stator leakage impedance, $z_1 = r_1 + j\,x_1$

Total equivalent impedance, $Z_{eq} = r_1 + j\,x_1 + R_f + jX_f + R_b + j\,X_b$

Stator current, $$I_1 = \frac{V_1}{Z_{eq}}$$

Stator power factor, $$\cos\theta_1 = \frac{R_{eq}}{Z_{eq}} = \frac{r_1 + R_f + R_b}{Z_{eq}}$$

$$\text{Power input} = V_1 I_1 \cdot \cos\theta_1$$

Power delivered to forward field, $P_{gf} = I_1^2 R_f$

Power delivered to backward field, $P_{gb} = I_1^2 R_b$

Net air-gap power, $P_g = P_{gf} - P_{gb} = I_1^2 (R_f - R_b)$

Internal mechanical power, $P_m = (1 - s) \cdot I_1^2 (R_f - R_b)$ ...(4.8)

$$\text{Shaft or output power} = P_m - (F \text{ and } W \text{ losses + core losses})$$

$$\text{Shaft or output torque} = \frac{P_m - \text{rotational losses}}{(1-s)\,\omega_s}$$

$$\text{Efficiency} = \frac{P_m - \text{rotational losses}}{V_1 I_1 \cos\theta_1}$$

Example 4.1. *A 230 V, 4-pole, 50 Hz, 1-phase induction motor has the following parameters and losses.*

$r_1 = 2.6\ \Omega,\quad x_1 = 3.8\ \Omega$

$r_2 = 4.4\ \Omega,\quad x_2 = 3.0\ \Omega,\ X_m = 90\ \Omega$

Core loss = 30 W, friction and windage loss = 10 W.

At rated voltage and frequency and for a slip of 0.04, determine (a) stator current (b) input power factor (c) power output (d) shaft torque and (e) efficiency, with auxiliary winding open.

Solution. For the equivalent circuit of Fig. 4.6 *(b)*,

$$\frac{r_2}{2s} + j\,\frac{x_2}{2} = \frac{4.4}{2 \times 0.04} + j\,\frac{3.0}{2} = 55 + j\,1.5 = 55.02\,\underline{/1.562^\circ}\ \Omega$$

$$\frac{r_2}{2(2-s)} + j\,\frac{x_2}{2} = \frac{4.4}{2(1.96)} + j\,\frac{3.0}{2} = 1.1224 + j\,1.5 = 1.873\,\underline{/53.194}\ \Omega$$

$$j\frac{X_m}{2} = j\,\frac{90}{2} = 45\ \underline{/90^\circ}\ \Omega$$

$$Z_f = R_f + j\,X_f$$

$$= \frac{j\dfrac{X_m}{2}\left[\dfrac{r_2}{2s} + j\dfrac{x_2}{2}\right]}{\dfrac{r_2}{2s} + j\left[\dfrac{x_2}{2} + \dfrac{X_m}{2}\right]}$$

$$= \frac{45\underline{/90^\circ}\,[55.02\underline{/1.562^\circ}]}{55 + j[1.5 + 45]}$$

$$= \frac{45 \times 55.02\underline{/91.562^\circ}}{72.02\underline{/40.213^\circ}} = 34.378\ \underline{/51.349}$$

$$= 21.472 + j\,26.85\ \Omega$$

$$Z_b = R_b + j\,X_b$$

$$= \frac{j\dfrac{X_m}{2}\left[\dfrac{r_2}{2(2-s)} + j\dfrac{x_2}{2}\right]}{\dfrac{r_2}{2(2-s)} + j\left[\dfrac{x_2}{2} + \dfrac{X_m}{2}\right]}$$

$$= \frac{45\underline{/90^\circ} \times 1.873\underline{/53.194^\circ}}{1.1224 + j46.5}$$

$$= \frac{45 \times 1.873\underline{/143.194^\circ}}{46.514\underline{/88.617^\circ}}$$

$$= 1.812\ \underline{/54.577} = 1.05 + j\,1.4766\ \Omega$$

Total equivalent impedance,

$Z_{aq} = r_1 + R_f + R_b + + j\,[x_1 + X_f + X_b] = 2.6 + 21.472 + 1.05 + j\,[3.8 + 26.85 + 1.4766]$

$= 25.122 + j\,32.127 = 40.783\ \underline{/51.976°}\ \Omega$

(a) Stator, or input, current, $I_1 = \dfrac{V_1}{Z_{eq}} = \dfrac{230}{40.783\underline{/51.976}} = 5.64\ \underline{/-51.976°}\ \text{A}$

(b) Power factor $= \cos 51.976 = 0.616$ lagging

Also, power factor, $\cos\theta = \dfrac{R_{eq}}{Z_{eq}} = \dfrac{25.122}{40.783} = 0.616$ lagging

(c) Internal mechanical power, $P_m = (1 - s)\ I_1^2\ [R_f - R_b]$

$= (1 - 0.04) \times (5.64)^2\ [21.522 - 1.05] = 625.16$ W

Power output or shaft power $= P_m - [F$ and W losses + core loss$]$

$= 625.16 - [10 + 30] =$ **585.13 W**

(d) Synchronous speed, $\omega_s = \dfrac{4\pi f}{P} = \dfrac{4\pi \times 50}{4} = 50\pi$ rad/sec.

∴ Shaft torque $= \dfrac{\text{Power output}}{(1 - s)\ \omega_s} = \dfrac{585.16}{0.96 \times 50\pi} =$ **3.88 Nm**

(e) Power input $V_1 I_1 \cos\theta_1 = 230 \times 5.64 \times 0.616 = 799.1$ W

∴ Efficiency $= \dfrac{\text{Power output}}{\text{Power input}} = \dfrac{585.16}{799.1} \times 100 =$ **73.227%**

4.6. DETERMINATION OF PARAMETERS

The equivalent circuit parameters of a single-phase induction motor can be determined from blocked-rotor and no-load tests and from stator winding resistance r_1. These tests are similar to those performed on a 3-phase induction motor.

4.6.1. Blocked-rotor Test

In this test, the rotor is kept at standstill. Single-phase voltage, applied to main winding, is gradually increased from zero till rated current flows in the main winding. Under these conditions, let V_{sc}, I_{sc} and W_{sc} be the voltmeter, ammeter and wattmeter readings respectively. Measure dc resistance of main winding by voltmeter-ammeter mothod. This dc resistance should be multiplied by a factor of 1.1 to 1.3 so as to obtain effective ac resistance r_1 at line frequency.

With the rotor blocked, slip $s = 1$. Also, voltage required to circulate full load current is very low. As a result, current through X_m is small as compared to the current in $(r_2 + j\,x_2)$, Fig. 4.5. Therefore, magnetizing reactance in Fig. 4.5 or Fig. 4.6 *(b)* can be neglected, leading to the blocked-rotor equivalent circuit of Fig. 4.7 *(a)*. Now, the equivalent impedance referred to stator is given by

$$Z_{sc} = \frac{V_{sc}}{I_{sc}} \quad ...(4.9)$$

From Fig. 4.7 *(a)*, equivalent resistance R_{sc} is given by

$$R_{sc} = r_1 + \left(\frac{r_2}{2}\right) \times 2 = r_1 + r_2 = \frac{W_{sc}}{I_{sc}^2} \quad ...(4.10)$$

Since effective stator winding resistance r_1 is already known, the effective rotor resistance r_2 at line frequency is

$$r_2 = R_{sc} - r_1 = \left[\frac{W_{sc}}{I_{sc}^2} - r_1\right] \quad ...(4.11)$$

From Fig. 4.7 *(a)*, equivalent reactance X_{sc} is given by

$$X_{sc} = x_1 + \left(\frac{x_2}{2}\right)2 = x_1 + x_2$$

Since the leakage reactances x_1 and x_2 cannot be separated out, it is common practice to assume $x_1 = x_2$.

$$\therefore \quad x_1 = x_2 = \frac{1}{2}\, X_{sc} = \frac{1}{2}\, \sqrt{Z_{sc}^2 - R_{sc}} \quad ...(4.12)$$

Thus, from blocked-rotor test, parameters r_2, x_1 and x_2 can be determined if r_1 is known.

4.6.2. No-load Test

For no-load test, single-phase induction motor is run at no load at rated voltage and frequency. Slip is very close to zero at no-load test, therefore $\frac{r_2}{2s}$ becomes very large as compared to $X_m/2$. Therefore, $\left[\frac{r_2}{2s} + j\frac{x_2}{2}\right]$ associated with forward field, may be neglected as shown in Fig. 4.7 *(b)*.

For almost zero slip, $\frac{r_2}{2(2-s)} \simeq \frac{r_2}{4}$, associated with backward field, becomes quite small as compared to $X_m/2$. Therefore, $X_m/2$ associated with backward field impedance can be neglected, Fig. 4.7 *(b)*. Therefore, Fig. 4.7 *(b)* gives the simplified equivalent circuit during no-load test.

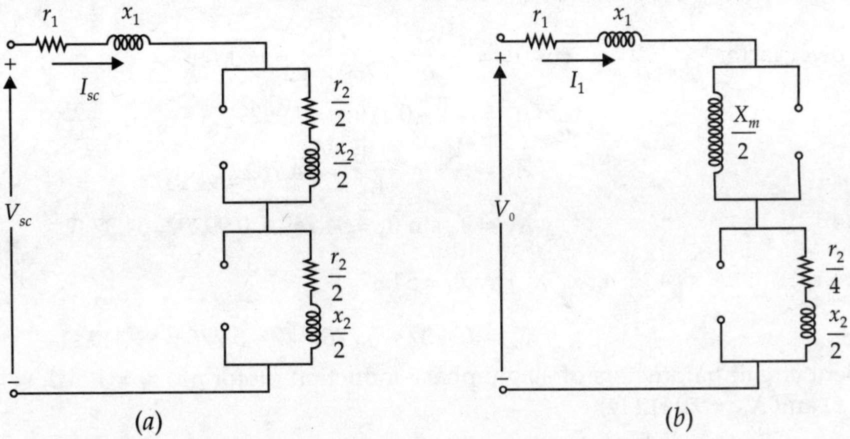

Fig 4.7: Simplified equivalent circuit for a single-phase induction motor during *(a)* blocked-rotor test and *(b)* no-load test.

During no-load test, let V_o, I_o, W_o be the voltmeter, ammeter and wattmeter readings respectively.

$$\therefore \text{ No load power factor,} \quad \cos\theta_o = \frac{W_o}{V_o I_o}$$

$$\text{No load equivalent impedance,} \quad Z_o = \frac{V_o}{I_o}$$

No load equivalent reactance, $X_o = Z_o\sqrt{1-\cos^2\theta_o} = Z_o \sin\theta_o$ ...(4.13)

From Fig. 4.7 *(b)*, the no load equivalent reactance X_o is

$$X_o = x_1 + \frac{1}{2}(x_2 + X_m) \quad ...(4.14)$$

From blocked-rotor test, x_1 and x_2 are already known. No load equivalent reactance X_o can be calculated from Eq. (4.13). This shows that magnetizing reactance X_m can be determined from Eq. (4.14). Thus no load test gives the value of magnetizing reactance X_m.

Example 4.2. *A 230 V, single-phase induction motor gave the following test results :*

Blocked-rotor test : 120 V, 9.6 A, 440 W

No-load test : 230 V, 4.2 A, 115 W

The stator winding reasistance is 1.5 Ω and during the blocked-rotor test, the auxiliary winding is kept open. Determine the equivalent circuit parameters. Also, find the core, friction and windage losses.

Solution. Blocked-rotor test : $V_{sc} = 120$ V, $I_{sc} = 9.6$ A, $W_{sc} = 440$ W.

From Eq. (4.9),
$$Z_{sc} = \frac{V_{sc}}{I_{sc}} = \frac{120}{9.6} = 12.5\ \Omega$$

From Eq. (4.10),
$$R_{sc} = \frac{W_{sc}}{I_{sc}^2} = \frac{440}{9.6^2} = 4.774\ \Omega$$

From Eq. (4.11),
$$r_2 = R_{sc} - r_1 = 4.774 - 1.5 = 3.274\ \Omega$$

$$X_{sc} = \sqrt{Z_{sc}^2 - R_{sc}^2} = \sqrt{12.5^2 - 4.774^2} = 11.552\ \Omega$$

$$x_1 = x_2 = \frac{1}{2}X_{sc} = \frac{1}{2} \times 11.552 = 5.776\ \Omega$$

No-load test : $V_o = 230$ V, $I_o = 4.2$ A, $W_o = 115$ W

No-load power factor,
$$\cos\theta_o = \frac{W_o}{V_o I_o} = \frac{115}{230 \times 4.2} = 0.119$$

$$\sin\theta_o = \sqrt{1 - 0.119^2} = 0.9929$$

$$Z_o = \frac{V_o}{I_o} = \frac{230}{4.2} = 54.762\ \Omega$$

From Eq. (4.13),
$$X_o = Z_o \sin\theta_o = 54.762 \times 0.9929 = 54.37\ \Omega$$

From Eq. (4.14),
$$x_1 + \frac{1}{2}(x_2 + X_m) = X_o = 54.37$$

$$\therefore \quad X_m = (54.37 - 5.776) \times 2 - 5.776 = 91.412\ \Omega$$

∴ Equivalent circuit parameters of single-phase induction motor are $r_1 = 1.5\ \Omega$, $r_2 = 3.274\ \Omega$, $x_1 = x_2 = 5.776\ \Omega$ and $X_m = 91.412\ \Omega$

Core, friction and windage losses = Power input to motor at no load – I^2R losses at no load

$$= W_o - I_o^2\left[r_1 + \frac{r_2}{4}\right]$$

$$= 115 - 4.2^2\left[1.5 + \frac{3.274}{4}\right] = 74.1\ \text{W}$$

4.7. STARTING METHODS OF SINGLE-PHASE INDUCTION MOTORS

It has been stated before that a single-phase induction motor with main stator winding alone has no inherent starting torque. It is because main winding produces stationary pulsating air-gap field.

For the development of starting torque, rotating air-gap field must be produced at the time of starting. Several methods have been developed for the starting of 1-phase induction motors. These are:

1. Split-phase starting
2. Shaded-pole starting

Here, only split-phase starting methods for 1-phase induction motors are described.

4.8. SPLIT PHASE STARTING METHODS

Single-phase induction motors using this method of starting are called **split-phase motors.** All split-phase motors have two stator windings, a **main (or running) winding** and an **auxiliary (or starting) winding**. Both these windings are space displaced from each other by 90° electrical as shown in Fig. 4.1. At the time of starting, both windings are in circuit. When the rotor has achieved about 75% of synchronous speed, auxiliary winding is disconnected from the supply by a centrifugal switch mounted on the shaft. The motor now runs on the main stator winding as a single-phase induction motor.

There are two important methods of phase splitting. These are *(i)* resistor phase splitting and *(ii)* capacitor phase splitting. Motors using resistor phase splitting are called **resistor-split phase motors** and those employing capacitor phase splitting are called **capacitor split-phase motors.**

The two types are now described below.

4.8.1. Resistor Split Phase Motors

The schematic diagram of a resistor split phase motor with two stator windings in quadrature is shown in Fig. 4.8 *(a)*. Here *M* and *A* denote main and auxiliary windings respectively. Subscripts *m* and *a* are used to denote main and auxiliary winding quantities respectively. *C S* is the centrifugal switch.

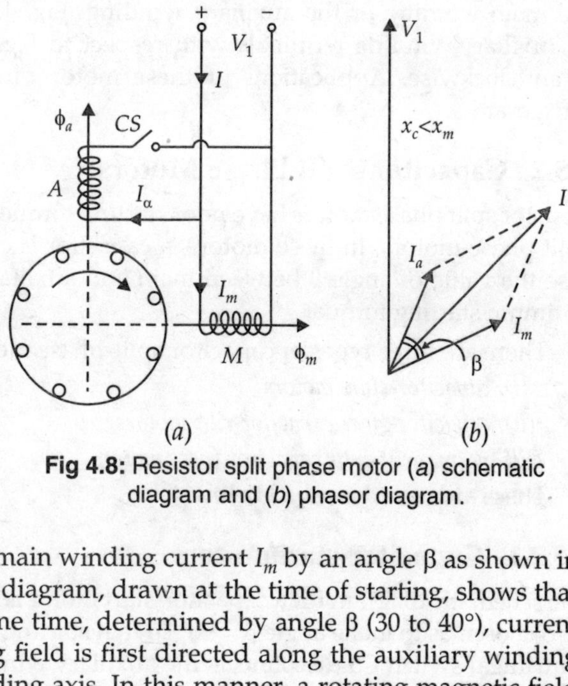

Fig 4.8: Resistor split phase motor *(a)* schematic diagram and *(b)* phasor diagram.

The current in the two windings can be made out of phase by having different impedances for main and auxiliary windings. For this purpose, main winding *M* is designed to have lower resistance (thick wire) and higher leakage reactance x_m. But the auxiliary winding is made to have high resistance (thin wire) and lower leakage reactance x_a. Since the auxiliary winding has lower leakage reactance as compared to main winding, *i.e.* $x_a < x_m$, auxiliary winding current I_a **leads** the main winding current I_m by an angle β as shown in the phasor diagram of Fig. 4.8 *(b)*. This phasor diagram, drawn at the time of starting, shows that current I_a reaches maximum first and after some time, determined by angle β (30 to 40°), current I_m reaches maximum. This means that rotating field is first directed along the auxiliary winding axis and sometimes later, along the main winding axis. In this manner, a rotating magnetic field is produced and rotor begins to rotate from auxiliary winding to main winding in the clockwise direction as shown in Fig. 4.8 *(a)*.

The two stator windings are 90° phase displaced as in Fig. 4.1, but the two currents I_a and I_m are not in quadrature (90° time displacement). Therefore, at the time of starting, motor behaves like an unbalanced two-phase induction motor.

Motor characteristics for this type of motor are shown in Fig. 4.9 *(a)*. The auxiliary winding *A* is disconnected by a centrifugal switch at about 75% of synchronous speed. After this, the motor runs only on main winding. Therefore, auxiliary winding is designed for short time use whereas main winding must be designed for continuous use.

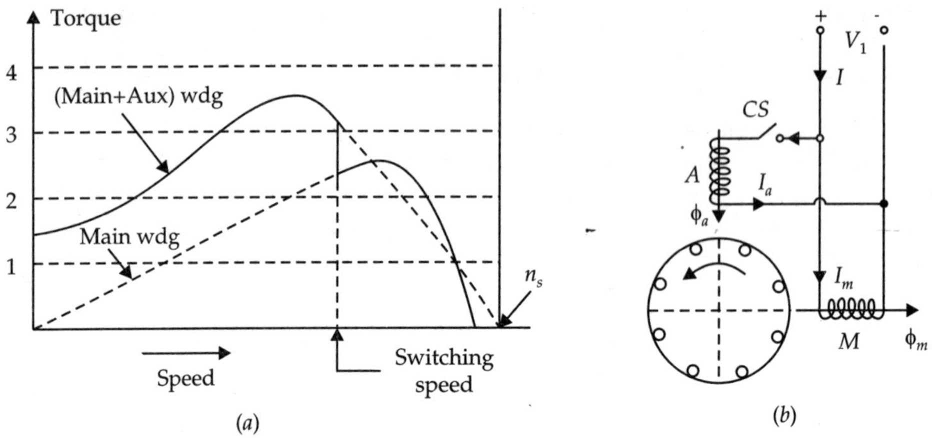

Fig 4.9: Resistor split-phase motor
(a) torque speed characteristics and *(b)* reversing the direction of rotation.

If the direction of rotation is to be reversed, interchange the supply to two terminals of either the main winding or the auxiliary winding. Fig. 4.9 *(b)* shows the interchange of supply leads to auxiliary winding terminals with respect to Fig. 4.8 *(a)* ; now the direction of rotor rotation is anticlockwise. Applications of these motors are for fans, blowers, centrifugal pumps and refrigerators.

4.8.2. Capacitor Split Phase Motors

Resistor split phase motors have poor starting torque. This problem is solved by the use of capacitor split phase motors. In these motors, a capacitor is connected in series with auxiliary winding. In case the value of angle β between main and auxiliary winding currents is 90°, it would result in optimum starting torque.

There are three types of capacitor split-phase motors. These are :

(i) capacitor-start motors,

(ii) capacitor-start capacitor run motors,

(iii) permanent split capacitor (psc) motors.

These are now described below.

4.8.2.1. Capacitor-start motors

The schematic diagram for a capacitor-start motor is shown in Fig. 4.10 *(a)*. The value of capacitor *C* is so chosen as to make angle $\beta = 90°$ so that starting torque, proportional to $I_a I_m \sin \beta$, is high. The centrifugal switch *CS* disconnects the auxiliary winding at about 75% of synchronous speed. The motor is named capacitor star motor because it uses the capacitor for the purpose of starting only.

Torque-speed characteristics of this motor is shown in Fig. 4.10 *(c)*. High starting torque, equal to 3 to 4.5 times the full-load torque, is an outstanding feature of this motor.

Capacitor *C* in the motor may be short-time rated. AC electrolytic capacitors are more commonly employed. The range of starting capacitor is 20 to 30 μ*F* for 100 W motors and 60 to 100 μ*F* for

750 W motors. These motors are used in refrigeration and air-conditioning equipment, compressors, reciprocating pumps etc.

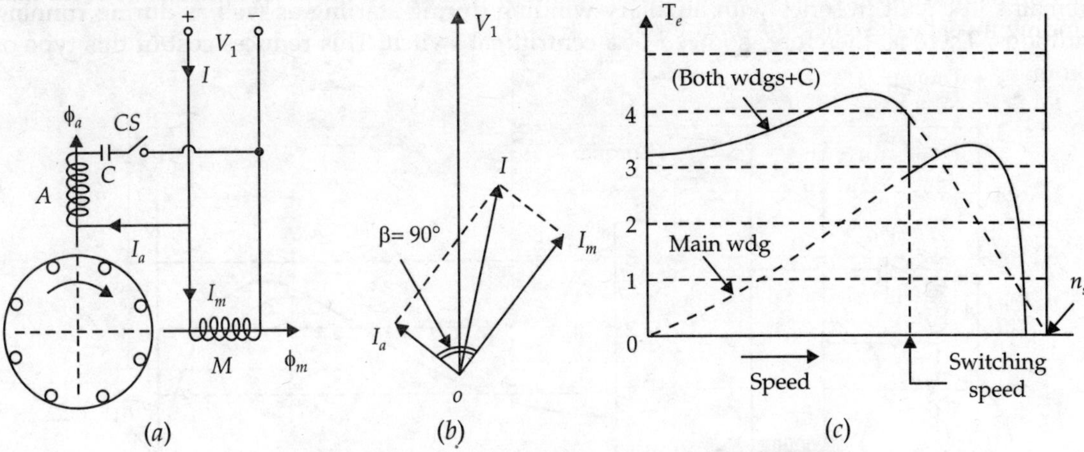

Fig 4.10: Capacitor-start motor *(a)* schematic diagram *(b)* phasor diagram at starting and *(c)* torque-speed characteristics.

4.8.2.2. Capacitor-start capacitor-run motors

Fig. 4.11 *(a)* gives the schematic diagram of this type of motor. Since two capacitors are used, this type of motor is also known as **two-value capacitor motor**. At the time of starting, large capacitor C_1 is connected in parallel with small capacitor C_2. Also, both the capacitors are in series with auxiliary winding. The centrifugal switch *CS* disconnected C_1 automatically at about 75% of synchronous speed, leaving behind C_2, a small capacitor, in series with the auxiliary winding. This shows that the best starting performance with high capacitance and optimum running performance with a low capacitance are obtained with this type of motor. Capacitor C_2 is so designed as to result in almost a balanced two-phase motor under running conditions. This leads to reduced torque pulsations and a quiet motor. Power factor and efficiency are also improved.

Starting capacitor C_1 is of ac electrolytic type, but **run-capacitor** C_2 is of ac paper foil and oil type. Rating of these motors is from 100 to 400 W. These are used for office equipment, fans etc.

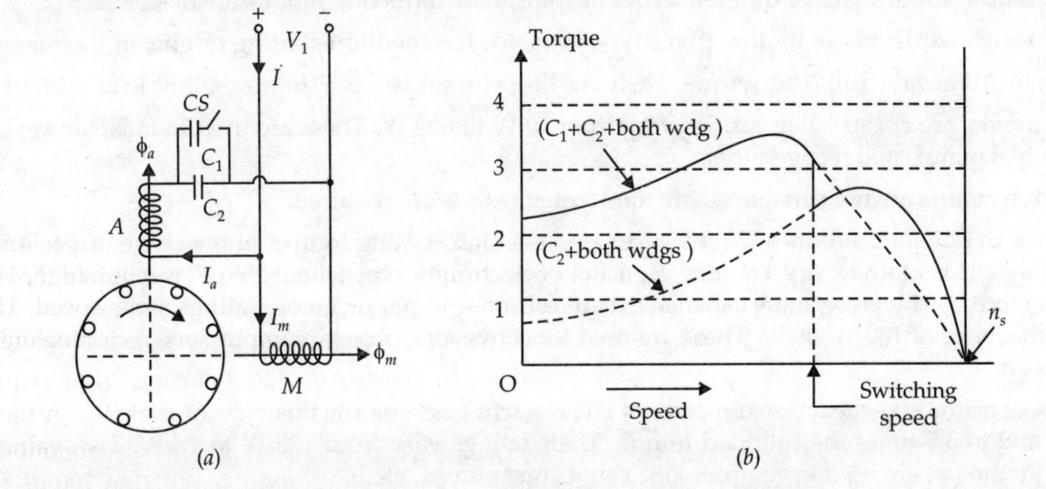

Fig 4.11: Capacitor-start capacitor-run motor *(a)* schematic diagram and *(b)* torque-speed characteristics.

4.8.2.3. Permanent-split capacitor motors

These are also called **capacitor-run motors.** Fig. 4.12 *(a)* gives its schematic diagram. The capacitor *C* remains in circuit in series with auxiliary winding during starting as well as during running conditions. There is, therefore, no need of a centrifugal switch. This reduces cost of this type of motors.

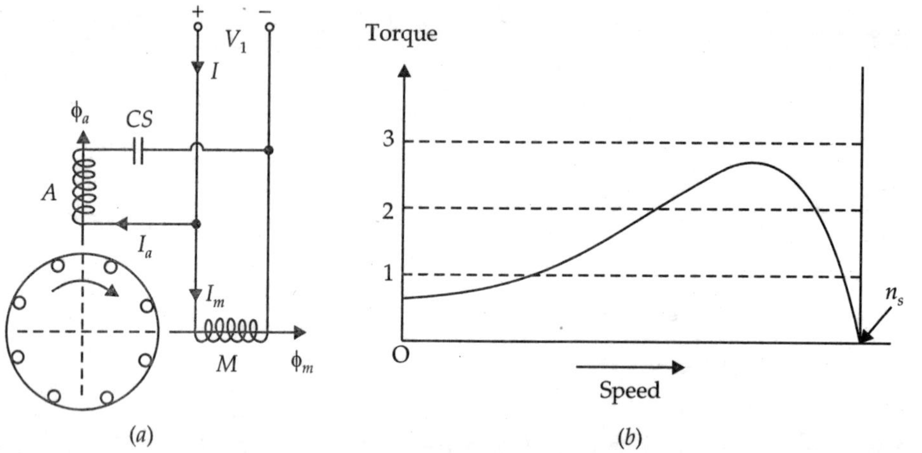

Fig 4.12: Permanent split capacitor motor *(a)* schematic diagram and *(b)* torque-speed characteristics.

In permanent split capacitor motors, the value of permanent capacitor is so chosen as to obtain a compromise between the best starting and optimum running conditions. Torque-speed characteristic of these motors is shown in Fig. 4.12 (*b*). It is seen from this curve that this type of motor has small starting torque.

These motors are used where quiet operation is essential, as in offices, classrooms, theatres etc. Ceiling fans are usually of permanent split-capacitor type, in which the value of capacitance varies from 2 to 3 μF.

4.9. APPLICATIONS

In this article, applications of different types of split-phase induction motors are described.

1. Resistor-split phase motors : This type of motor has medium starting torque, in the range of $1\frac{1}{2}$ to 2 times the full load torque. Their starting current is 5 to 7 times the full load current. These motors are cheap. Their ratings vary from 10 W to 600 W. These are used in fans, blowers, centrifugal pumps and refrigerators.

These motors are not suitable where too-frequent starts are required.

2. Capacitor start motors : These motors possess high starting torque, in the range of 3 to 4.5 times the full load torque. A VAr rating capacitor of electrolytic type (about 250 μF) is required. This type of motor is, therefore, more expensive than resistor-split phase motor. Ratings of these motors are in the range of 100 to 800 W. These are used for conveyors, pumps, compressors, reciprocating pumps etc.

3. Capacitor star-capacitor run motors : The starting torque for this type of motor is in the range of 2 to 3.5 times the full load torque. Their ratings vary from 125 W to 1 kW. Two-value capacitor motors are used in compressors, conveyors, pumps, etc.

4. Permanent-split capacitor motors : These motors possess low starting torque, less than the full load torque. These are manufactured in the range of 40 W to 600 W. These are used in direct-connected fans, blowers, centrifugal pumps, office equipment, class-room fans, blowers in heaters etc.

PROBLEMS

4.1. Give the constructional features of a single-phase induction motor. Show the basic arrangement of main and auxiliary windings and indicate the space angle between these two windings.

4.2. *(a)* Prove that a single-phase induction motor has no inherent starting torque.

(b) In a single-phase induction motor, derive expressions for slip with respect to forward rotating field and also with respect to backward rotating field.

4.3. Write an expression for the stationary pulsating stator mmf wave when main winding of a single-phase induction motor is fed from single-phase supply. Discuss about the various terms involved in it.

Explain how this pulsating mmf wave can be resolved into two counter rotating mmf waves. Hence draw typical torque-speed characteristics of this motor based on double revolving field theory.

4.4. Draw equivalent circuit for a single-phase induction motor at standstill. Discuss about the various parameter involved in it. Hence, derive the equivalent circuit of this motor based on double revolving field theory when running with a slip *s*.

4.5. Draw the equivalent circuit of a single-phase induction motor based on double revolving field theory. Explain how this circuit can be used to obtain performance calculations of this motor at any slip *s*.

4.6. Based on double revolving field theory, draw equivalent circuit of a single-phase induction motor at any slip *s*. From this, derive expressions for forward field impedance, backward field impedance and internal mechanical power developed in terms of forward and backward field resistances.

4.7. A 230 V, 4-pole, 50 Hz, single-phase induction motor has the following parameters and losses:

$r_1 = 2.3\ \Omega$, $x_1 = 3.2\ \Omega$, $r_2 = 4.2\ \Omega$, $x_2 = 3.2\ \Omega$, $X_m = 74\ \Omega$

Core loss = 90 watts, Friction and windage loss = 30 watts.

The motor is running at rated voltage and frequency with a slip of 0.05. Calculate the stator current, pf, power output, shaft torque and efficiency with auxiliary winding open.

[**Ans.** 6.95 A, 0.637 lag, 645 W, 4.32 Nm, 63.235%]

4.8. Explain the procedure for determining the equivalent circuit parameters of a single-phase induction motor from its no-load and blocked rotor tests and stator winding resistance.

4.9. The following test results were obtained on a 230 V, 50 Hz, 6-pole, single-phase induction motor :

Stator winding resistance = 2.0 Ω

No load test : 230 V, 4 A, 120 W

Blocked-rotor test : 120 V, 10 A, 450 W.

Determine the equivalent circuit parameters of this motor. Also, find the core, friction and windage losses. [**Ans.** $r_1 = 2\ \Omega$, $r_2 = 2.5\ \Omega$, $x_1 = x_2 = 5.562\ \Omega$, $X_m = 97.334\ \Omega$; 78 W]

4.10. List the various split-phase starting methods for single-phase induction motors.

Describe resistor-split phase starting of a single-phase induction motor with the help of its circuit diagram, phasor diagram and torque-speed characteristic.

4.11. Describe the various starting methods for single-phase induction motor employing capacitor-split phase technique. Draw suitable circuit diagrams, phasor diagrams and torque-speed characteristics for each method.

4.12. (*a*) Give the applications of various types of split-phase single-phase induction motors.

(*b*) In a 4-pole, 50 Hz, single-phase induction motor, the power delivered to forward and backward rotating fields are 200 W and 40 W respectively at a speed of 1425 rpm. If no-load rotational losses are 60 W, find the shaft torque. **[Ans.** (*b*) 0.6165 Nm]

Objective Type Questions

1. In a single-phase induction motor,

(*a*) stator has one winding (*b*) rotor is wound-rotor type

(*c*) stator has two windings (*d*) stator and rotor windings are in series.

2. Read the following statements about a single-phase induction motor,

(*a*) the starting winding is placed on rotor (*b*) the main winding is placed on stator

(*c*) this motor is a self-starting motor (*d*) this motor can run in one direction only.

3. In a single-phase induction motor driving a fan load, the reason for having a high resistance rotor is to achieve

(*a*) low starting torque (*b*) quick acceleration

(*c*) high efficiency (*d*) reduced size [*GATE*, 2005]

4. In a capacitor-split motor, if C_1 is the capacitance required for best starting torque and C_2 for best running performance, then

(*a*) C_1 is much smaller than C_2 (*b*) C_1 is almost equal to C_2

(*c*) C_1 is much larger than C_2

(*d*) nothing can be specified about their relative values.

5. The direction of rotation of a single-phase induction motor can be reversed by

(*a*) reversing the leads of the main supply

(*b*) reversing the leads of both windings

(*c*) reversing the leads of auxiliary winding only

(*d*) either (*a*) or (*c*).

6. In a capacitor start single-phase induction motor, the current in the auxiliary winding

(*a*) lags the current I_m in the main winding

(*b*) is in phase with I_m

(*c*) leads I_m by 90°

(*d*) leads I_m by about 80°.

7. When main winding of a single-phase induction motor is connected to 220 V, 50 Hz source, it takes a current off 55 $\angle -60°$ A at standstill. Neglecting stator leakage impedance and magnetizing current, the rotor circuit parameters r_2 and x_2 in ohms are respectively

(*a*) 2, 3.464 (*b*) 3.464, 2 (*c*) 4, 6.928 (*d*) 6.928, 4

8. In case of resistor-split phase motor, the phase shift between the currents in the two windings is around,

(*a*) 30° (*b*) 70° (*c*) 90° (*d*) 120° [*GATE*, 1996]

9. In a capacitor-start single-phase induction motor, if the capacitor fails to open as the speed picks up, then

   (a) the motor will stop
   (b) the auxiliary winding will be damaged
   (c) main winding will be damaged
   (d) capacitor will be damaged.

10. In a capacitor-start induction motor, the value of capacitor is decided by its

   (a) speed
   (b) efficiency
   (c) starting torque
   (d) power factor

11. In the torque-slip characteristic of a single-phase induction motor will only main winding energised, it is found that

   1. torque is zero when slip is zero
   2. torque is zero when slip = 1
   3. torque is zero with slip a little less than one
   4. torque is negative when slip is zero

   From above, the correct statements are

   (a) 1, 2, 3, 4
   (b) 1, 2, 3
   (c) 2, 3, 4
   (d) 1, 2, 4

Answers

1. (c)	**2.** (b)	**3.** (b)	**4.** (c)	**5.** (c)
6. (d)	**7.** (a)	**8.** (a)	**9.** (d)	**10.** (c)
11. (c)				

Chapter 5

Synchronous Machines

Large ac power networks operate at constant frequency of 60 Hz or 50 Hz. These power networks rely primarily on synchronous generators for electrical energy.

Like other rotating electrical machines, a synchronous machine has a rotor and a stator. Its rotor always runs at synchronous speed. This machine can work as a synchronous generator or a synchronous motor. A synchronous generator, also called **ac generator** or **alternator**, converts mechanical energy of prime-mover into electrical energy. A synchronous motor converts ac electrical energy into mechanical energy. Since ac networks are always 3-phase power systems, three-phase synchronous machines are invariably used. In a synchronous generator, frequency of ac output voltage depends on the number of poles and speed. Similarly, the rotating speed of rotor in a synchronous motor is dependent on number of poles and frequency. A rotating machine that operates at a speed fixed by the number of poles and frequency is called a synchronous machine.

Synchronous generators have ratings varying from a few kVA to very large sizes. The biggest size in India has a rating of 500 MVA used in super thermal plants. A single largest unit of synchronous generator having rating of about 1500 MVA are being produced at present. These ratings may grow to several thousand MVA in the near future. At present, synchronous generators are used universally for the generation of three-phase power in the whole world.

Like dc machines, all synchronous machines have one field winding and one armature winding. A synchronous machine may have stationary field and rotating armature or rotating field and stationary armature. In small sizes, up to about 10 kVA or so, a synchronous machine may have stationary field and rotating armature. But in large rated machines, field winding is on rotor and armature winding on stator. For large synchronous machines, the stator windings are designed to handle voltages up to 33 kV.

5.1. CONSTRUCTIONAL FEATURES OF SYNCHRONOUS MACHINES

Here, the armature winding is taken on the stator and field winding on rotor. Depending upon the rotor structure, there are two types of synchronous machines; these are (*a*) cylindrical-rotor, round-rotor or non-salient type and (*b*) salient-pole type. The constructional features of both types are now described.

5.1.1. Stator Construction

Stator structure of both types of synchronous machines is similar. A synchronous machine stator consists of frame, core, slots, teeth and armature winding. For small size machines, stator frame is made from cast-iron. For large size machines, stator frame is fabricated from mild steel plates welded together. Inside the frame, there is stator core made from high-grade steel laminations. Inner periphery of the stator core is slotted to house the three-phase armature winding. Usually, double layer fractional slot (slots per pole per phase not an integer) windings are used. The three-phase winding is uniformly distributed in slots. The armature is always star-connected.

The three-phase armature winding is so designed as to generate an output voltage as nearly sinusoidal as possible. In a synchronous motor, the 3-phase armature winding would produce rotating magnetic field almost sinusoidal in nature. Fig. 5.1 illustrates the constructional features of stator of both types of synchronous machines. In this figure, stator frame, stator core, stator teeth, stator slots and armature winding are clearly indicated.

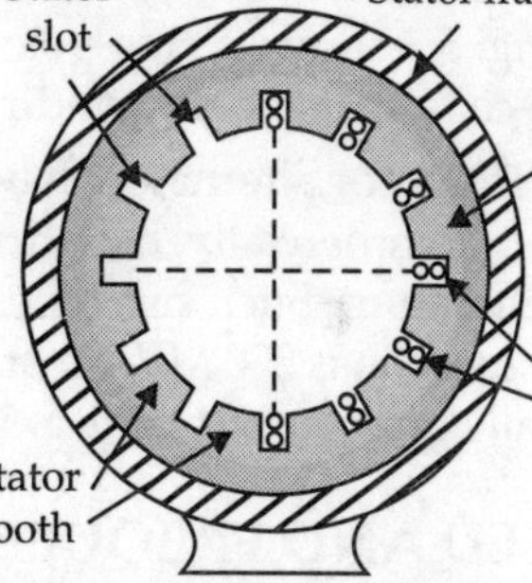

Fig 5.1: Stator structure of a synchronous machine.

5.1.2. Rotor Construction

As stated before, there are two types of rotor structures, salient-pole type and cylindrical-rotor type. These two types are now described.

5.1.2.1. Salient-pole rotor

The rotor consists of shaft, steel spider, even number of **salient or projecting poles,** concentric field winding, **damper bars** etc. The poles are made of a stack of mild steel laminations about 2 mm thick. These laminations are pressed between two thick steel-end plates by rivets or bolts. Now concentric field winding is put on the pole core. The poles are then fitted to steel spider by bolts or by dove-tail joints as shown in Fig. 5.2. Slots are prepared in the pole shoes to house damper bars. The function of damper bars is to damp out rotor oscillations during sudden changes in load conditions. The pole shoes are so shaped as to have minimum air gap at the pole centre and more air gap at the pole tips. This is done to obtain sinusoidal flux distribution under the poles.

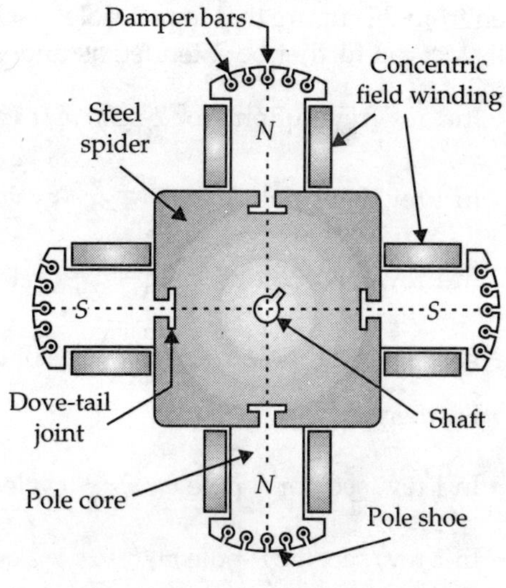

Fig 5.2: Four-pole salient-pole rotor.

The field windings on various poles are connected in series to produce alternate north and south poles on the rotor. The field winding terminals are fed from a dc source through brushes and two slip rings. The slip rings are mounted on the shaft but are insulated from it.

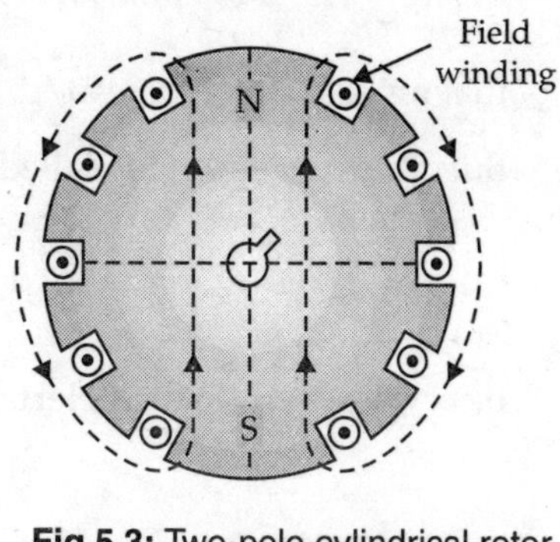

Fig 5.3: Two-pole cylindrical rotor.

Salient pole synchronous machines have small length but larger rotor diameter to accommodate large number of salient poles.

Salient-pole alternators driven by impulse turbines have horizontal configuration and those driven by Kaplan turbines have vertical configuration. Commercially, salient-pole alternators driven by water turbines are called **hydro-alternators** or **hydro-generators.**

5.1.2.2. Cylindrical rotor

Cylindrical rotor is made from steel forgings of high grade steel nickel-chrome-molybdenum steel. Outer periphery of the rotor has slots to house the field winding. About two-third of rotor periphery is slotted. Fig. 5.3 shows a two-pole cylindrical rotor. In this figure, there are five concentric field coils. These coils, called field winding, creates two poles in the unslotted rotor portion as shown.

Cylindrical-rotor alternators have two or four poles on the rotor. These are driven by steam or gas turbines. Commercially, cylindrical-rotor synchronous generators are called **turbo-alternators** or **turbo-generators**. Such machines are built in sizes varying from 10 MVA to 1500 MVA. The biggest size in India is 500 MVA installed at a superthermal power plant. Turbo-generators usually possess small diameter but large axial length.

5.2. SPEED AND FREQUENCY

Consider a 2-pole machine as shown in Fig. 5.4 (*a*). When the rotating conductor is at *'a'*, zero emf (= *Blv*) is generated in it, because flux density at *'a'* is zero. When the conductor rotates to position *b*, maximum emf is generated, at *c* zero emf, at *d* maximum emf though negative and further at *'a'* again, zero emf is generated. This variation of generated emf is shown sinusoidal in Fig. 5.4 (*b*). It is seen from this figure that for a 2-pole machine, 1 $\left(=\frac{2}{2}\right)$ cycle of emf is generated in one revolution. This fact can further be extended as under :

In 1 rev (revolution), for 2-pole *m/c* (machine 1 $\left(=\frac{2}{2}\right)$ cycle of emf is generated.

In 1 rev, for 4-pole *m/c*, 2 $\left(=\frac{4}{2}\right)$ cycles of emf would be generated.

In 1 rev, for 6 pole *m/c*, 3 $\left(=\frac{6}{2}\right)$ cycles of emf would be generated.

In 1 rev, for P-pole *m/c*, $\frac{P}{2}$ cycles of emf would be generated.

Further,

In 1 rev/sec, for *P*-pole *m/c*, $\frac{P}{2}$ cycles/sec of emf would be generated.

In 2 rev/sec, for *P*-pole *m/c*, $\frac{P}{2} \times 2$ cycles/sec of emf would be generated.

In 3 rev/sec, for *P*-pole *m/c*, $\frac{P}{2} \times 3$ cycles/sec of emf would be generated.

In *n* rev/sec, for *P*-pole *m/c*, $\frac{P}{2} \times n$ cycles/sec of emf would be generated.

But cycles per second is called frequency. Therefore, it can be stated that frequency of generated emf is given by

$$f = \frac{P \cdot n}{2} \text{ cycles/sec} \qquad \text{...(5.1a)}$$

But cycles/sec is called Hertz.

$$\therefore \qquad f = \frac{P \cdot n}{2} \text{ Hz}$$

Here n = speed in rps. In case speed is in rpm, then $n = \frac{N}{60}$ where N is in rpm.

$$\therefore \qquad f = \frac{P \cdot N}{2 \times 60} = \frac{PN}{120} \qquad \text{...(5.1}b\text{)}$$

Synchronous speed : If supply frequency is f Hz in a synchronous machine and P is the number of poles, then from Eq. (5.1),

$$N_s = \frac{120f}{P} \text{ rpm} \qquad \text{...(5.2)}$$

The speed given by Eq. (5.2) is called **synchronous speed**. For an alternator operation, the prime-mover must rotate the rotor at synchronous speed. For a synchronous motor, the rotor would always run at synchronous speed.

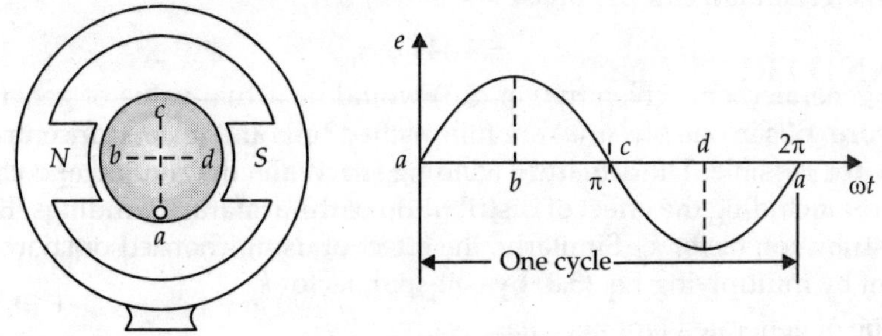

Fig 5.4: Pertaining to two-pole machine with one conductor.

5.3. GENERATED EMF IN AN ALTERNATOR

In an alternator, rotor is driven by a prime-mover at synchronous speed. With relative motion between field flux and armature conductors, emfs are generated in the armature windings of alternator. The purpose of this article is to derive an expression for the emf generated in a synchronous generator.

5.3.1. Emf Equation of an Alternator

Let $\quad Z$ = series armature conductors per phase

N_{ph} = series armature turns per phase = $\frac{Z}{2}$

P = number of poles

ϕ = flux per pole, Wb

N = rotor speed in rpm

f = frequency of generated voltage, Hz

Since flux per pole is ϕ, each stator conductor cuts a total field flux of $P\phi$ webers in one revolution. Here rotor speed is N revolutions per minute or N revolutions per 60 seconds.

$$\therefore \qquad \text{Time for one revolution} = \frac{60}{N} \text{ sec.}$$

Average emf generated in one conductor E_z is given by

$$E_z = \frac{\text{Total field flux cut by one conductor in one revolution}}{\text{Total time for one revolution}}$$

$$= \frac{P\phi}{60/N} = \frac{P\phi N}{60}$$

From Eq. (5.1), frequency $f = \frac{PN}{120}$ or $N = \frac{120f}{P}$.

Substituting this value of speed N in above expression, we get average emf per conductor,

$$E_z = \frac{P\phi}{60} \times \frac{120f}{P} = 2f\,\phi \text{ volts}$$

There are Z conductors in series per phase, therefore, average generated emf per phase = $2f\,\phi\,Z$ = $2f\,\phi\,(2\,N_{ph}) = 4\,f\,\phi\,N_{ph}$ volts. For sine voltage wave generated in armature,

$$\frac{\text{rms value}}{\text{average value}} = 1.11$$

$\therefore$ Rms value of generated emf per phase = $1.11 \times 4\,f\,\phi\,N_{ph}$

$$= 4.44\,f\,\phi\,N_{ph} \qquad ...(5.3)$$

The value of generated emf given by Eq. (5.3) would be actual value of generated voltage in case all the armature coils in one phase (*a*) are full-pitched coils and (*b*) are concentrated in one slot. This, however, is not possible. The armature winding is actually distributed and chorded coils are used. Therefore, for including the effect of distribution of the armature windings, Eq. (5.3) must be multiplied by distribution factor k_d. Similarly, the effect of using chorded or short pitched coils is taken into account by multiplying Eq. (5.3) by coil-span factor k_p.

$\therefore$ Actual value of generated emf per phase is given by

$$E_{ph} = 4.44 \times k_d \times k_p \times f\,\phi\,N_{ph}$$
$$= 4.44\,k_w \cdot f\,\phi\,N_{ph} \qquad ...(5.4)$$

where $k_w = k_d \times k_p$ is called winding factor for armature winding. Distribution factor, coil-span factor and winding factor are already described in Chapter 1. Note that $\sqrt{2} \cdot \pi = 4.442833 \cong 4.44$, therefore E_{ph} can also be written as

$$E_{ph} = \sqrt{2} \cdot \pi\,f\,\phi\,k_w \cdot N_{ph} \qquad ...(5.4\,a)$$

For star-connected alternator, line voltage

$$E_L = \sqrt{3} \cdot E_{ph} = \sqrt{3} \times \sqrt{2} \cdot \pi\,f\,\phi\,k_w\,N_{ph}.$$

and for delta-connected alternator, $E_L = E_{ph} = \sqrt{2} \cdot \pi\,f\,\phi\,k_w \cdot N_{ph}$.

The per-phase voltage generated in a 3-phase alternator is usually written as

$$E_f = E_{ph} = 4.44\,f\,\phi\,k_w \cdot N_{ph} = \sqrt{2} \cdot \pi\,f\,\phi\,k_w \cdot N_{ph} \qquad ...(5.4\,b)$$

Here E_f is called open-circuit voltage per phase, per-phase generated voltage at no load, **excitation emf per phase** or excitation voltage per phase.

Example 5.1. *A 3-phase, 50 Hz, 10 pole alternator has the following data :*

Slots per pole per phase = 3, Conductors per slot = 12

Flux per pole = 0.05 Wb.

Coils are chorded by one slot. If all the conductors per phase are connected in series, calculate the generated emf per phase and its line value.

Solution. Here slots per pole per phase, $q = 3$

Total number of slots, $S = q \times \text{poles} \times \text{phases} = 3 \times 10 \times 3 = 90$

Slot angular pitch, $\gamma = \frac{P \times 180}{\text{number of slots}} = \frac{10 \times 180}{90} = 20°$

Distribution factor, $k_d = \frac{\sin\frac{q\gamma}{2}}{q\sin\frac{\gamma}{2}} = \frac{\sin\frac{3 \times 20}{2}}{3\sin\frac{20}{2}} = 0.9598.$

Coils are chorded by one slot. Therefore, chording angle ε = one slot pitch or one slot angle $\gamma = 20°$.

$\therefore$ Coil-span factor, $\quad k_p = \cos\frac{\varepsilon}{2} = \cos\frac{20}{2} = 0.9848.$

Winding factor, $\quad k_w = k_d \times k_p$

$$= 0.9598 \times 0.9848 = 0.9452.$$

Number of turns per phase, $\quad N_{ph} = \frac{90 \times 12}{2 \times 3} = 180$

From Eq. (5.4), per-phase generated emf is given by

$$E_{ph} = E_f = \sqrt{2}\,\pi f \phi\, k_w \cdot N_{ph}$$

$$= \sqrt{2} \cdot \pi \times 50 \times 0.05 \times 0.9452 \times 180 = \mathbf{1889.45}\text{ V}$$

$\therefore$ Line voltage $\quad = \sqrt{3} \times 1889.45 = \mathbf{3272.53}$ V

5.4. ALTERNATOR ON LOAD

At no load, generated voltage in armature is E_f; it is also called excitation emf. When alternator is loaded, its terminal voltage changes as the load on the alternator is varied. This variation in the terminal voltage V_t is due to the following reasons:

(*a*) Voltage drop due to armature resistance r_a.

(*b*) Voltage drop due to armature leakage reactance x_{al}.

(*c*) Voltage drop due to armature reaction.

This shows that no-load generated voltage is given by

E_f = terminal voltage V_t + sum of voltage drops due to r_a, x_{al} and armature reaction.

(*a*) **Armature resistance drop:** Per-phase armature resistance r_a causes a voltage drop $I_a\,r_a$. Here I_a is the armature current per phase. The voltage drop $I_a\,r_a$ is in phase with armature current.

(*b*) **Armature leakage reactance drop:** When current flows in armature winding, armature flux is set up. The flux which links both armature and field windings is useful flux. Some flux may link only the armature winding, this flux is called **armature leakage flux**. This leakage flux induces an emf in armature winding. The emf established by armature leakage flux is taken care of by voltage drop $I_a{\cdot}x_{al}$, just like a transformer. Here armature winding is assumed to have leakage reactance x_{al}. The voltage drop $I_a \cdot x_{al}$ leads the armature current I_a by 90° as in any inductive reactance. The phasor sum of V_t, $I_a\,r_a$ and $I_a \cdot x_{al}$ is shown in phasor diagram of Fig. 5.5. In this figure, I_a lags V_t by power factor angle θ. As stated before, $I_a\,r_a$ is drawn parallel to I_a and $I_a \cdot x_{al}$ perpendicular to I_a. From this phasor diagram,

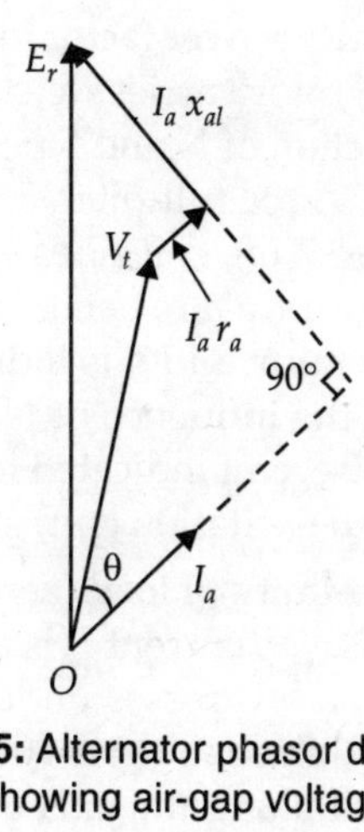

Fig 5.5: Alternator phasor diagram showing air-gap voltage.

$$\bar{E}_r = \bar{V}_t + \bar{I}_a\,(r_a + j\,x_{al}) \qquad ...(5.5)$$

This emf E_r is called **air-gap voltage, internal emf** or **voltage behind leakage impedance.**

5.5. ALTERNATOR AT NO LOAD

Run at synchronous generator at synchronous speed with the help of a prime-mover. Now excite its field winding from a dc source. The alternator terminal voltage is made equal to rated voltate at no load by adjusting its field current. The per phase generated emf at no load, as per Eq. (5.4), is

$$E_f = \sqrt{2} \cdot \pi f k_w \cdot \phi \cdot N_{ph} \qquad ...(5.4)$$

It is already known that generated emf lags by 90° the flux that generates it. This is shown in Fig. 5.6.

In this figure, field mmf $F_f = I_f \cdot N_f$ is taken horizontal just for convenience. Axis of field is along field flux ϕ_f. Excitation emf E_f lags ϕ_f by 90° in Fig. 5.6.

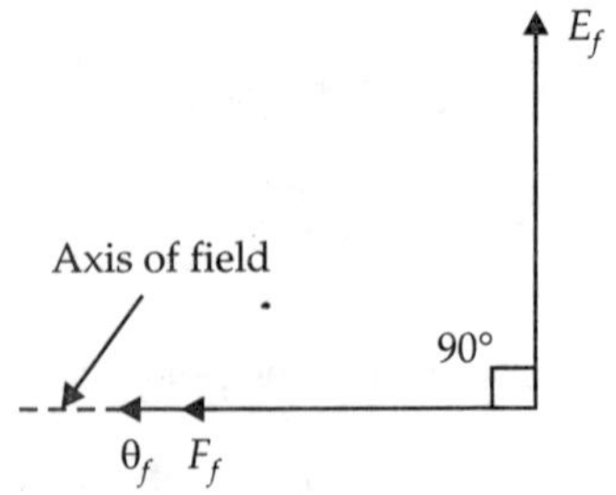

Fig 5.6: Alternator phasor diagram at no load.

5.6. ARMATURE REACTION

When alternator is loaded, current flows in 3-phase armature winding. These currents establish armature mmf and therefore armature flux. This armature flux reacts with the main field flux and may cause the resultant flux to decrease, increase or distort. The effect of armature flux on the flux produced by main field winding is called **armature reaction.**

In a synchronous machine, the effect of armature flux on the main field flux depends on (*i*) the magnitude of armature current and (*ii*) the operating power factor. Here, three extreme conditions of unity power factor, zero pf lagging and zero pf leading would be considered. The results can then be generalized for different operating power factors. For the sake of convenience, a cylindrical-rotor synchronous machine with two field poles is considered.

5.6.1. Armature Reaction in Alternators

Here, we shall first take unity power factor load, then zero pf lagging load, zero pf leading load and finally lagging pf load.

Unity power factor load : In Fig. 5.7 (*a*), a 3-phase synchronous machine is shown. Field winding on the rotor carries dc current indicated by crosses and dots. Right-hand grip rule indicates the production of *N* and *S* poles on the rotor. Rotor is assumed to rotate anticlockwise at synchronous speed. Three full-pitch coils *aa′*, *bb′*, *cc′* on the stator represent three-phase winding in all respects. In Fig. 5.7 (*a*), coil sides *a*, *a′* are located under the influence of *N*, *S* poles respectively. Therefore, coil-sides *a*, *a′* are being cut by peak flux density. As a result, emf generated (= *Blv*) in coil-sides *aa′* is maximum and it is indicated by dot in *a* and cross in *a′* in Fig. 5.7 (*a*). Further, coil-sides *b′*, *c′* are under the influence of N pole, therefore emf induced in these two coil-sides is indicated by dot. Likewise, emf indicated in coil-sides *b*, *c* is shown by cross. This emf generated by field flux ϕ_f alone is called excitation emf, given by Eq. (5.4).

For unity pf load (zero degree angle between E_f and armature current I_a), when E_f is maximum in phase *'a'*, current I_a is also maximum in phase *'a'*. These currents are indicated by dots under *N* pole and by crosses under *S* pole in Fig. 5.7 (*b*). These three armature currents establish armature mmf. Right-hand grip rule for stator armature currents indicates that armature mmf F_a is vertically upward along the axis of phase *a*. Note that armature mmf F_a is due to the combined action of 3-phase mmfs. The phasor sum of F_f and F_a gives resultant air-gap mmf F_r. In Fig. 5.7 (*b*), F_f is leading F_a by 90°, this is indicated in space phasor diagram of Fig. 5.7 (*c*). In Figs. 5.7 (*b*) and (*c*), $\overline{F}_r = \overline{F}_f + \overline{F}_a$ is also shown.

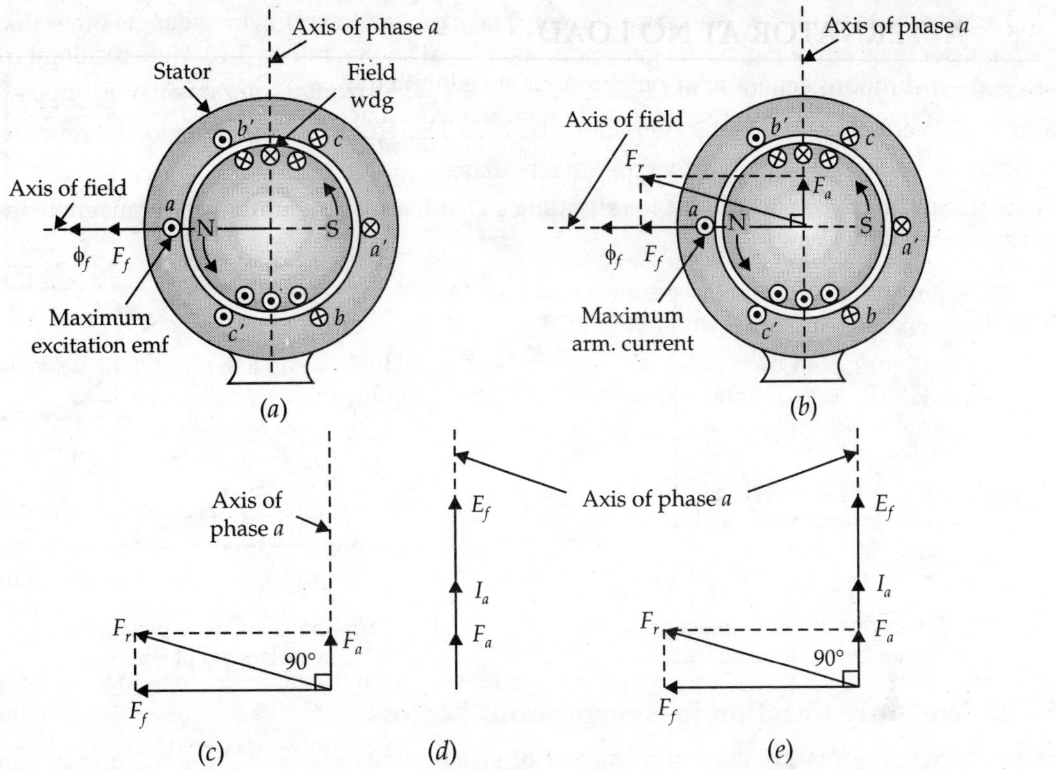

Fig 5.7: (*a*) Generation of emf (*b*) space position of field, armature and resultant mmf (*c*) space-phasor diagram (*d*) time-phasor diagram (*e*) combined space and time phasor diagram.

Armature mmf F_a is proportional to I_a and is also in phase with I_a. In Fig. 5.7 (*c*), F_a is shown vertical as in Fig. 5.7 (*b*). Therefore I_a must be drawn parallel to F_a, *i.e.* along the vertical axis in Fig. 5.7 (*d*). As internal power factor is unity, E_f must be drawn parallel with I_a, in the time phasor diagram of Fig. 5.7 (*d*). Therefore, in Fig. 5.7 (*d*), E_f, I_a and F_a in phase with each other. Space-phasor diagram of Fig. 5.7 (*c*) and time phasor diagram of Fig. 5.7 (*d*) can be superimposed to give the combined space and time phasor diagram of Fig. 5.7 (*e*).

Note from Fig. 5.7 (*b*) that armature mmf F_a is perpendicular to field mmf F_f or field flux ϕ_f, therefore armature mmf at unity power factor is **cross-magnetizing** in nature.

Zero pf lagging load : For zero pf lagging load, the internal pf angle ψ is 90°, *i.e.* the armature current I_a lags the excitation emf E_f by 90°. For zero pf lagging load with $\psi = 90°$, Fig. 5.7 (*e*) gets modified to that shown in Fig. 5.8. As F_a is in phase with I_a, F_a is shown lagging E_f by 90°.

It is observed from Fig. 5.8 that F_a is opposite to F_f and the resultant air-gap mmf $F_r = F_f - F_a$ (numerical difference between F_f and F_a). Since armature mmf opposes field flux, armature mmf under zero pf lagging load is entirely demagnetizing in nature.

Zero leading load : For zero pf leading load, I_a leads E_f by 90°, armature mmf F_a also leads E_f by 90° ; this is shown in Fig. 5.9. It is seen from this figure that F_a aids F_f so that resultant air-gap mmf $F_r = F_f + F_a$ (arithmetic sum of F_f and F_a). Since armature mmf F_a aids the field mmf or field flux, armature mmf under zero pf leading conditions is entirely **magnetizing** in nature.

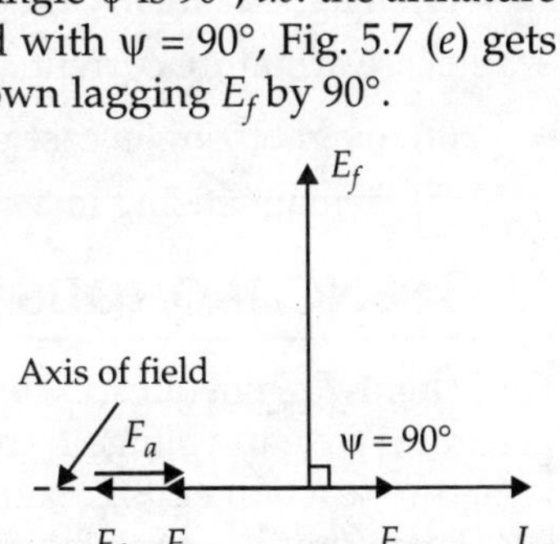

Fig 5.8: Space and time phasor diagram for zero pf lagging load.

Lagging pf load : When armature current I_a lags excitation emf E_f by an angle other than 90°, then phasor diagram of Fig. 5.7 (*e*) gets modified to that shown in Fig. 5.10. Here resultant mmf F_r is equal to the phasor sum of F_f and F_a, *i.e.* $\overline{F}_r = \overline{F}_f + \overline{F}_a$. Horizontal component of F_a opposes field mmf F_f. Its vertical component is perpendicular to F_f. Therefore, for lagging pf load, armature mmf is partly demagnetizing and partly cross-magnetizing.

Similarly, it can be shown that for a leading pf load, armature mmf is partly magnetizing and partly cross-magnetizing.

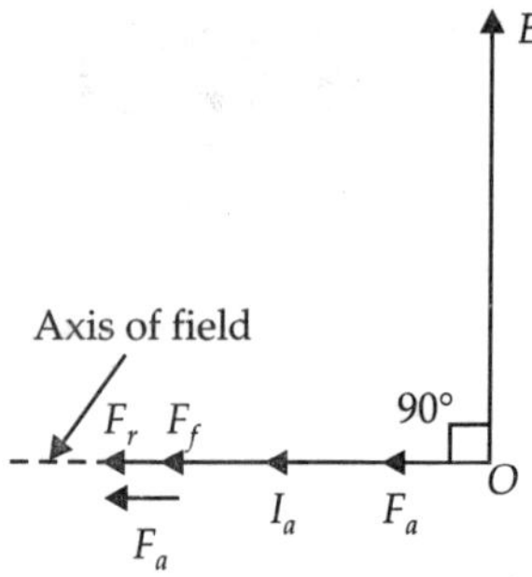

Fig 5.9: Space and time-phasor diagram for zero pf leading load.

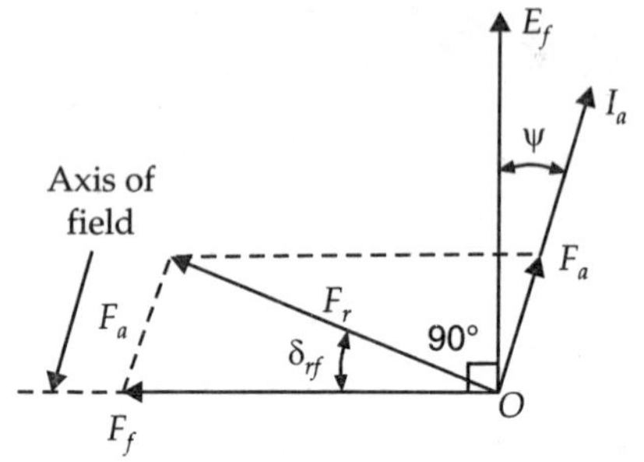

Fig 5.10: Space and time-phasor diagram for a lagging pf load.

5.6.2. Armature Reaction in Synchronous Motors

In an alternator, armature current flows **out** of synchronous machine. In a synchronous motor, armature current flows **into** the synchronous machine. This means that nature of armature mmf in a motor is just the opposite of that in an alternator. As a result, the following conclusions can be derived for a cylindrical-rotor synchronous motor:

(*a*) With synchronous motor working at a lagging pf, the armature mmf is partly magnetizing and partly cross-magnetizing.

(*b*) With synchronous motor working at a leading pf, the armature mmf is partly demagnetizing and partly cross-magnetizing.

It may be summarised from above that if armature current lags the excitation emf E_f by 90°, the nature of armature mmf F_a is

(*a*) demagnetizing in an alternator and

(*b*) magnetizing in case of synchronous motor.

In case armature current I_a leads E_f by 90°, the nature of armature mmf F_a is

(*a*) magnetizing in case of alternator and

(*b*) demagnetizing in a synchronous motor.

5.7. SYNCHRONOUS IMPEDANCE

Field mmf F_f generates excitation emf E_f lagging it by 90°, resultant mmf, or air-gap mmf F_r generates air-gap voltage E_r lagging it by 90°. Similarly, armature reaction mmf F_a must generate armature reaction emf E_{ar} lagging F_a by 90°. This all is shown in Fig. 5.11. Here E_{ar} lags F_a or I_a by 90°. Therefore, E_{ar} is related to current I_a through an inductive reactance. Since E_{ar} lags I_a by 90°, this can be expressed as

$$\overline{E}_{ar} = -j\,X_{ar}\,\overline{I}_a \quad ...(5.6)$$

Here armature reaction mmf F_a is considered equivalent to reactance drop $I_a \cdot X_{ar}$. Here X_{ar} is the fictitious reactance. Since X_{ar} takes care of armature reaction effect, X_{ar} is called **armature reaction reactance** or **armature magnetizing reactance.**

From Fig. 5.11, $\overline{F}_r = \overline{F}_f + \overline{F}_a$

or $\overline{E}_r = \overline{E}_f + \overline{E}_{ar}$ ...(5.7)

or $\overline{E}_f = \overline{E}_r - \overline{E}_{ar}$

From Eq. (5.6), $\overline{E}_{ar} = -j X_{ar} \cdot \overline{I}_a$

$\therefore$ $\overline{E}_f = \overline{E}_r + j\, \overline{I}_a \cdot X_{ar}$

From Eq. (5.5), $\overline{E}_r = \overline{V}_t + \overline{I}_a\, (r_a + j\, x_{al})$

$\therefore$ $\overline{E}_f = \overline{V}_t + \overline{I}_a r_a + j\, \overline{I}_a\, (x_{al} + X_{ar})$

$= \overline{V}_t + \overline{I}_a r_a + j\, \overline{I}_a \cdot X_s$ ...(5.8)

where $X_s = (x_{al} + X_{ar})$ is called **synchronous reactance.**

Also $\overline{E}_f = \overline{V}_t + \overline{I}_a\, (r_a + j\, X_s)$

$= \overline{V}_t + \overline{I}_a \overline{Z}_s$

where $Z_s = (r_a + j\, X_s) = \sqrt{r_a^2 + X_s^2}$ ...(5.9)

The impedance Z_s is called **synchronous impedance.**

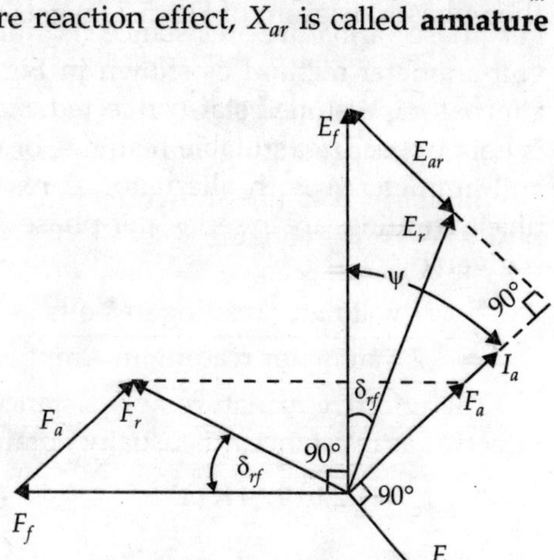

Fig 5.11: Alternator phasor diagram for a lagging pf load showing armature reaction emf E_{ar}

5.8. EQUIVALENT CIRCUIT OF CYLINDRICAL ROTOR ALTERNATOR

Eqs. (5.5) and (5.8) give the equivalent circuit of a cylindrical-rotor alternator as shown in Fig. 5.12 (*a*). In this figure, air-gap emf $\overline{E}_r = \overline{V}_t + \overline{I}_a\, (r_a + j\, x_{al})$. Also excitation emf is equal to the phasor sum of E_r and $I_a X_{ar}$, *i.e.* $\overline{E}_f = \overline{E}_r + j\, \overline{I}_a X_{ar}$. Fig. 5.12 (*a*) is redrawn in Fig. 5.12 (*b*) by taking synchronous reactance X_s = armature leakage reactance x_{al} + armature reaction reactance X_{ar}. Here phasor sum of V_t and $I_a\, (r_a + j\, X_s)$ gives the excitation emf E_f.

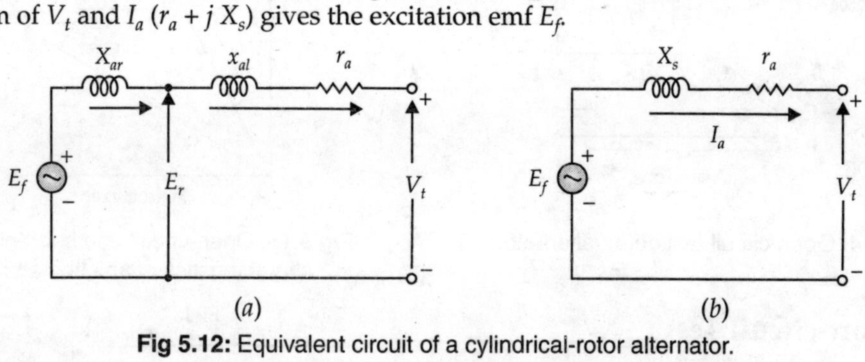

Fig 5.12: Equivalent circuit of a cylindrical-rotor alternator.

5.9. MEASUREMENT OF SYNCHRONOUS IMPEDANCE

Synchronous impedance Z_s and synchronous reactance X_s can be determined by performing the following tests on a synchronous machine:

(*a*) DC resistance test

(*b*) open-circuit test and

(*c*) short-circuit test.

5.9.1. DC Resistance Test

Per-phase armature resistance is measured by volt-ammeter method as shown in Fig. 5.13. Here alternator is assumed star-connected. Field winding is kept open. Take suitable readings of voltmeter V and ammeter A with alternator at rest. Since two phase windings are in series, per-phase dc resistance is given by

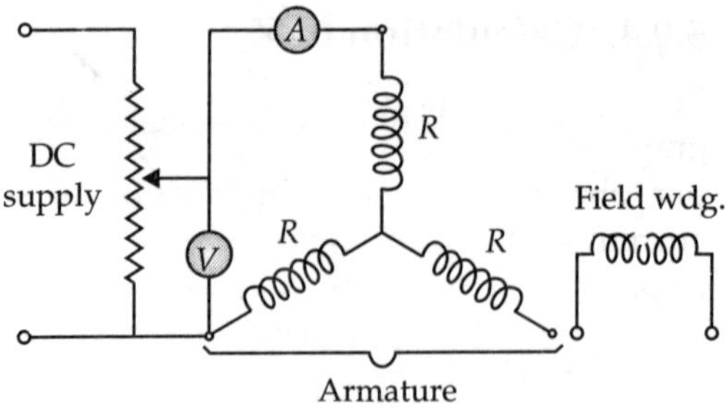

Fig 5.13: Measurement of armature resistance.

$$R = \frac{\text{voltmeter reading in Volts}}{2 \times \text{ammeter reading in Amps}}$$

The effective armature ac resistance is more than its dc resistance R because of spin effect. Effective ac resistance r_a is usually obtained by multiplying dc resistance R by a factor of 1.2 to 1.3.

$\therefore \quad r_a = (1.2 \text{ to } 1.3)\, R\ \Omega.$

5.9.2. Open Circuit Test

The connections are made as shown in Fig. 5.14. The rotor is run at synchronous speed by a prime-mover. Initially, field current is set to zero value.

Now field current is gradually increased in steps. At each step, readings of field current I_f and open circuit emf E_f upto about 1.25 times the rated phase voltage are taken. Now a gaph is plotted between per-phase excitation emf E_f and dc field current I_f as shown in Fig. 5.15. The characteristic curve so obtained is called **open-circuit characteristic** (OCC) or **magnetization curve** of alternator. The extension of linear portion of OCC is called **air-gap line** as shown in Fig. 5.15.

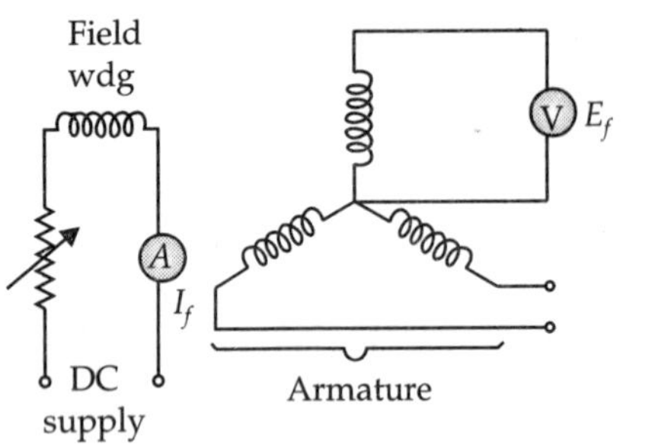

Fig 5.14: Open-circuit test on an alternator.

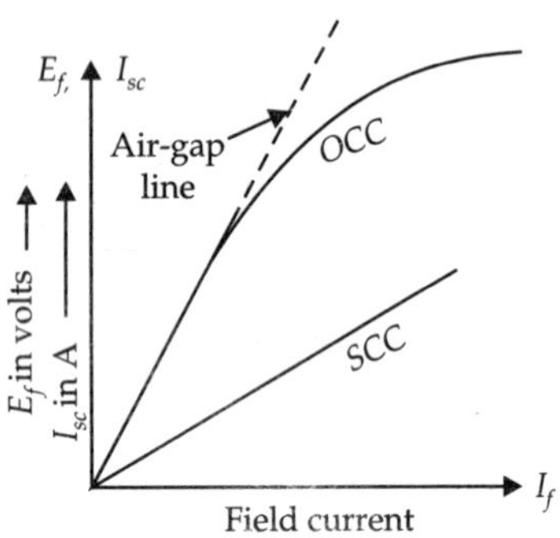

Fig 5.15: Open-circuit and short-circuit characteristics of an alternator.

5.9.3. Short-circuit Test

For this test, connections are made as shown in Fig. 5.16. Initially, the field current is set to zero. The alternator is driven at synchronous speed by a prime-mover.

Now field current is gradually increased in steps. At each step, take readings of field current I_f and short circuit armature current till I_{sc} is about 1.25 to 1.5 times it rated armature current. Now plot a graph between short-circuit armature current I_{sc} and field current I_f. This plot, shown in Fig. 5.15, is a straight line and is called short-circuit characteristic (SCC).

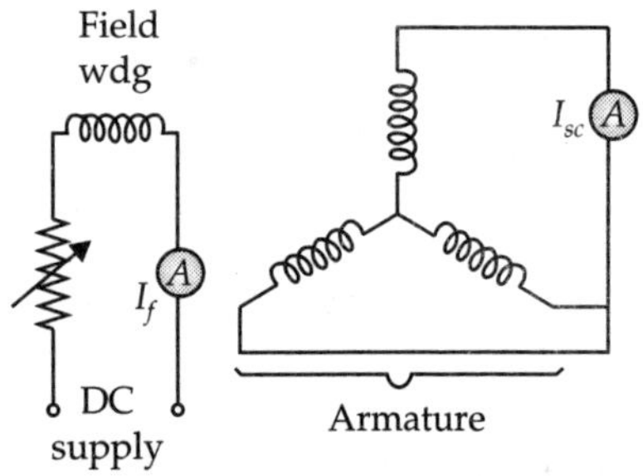

Fig 5.16: Short circuit test on an alternator.

5.9.4. Calculation of Z_s

Plot open-circuit and short-circuit characteristics on the same graph sheet as shown in Fig. 5.17. For rated alternator voltage per phase = *AB*, obtain the value of short-circuit armature current = *BC* for the same field current *OB*. Now synchronous impedance is given by

$$Z_s = \left[\frac{\text{Open-circuit voltage per phase}}{\text{Short-circuit current per phase}}\right]$$

for the same field current.

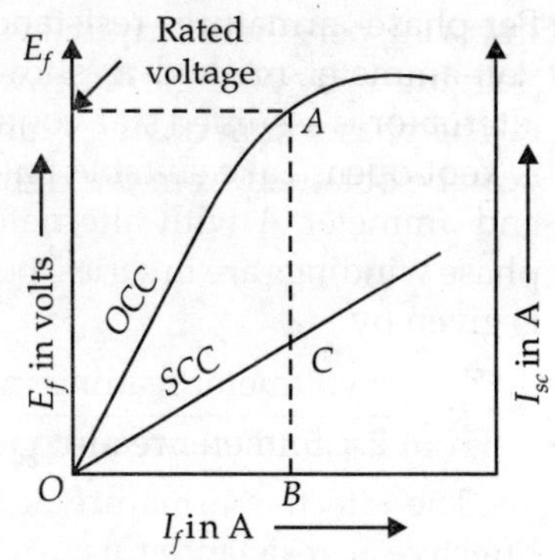

Fig 5.17: Calculation of Z_s

Armature circuit resistance per phase is already calculated. Therefore, synchronous reactance X_s per phase can be obtained as under.

$$X_s = \sqrt{Z_s^2 - r_a^2}$$

After per-phase value of r_a and X_s are known, alternator voltage phasor diagram can be drawn for the analysis of synchronous machine.

5.10. EQUIVALENT CIRCUIT OF CYLINDRICAL-ROTOR SYNCHRONOUS MOTOR

For an alternator, armature current is **output current**. For a synchronous motor, armature current is **input current**, opposite to the flow of current in an alternator. In other words, armature current in a synchronous motor gets reversed. As a result, equivalent circuit of Fig. 5.12 (*b*) gets modified to that shown in Fig. 5.18 (*a*) for a cylindrical-rotor synchronous motor. Equivalent circuit of Fig. 5.18 (*a*) can be redrawn as illustrated in Fig. 5.18 (*b*). This circuit shows that voltage V_t is applied and armature current I_a flows into the synchronous motor. Here E_f is the generated emf in the motor and is again called excitation emf.

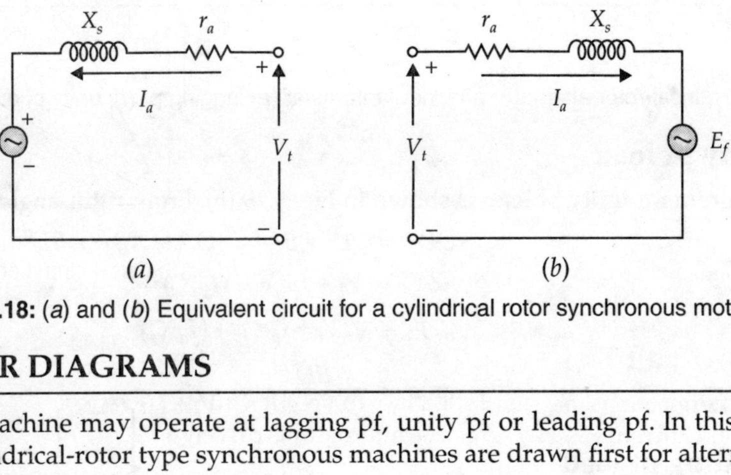

Fig 5.18: (*a*) and (*b*) Equivalent circuit for a cylindrical rotor synchronous motor.

5.11. PHASOR DIAGRAMS

A synchronous machine may operate at lagging pf, unity pf or leading pf. In this article, phasor diagrams for cylindrical-rotor type synchronous machines are drawn first for alternators and then for synchronous motors.

5.11.1. Cylindrical-rotor Alternators

Here phasor diagram for cylindrical-rotor alternator are drawn for the three operating power factors with the help of equivalent circuit of Fig. 5.12 (*b*). This equivalent circuit reveals that terminal voltage plus synchronous-impedance voltage drop gives the excitation emf. For the sake of convenience, per-phase terminal voltage V_t is taken vertical.

5.11.1.1. Lagging pf load

First of all, per-phase terminal voltage V_t is drawn vertical as assumed. Now draw armature current I_a lagging V_t by pf angle θ. Draw $I_a r_a$ parallel to I_a and $I_a X_s$ perpendicular to I_a as shown in Fig. 5.19 (*a*). The phasor sum of V_t, $I_a r_a$ and $I_a X_s$ gives excitation voltage E_f. In Fig. 5.19 (*a*), the magnitude of E_f can be obtained from the right-angled triangle *OBD*.

∴ $$OD^2 = OB^2 + BD^2 = (OA + AB)^2 + (BC + CD)^2$$

$$= (V_t \cos\theta + I_a r_a)^2 + (V_t \sin\theta + I_a X_s)^2$$

or $$E_f = \sqrt{(V_t \cos\theta + I_a r_a)^2 + (V_t \sin\theta + I_a X_s)^2} \quad \text{...(5.10)}$$

From Eq. 5.19 (*a*), we also get

$$\tan\psi = \tan(\theta + \delta) = \frac{BC + CD}{OA + AB} = \frac{V_t \sin\theta + I_a X_s}{V_t \cos\theta + I_a r_a} \quad \text{...(5.11)}$$

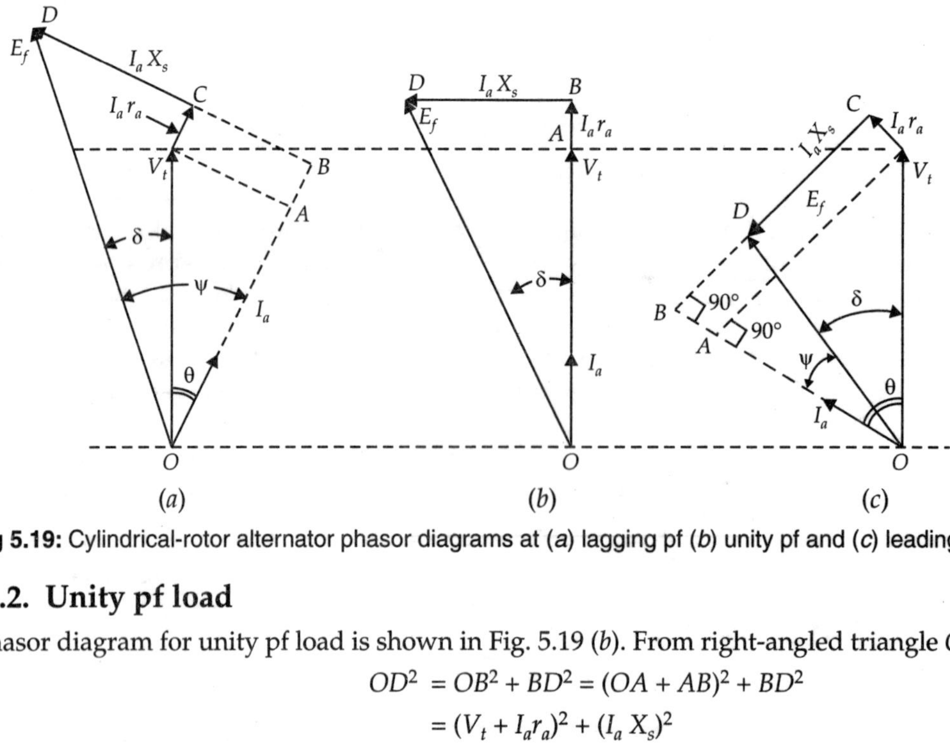

Fig 5.19: Cylindrical-rotor alternator phasor diagrams at (*a*) lagging pf (*b*) unity pf and (*c*) leading pf.

5.11.1.2. Unity pf load

The phasor diagram for unity pf load is shown in Fig. 5.19 (*b*). From right-angled triangle *OBD*,

$$OD^2 = OB^2 + BD^2 = (OA + AB)^2 + BD^2$$

$$= (V_t + I_a r_a)^2 + (I_a X_s)^2$$

∴ $$E_f = \sqrt{(V_t + I_a r_a)^2 + (I_a X_s)^2} \quad \text{...(5.12)}$$

Also, $$\tan\delta = \frac{BD}{OA + AB} = \frac{I_a X_s}{V_t + I_a r_a} \quad \text{...(5.13)}$$

5.11.1.3. Leading pf load

Here I_a leads terminal voltage V_t by pf angle θ. The phasor diagram for leading pf load is shown in Fig. 5.19 (*c*). From right-angled triangle *OBD*,

$$OD^2 = OB^2 + BD^2 = (OA + AB)^2 + (BC - CD)^2$$

$$= (V_t \cos\theta + I_a r_a)^2 + (V_t \sin\theta - I_a X_s)^2$$

∴ $$E_f = \sqrt{(V_t \cos\theta + I_a r_a)^2 + (V_t \sin\theta - I_a X_s)^2} \quad \text{...(5.14)}$$

Also, $$\tan\psi = (\theta - \delta) = \frac{BC - CD}{OA + AB} = \frac{V_t \sin\theta - I_a X_s}{V_t \cos\theta + I_a r_a} \quad ...(5.15)$$

The angle δ between E_f and V_t is called load angle or power angle.

5.11.2. Cylindrical-rotor Synchronous Motors

Here phasor diagrams for cylindrical rotor synchronous motor are drawn for the three operating power factors with the help of equivalent circuit of Fig. 5.18 (*b*). In this figure, excitation voltage E_f plus synchronous-impedance voltage drop gives the motor terminal voltage V_t. For the sake of convenience, per-phase terminal voltage V_t is taken vertical.

5.11.2.1. Lagging pf load

First of all, draw per phase excitation voltage E_f lagging behind vertical line by load angle δ. Draw I_a lagging E_f by internal pf angle ψ. Now draw $I_a r_a$ parallel to I_a and $I_a X_s$ perpendicular to I_a as shown in Fig. 5.20 (*a*). The phasor sum of E_f, $I_a r_a$ and $I_a X_s$ gives terminal voltage V_t. In Fig. 5.20 (*a*), the magnitude of E_f can be obtained from right-angled triangle *OBD*.

$$E_f^2 = OB^2 + BD^2 = (OA - AB)^2 + (AH - CD)^2$$

$$= (V_t \cos\theta - I_a r_a)^2 + (V_t \sin\theta - I_a X_s)^2$$

or $$E_f = \sqrt{(V_t \cos\theta - I_a r_a)^2 + (V_t \sin\theta - I_a X_s)^2} \quad ...(5.16)$$

Also, from Fig. 5.20 (*a*), $$\tan\psi = \tan(\theta - \delta) = \frac{BD}{OB} = \frac{AC}{OB} = \frac{V_t \sin\theta - I_a X_s}{V_t \cos\theta - I_a r_a} \quad ...(5.17)$$

From Eq. (5.17), $(\theta - \delta)$ can be calculated. Load angle δ can now be obtained.

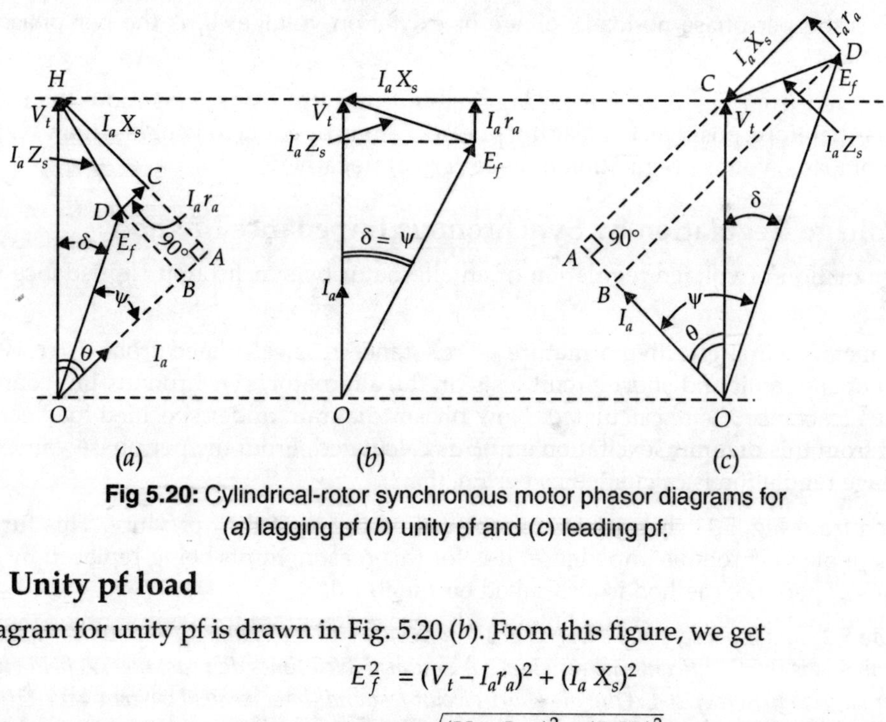

Fig 5.20: Cylindrical-rotor synchronous motor phasor diagrams for (*a*) lagging pf (*b*) unity pf and (*c*) leading pf.

5.11.2.2. Unity pf load

Phasor diagram for unity pf is drawn in Fig. 5.20 (*b*). From this figure, we get

$$E_f^2 = (V_t - I_a r_a)^2 + (I_a X_s)^2$$

or $$E_f = \sqrt{(V_t - I_a r_a)^2 + (I_a X_s)^2} \quad ...(5.18)$$

Also, $$\tan \psi = \tan \delta = \frac{I_a X_s}{V_t - I_a r_a} \quad ...(5.19)$$

Load angle can be obtained from this equation.

5.11.2.3. Leading pf load

For leading power factor operation of the synchronous motor, Fig. 5.20 (c) shows the phasor diagram. From this figure,

$$E_f = \sqrt{(V_t \cos\theta - I_a r_a)^2 + (V_t \sin\theta + I_a X_s)^2} \quad ...(5.20)$$

Also, $$\tan \psi = \tan (\delta + \theta) = \frac{BD}{OB} = \frac{V_t \sin\theta + I_a X_s}{V_t \cos\theta - I_a r_a} \quad ...(5.21)$$

Load angle can be obtained from Eq. (5.21).

5.12. VOLTAGE REGULATION

Voltage regulation of an alternator is defined as the change in terminal voltage, expressed as a percentage (or per unit) of the rated voltage, when the load at a given pf is removed, with speed and field current remaining constant.

$$\therefore \quad \text{Voltage regulation} = \frac{E_f - V_t}{V_t} \text{ in per unit}$$
$$= \frac{E_f - V_t}{V_t} \times 100 \text{ in percentage} \quad ...(5.22)$$

Here E_f is the per-phase no-load voltage or excitation voltage, V_t is the per phase full-load terminal voltage.

It is observed from Fig. 5.19 that for lagging and unity pf loads, E_f is more than V_t, voltage regulation is, therefore, positive. For leading pf load, E_f may be equal to V_t or less than V_t. Therefore, for leading pf loads, voltage regulation may be zero or negative.

5.12.1. Voltage Regulation by Synchronous Impedance Method

Here determination of voltage regulation of an alternator by synchronous impedance method is described.

In this method, first effective armature ac resistance r_a is calculated from dc resistance test. Then, from open-circuit and short-circuit tests on the alternator, synchronous impedance Z_s and synchronous reactance X_s are calculated. Now phasor diagram under specified load conditions is drawn and from this diagram, excitation emf E_f is calculated. From the per phase values of E_f and V_t, the voltage regulation is calculated as per Eq. (5.22).

It is seen from Fig. 5.11 that mmfs are replaced by the emfs they produce. This further leads to the concept of synchronous impedance. It is for this reason, mmfs being replaced by emfs, that synchronous impedance method is also called **emf method**.

Example 5.2. *In a 3-phase, 1500 kVA, 3300 V, star-connected alternator, dc resistance measured across any two terminals is 0.4 Ω. Effective ac resistance is assumed 1.25 times dc resistance. A field current of 10 A gave an armature current of 264 A during short-circuit test and the same field current gave 1100 V during open-circuit test. Calculate synchronous reactance and the voltage regulation at full load 0.8 pf lagging. Find the value of load angle also.*

Solution. Armature resistance per phase, $R = \dfrac{0.4}{2} = 0.2\ \Omega$

Effective armature resistance per phase, $r_a = 1.25 \times 0.2 = 0.25\ \Omega$

Synchronous impedance,

$$Z_s = \left[\frac{\text{open-circuit voltage per phase}}{\text{short-circuit armature current per phase}}\right] \text{for the same field current}$$

$$\therefore \quad X_s = \frac{1100 \times 1}{\sqrt{3} \times 264} = 2.405\ \Omega$$

$\therefore$ Synchronous reactance, $X_s = \sqrt{2.405^2 - 0.25^2} = 2.392\ \Omega$

Rated voltage per phase, $V_t = \dfrac{3300}{\sqrt{3}} = 1905.3$ V

Rated per phase current, $I_a = \dfrac{1500 \times 100°}{\sqrt{3} \times 3300} = 262.44$ A

Power factor, $\cos\theta = 0.8$ and $\sin\theta = \sqrt{1 - 0.8^2} = 0.6$

Phasor diagram for this problem is shown in Fig. 5.19 (*a*). From Eq. (5.10), per-phase excitation voltage is given by

$$E_f^2 = (V_t \cos\theta + I_a r_a)^2 + (V_t \sin\theta + I_a X_s)^2$$
$$= (1905.3 \times 0.8 + 262.44 \times 0.25)^2 + (1905.3 \times 0.6 + 262.44 \times 2.392)^2$$
$$= (1589.85)^2 + (1770.94)^2$$
$$\therefore \quad E_f = 2379.88 \text{ V}$$

$$\text{Percentage voltage regulation} = \frac{E_f - V_t}{V_t} \times 100 = \frac{2379.88 - 1905.3}{1905.3} \times 100$$
$$= 24.908\%$$

From Eq. (5.11), $\tan(\theta + \delta) = \dfrac{V_t \sin\theta + I_a X_s}{V_t \cos\theta + I_a r_a} = \dfrac{1770.94}{1589.85}$

$$\therefore \quad \theta + \delta = 48.08°$$

But pf angle $\theta = \cos^{-1}(0.8) = 36.87°$

$\therefore$ Load angle $\delta = 48.08 - 36.87 = 11.21°$

Example 5.3. *A 3-phase, 1000 kVA, 6.6 kV, star-connected alternator has per phase synchronous impedance $Z_s = 1 + j\,15\ \Omega$. Calculate voltage regulation and load angle for a load of 1000 kW at power factors of (a) 0.8 lagging (b) unity pf and (c) 0.8 leading.*

Solution. Here $Z_s = 1 + j\,15$, $\therefore r_a = 1\ \Omega$ and $X_s = 15\ \Omega$

Line voltage, $V_L = 6600$ V

Per-phase rated voltage, $V_t = \dfrac{6600}{\sqrt{3}} = 3810.6$ V

(*a*) **Power factor = 0.8 lagging :** Here $\sqrt{3}\ V_L I_L \cos\theta = 1000$ kW

$\therefore$ Line current = per-phase current, $I_a = \dfrac{1000 \times 1000}{\sqrt{3} \times 6600 \times 0.8} = 109.35$ A

From Eq. (5.10), the excitation voltage per phase is

$$E_f = \sqrt{(V_t \cos\theta + I_a r_a)^2 + (V_t \sin\theta + I_a X_s)^2}$$

$$= \sqrt{(3810.6 \times 0.8 + 109.35 \times 1)^2 + (3810.6 \times 0.6 + 109.35 \times 15)^2}$$

$$= \sqrt{(3157.83)^2 + (3926.61)^2} = 5038.86 \text{ V}$$

$\therefore$ Percentage voltage regulation $= \dfrac{E_f - V_t}{V_t} \times 100$

$$= \frac{5038.86 - 3810.6}{3810.6} \times 100 = 32.233\%$$

From Eq. (5.11), $\tan(\theta + \delta) = \dfrac{V_t \sin\theta + I_a X_s}{V_t \cos\theta + I_a r_a} = \dfrac{3926.61}{3157.83}$

$\therefore$ $\theta + \delta = 51.193°$

But pf angle $\theta = \cos^{-1}(0.8) = 36.87°$

$\therefore$ Load angle $= 51.193 - 36.87 = 14.323°$

(*b*) **Unity power factor :** $\sqrt{3}\ V_L I_L \cos\theta = 1000$ kW

$\therefore$ Line current = per-phase current, $I_a = \dfrac{1000 \times 1000}{\sqrt{3} \times 6600 \times 1} = 87.48$ A

From Eq. (5.12), excitation voltage per phase is

$$E_f = \sqrt{(V_t + I_a r_a)^2 + (I_a X_s)^2}$$

$$= \sqrt{(3810.6 + 87.48 \times 1)^2 + (87.48 \times 15)^2}$$

$$= \sqrt{(3898.1)^2 + (1312.2)^2} = 4113.03 \text{ V}$$

$\therefore$ Voltage regulation $= \dfrac{4113.03 - 3810.6}{3810.6} \times 100 = 7.937\%$

From Eq. (5.13), $\delta = \tan^{-1}\left[\dfrac{I_a X_s}{V_t + I_a r_a}\right]$

$$= \tan^{-1}\left[\frac{1312.2}{3898.1}\right] = 18.605°$$

(*c*) **Power-factor = 0.8 leading :** Here $I_L = I_a = 109.35$ A (as in part (*a*)).

From Eq. (5.14), $E_f^2 = (V_t \cos\theta + I_a r_a)^2 + (V_t \sin\theta - I_a X_s)^2$

$\therefore$ $E_f = \sqrt{(3810.6 \times 0.8 + 109.35 \times 1)^2 + (3810.6 \times 0.6 - 109.35 \times 15)^2}$

$$= \sqrt{(3157.83)^2 + (646.11)^2} = 3223.25 \text{ V}$$

$\therefore$ Voltage regulation $= \dfrac{E_f - V_t}{V_t} = \dfrac{3223.25 - 3810.6}{3810.6} \times 100 = -15.414\%$

From Eq. (5.15), $\tan(\theta - \delta) = \dfrac{V_t \sin\theta - I_a X_s}{V_t \cos\theta + I_a r_a} = \dfrac{646.11}{3157.83}$

$\therefore$ $(\theta - \delta) = 11.563°$

But $\theta = 36.87°$ $\therefore$ Load angle $\delta = 36.87 - 11.563 =$ **25.307°**

Part (*a*) can alternatively be solved as under.

In Fig. 5.19 (*a*), take V_t as the reference phasor. $\therefore\ V_t = 3810.6\ \angle 0°$

For lagging power factor load, $I_a = 109.35\ \angle -\cos^{-1} 0.8$

$= 109.35\ \angle -36.87°$ A

Synchronous impedance $Z_s = 1 + j\,15\ \Omega = 15.033\ \angle 86.186°\ \Omega$

$$\therefore \quad \overline{E}_f = \overline{V}_t + \overline{I}_a\, \overline{Z}_s$$

$$= 3810.6\ \angle 0° + 109.35\ \angle -36.87° \times 15.033\ \angle 86.186°\ \Omega$$

$$= 3810.6 + 1643.86\ \angle 49.316°$$

$$= 3810.6 + 1643.86\,[\cos 49.316° + j \sin 49.316°]$$

$$= 3810.6 + 1071.61 + j\,1246.57$$

$$= 4882.21 + j\,1246.57 = 5038.84\ \angle 14.323°$$

Here E_f leads V_t by 14.323°. Therefore, E_f = 5038.84 V and load angle δ = 14.323°.

5.13. SALIENT POLE MACHINES–TWO REACTION THEORY

So far, we have studied only cylindrical-rotor synchronous machines in which the air gap is uniform. Reluctance seen by field mmf is the same in all orientations of the rotor. As a result, field mmf and armature mmf can be combined together for analysis purposes. This, however, is not possible in salient-pole synchronous machines. In these machines, reluctance of the magnetic circuit along field or polar axis is different from its value along interpolar or quadrature axis. This difficulty can, however, be overcome by the use of two-reaction theory of salient-pole machines.

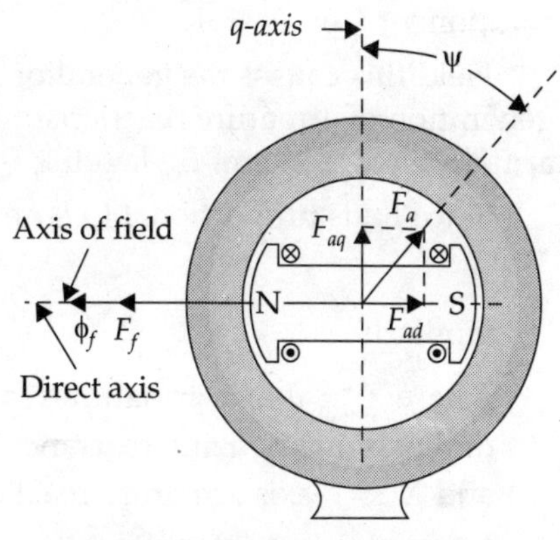

Fig 5.21: Salient-pole synchronous machine.

Refer to Fig. 5.21, where two-pole salient-pole synchronous machine is shown. Field winding on the rotor produces field flux ϕ_f as shown. Axis of field winding is called **direct axis** (*d*-axis). An axis 90° away from *d*-axis is called **quadrature axis** (*q*-axis) as indicated in Fig. 5.21.

Three-phase currents in 3-phase winding produce armature mmf F_a. In Fig. 5.29, armature mmf F_a is shown lagging *q*-axis by an angle ψ. In this figure, if $\psi = 0$, mmf F_a would be along *q*-axis and the reluctance offered to F_a would be maximum due to two long air-gaps. In case $\psi = 90°$, the mmf F_a would be along *d*-axis and the reluctance offered to F_a would be minimum due to two small air gaps. This difficulty of seeing different reluctances by F_a, as angle ψ varies, can be overcome by using two **reaction theory**.

The two reaction theory was proposed by Andre Blondel. According to two reaction theory, armature mmf F_a can be resolved (or decomposed) into two components, one F_{ad} along *d*-axis and the other F_{aq} along *q*-axis as shown in Fig. 5.21. In this figure, F_{ad} experiences minimum reluctance along *d*-axis, whereas F_{aq} sees minimum reluctance along *q*-axis.

The phasor diagram of Fig. 5.22 is drawn to illustrate two reaction theory. Here field flux ϕ_f is drawn along *d*-axis as in Fig. 5.21. Now draw *q*-axis 90° away from *d*-axis. Excitation voltage E_f lags ϕ_f by 90° as in cylindrical-rotor alternator. Here E_f is along *q*-axis. Take armature current I_a lagging E_f (or *q*-axis) by an angle ψ. Here cos ψ is called internal power factor. Armature current sets up armature mmf F_a in phase with I_a. As per two-reaction theory, now F_a is resolved into two components, F_{ad} along d-axis and F_{aq} along q-axis, Fig. 5.22. These two component mmfs produce flux ϕ_{ad} and ϕ_{aq} as shown. Reluctance along d-axis Rl_d is low, but along q-axis, reluctance Rl_q is high.

Here $\qquad \phi_{ad} = \dfrac{F_{ad}}{Rl_d}$ and $\phi_{aq} = \dfrac{F_{aq}}{Rl_q}$

Since $Rl_d < Rl_q$, the ratio $\dfrac{\phi_{ad}}{F_{ad}} \left(= \dfrac{1}{Rl_d}\right)$ is more than the ratio $\dfrac{\phi_{aq}}{F_{aq}} \left[= \dfrac{1}{Rl_q}\right]$. As a result, resultant armature flux ϕ_a is not in phase with armature mmf F_a but it lags behind F_a. The flux ϕ_{ad} opposes field flux ϕ_f because the internal pf is lagging. For a leading internal pf, ϕ_{ad} would be aiding the field flux ϕ_f. The q-axis flux ϕ_{aq} is cross-magnetizing in nature.

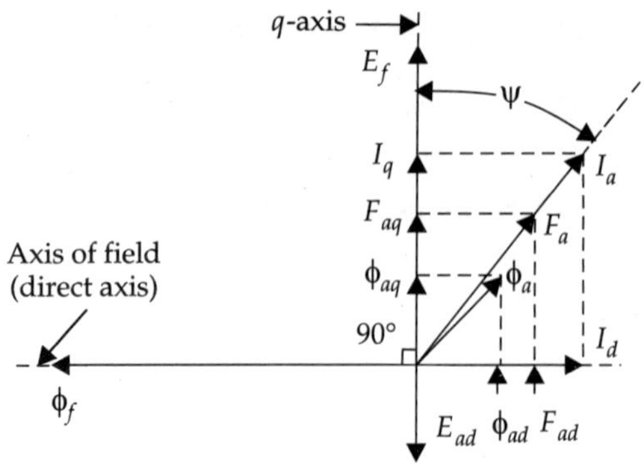

Fig 5.22: Phasor diagram illustrating two-reaction theory of salient-pole machines.

Now armature current I_a is in phase with F_a. Similarly, armature-current component I_d is in phase with F_{ad}. Same is true for I_q. Therefore, armature current I_a = d-axis component I_d + q-axis component I_q or $\bar{I}_a = \bar{I}_d + \bar{I}_q$.

Field flux causes the generation of excitation emf E_f lagging ϕ_f by 90°. Similarly, ϕ_{ad} causes the generation of armature reaction emf E_{ad} lagging ϕ_{ad} by 90° as shown in Fig. 5.22. Also, ϕ_{aq} sets up armature reaction emf E_{aq} lagging F_{aq} by 90° (not shown in Fig. 5.22).

Since E_{ad} is proportional to I_d and lags it by 90°, it is possible to write (as in Eq. (5.6)),

$$\bar{E}_{ad} = -j\,X_{ad} \cdot \bar{I}_d$$

Similarly,

$$\bar{E}_{aq} = -j\,X_{aq} \cdot \bar{I}_q$$

where X_{ad} = d-axis armature-reaction reactance
or d-axis magnetizing reactance
and X_{aq} = q-axis armature-reaction reactance.

In a cylindrical-rotor alternator, $\bar{E}_f + \bar{E}_{ar} = \bar{E}_r$, air-gap voltage, Eq. (5.7). Similarly, in a salient-pole alternator, phasor sum of excitation emf E_f and armature reaction emfs E_{ad} and E_{aq} gives air-gap voltage E_r.

$$\therefore \quad \left.\begin{aligned} \bar{E}_r &= \bar{E}_f + \bar{E}_{ad} + \bar{E}_{aq} \\ &= \bar{E}_f - j\,I_d\,X_{ad} - j\,\bar{I}_q \cdot X_{aq} \end{aligned}\right\} \qquad ...(5.23)$$

Like cylindrical-rotor alternator, air-gap voltage E_r is given by

$$\bar{E}_r = \bar{V}_t + \bar{I}_a\,(r_a + j\,x_{al})$$

Substituting this value of $\bar{E}_r$ in Eq. (5.23) gives

$$\bar{V}_t + \bar{I}_a\,(r_a + j\,x_{al}) = \bar{E}_f - j\,\bar{I}_d \cdot X_{ad} - j\,I_q \cdot X_{aq}$$

or

$$\bar{E}_f = \bar{V}_t + \bar{I}_a r_a + j\,\bar{I}_a \cdot x_{al} + j\,\bar{I}_d \cdot X_{ad} + j\,I_q \cdot X_{aq}$$

But

$$\bar{I}_a = \bar{I}_d + \bar{I}_q$$

$$\therefore \quad \begin{aligned} \bar{E}_f &= \bar{V}_t + \bar{I}_a r_a + j\,x_{al}\,(\bar{I}_d + \bar{I}_q) + j\,X_{ad}\,\bar{I}_d + j\,X_{aq}\,\bar{I}_q \\ &= \bar{V}_t + \bar{I}_a r_a + j\,(x_{al} + X_{ad})\,\bar{I}_d + j\,(x_{al} + X_{aq})\,\bar{I}_q \\ &= \bar{V}_t + \bar{I}_a r_a + j\,X_d \cdot \bar{I}_d + j\,X_q\,\bar{I}_q \end{aligned} \qquad ...(5.24)$$

where $X_d = X_{ad} + x_{al}$ = d-axis synchronous reactance
and $X_q = X_{aq} + x_{al}$ = q-axis synchronous reactance.

Note that armature leakage reactance x_{al} is assumed to be the same for both d-axis and q-axis currents.

Thus, the voltage equation for a 3-phase salient-pole alternator is given by Eq. (5.24), where all values are per phase.

5.13.1. Phasor Diagram

With the help of Eq. (5.24), the complete phasor diagram of a salient pole alternator, based on two-reaction theory, is drawn in Fig. 5.23. Here θ = power factor angle by which I_a lags terminal voltage V_t. Armature current is resolved into two components I_d which is perpendicular to E_f and I_q in phase with E_f. Phasor sum of V_t, $I_a r_a$, $I_d X_d$ and $I_q X_q$ gives the excitation emf E_f. Here $I_a r_a$ is drawn parallel to I_a, $j I_d X_d$ perpendicular to I_d and $j I_q X_q$ perpendicular to I_q.

In order to use the phasor diagram of Fig. 5.23, armature currents I_a must be resolved into its d-q components. For this purpose, draw Fig. 5.23 again as shown in Fig. 5.24. From A, draw ABC perpendicular to I_a. From C, draw CD perpendicular to E_f or OK. In the right angled triangle OAC, $\angle OCA = 90 - \psi$. In ΔBCD, $\angle BCD = \psi°$. Now in ΔBCD,

$$CD = BC \cos \psi \quad \text{...(5.25)}$$

or

$$BC = \frac{CD}{\cos \psi}$$

But $CD = KF = I_q X_q$ and $I_q = I_a \cos \psi$ or $\cos \psi = \dfrac{I_q}{I_a}$

$$\therefore \quad BC = \frac{I_q \cdot X_q}{I_q / I_a} = I_a \cdot X_q$$

This shows that BC, perpendicular to I_a, is equal to $I_a \cdot X_q$.

$$\therefore \text{ Voltage} \quad OC = \bar{E}_f' = \bar{V}_t + \bar{I}_a r_a + j\, \bar{I}_a X_q \quad \text{...(5.26)}$$

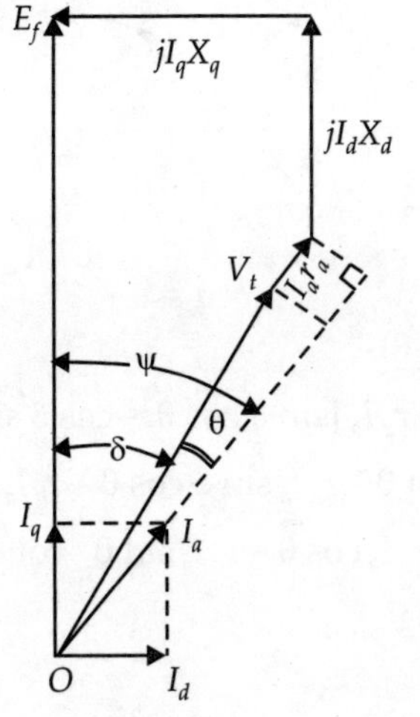

Fig 5.23: Phasor diagram of salient-pole alternator.

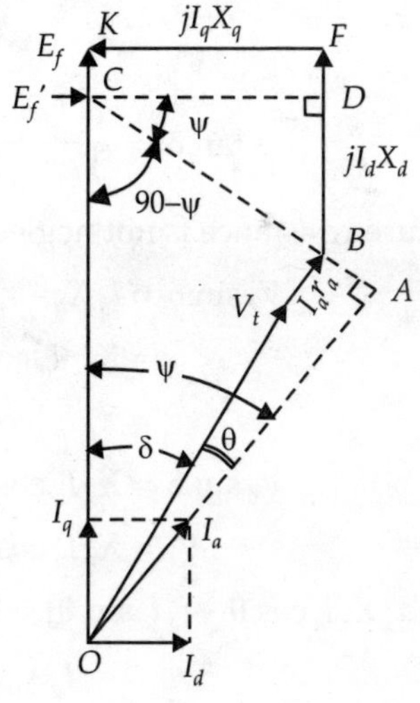

Fig 5.24: Resolution of armature current I_a into I_d and I_q.

From Eq. (5.26), $E_f' = OC$ can be calculated and therefore power angle δ can be obtained. Power factor angle θ is already known. Therefore, internal power factor angle $\psi = \theta + \delta$ can be determined and the currents I_d and I_q can be obtained as under.

$$I_d = I_a \sin \psi = I_a \sin (\delta + \theta)$$

$$I_q = I_a \cos \psi = I_a \cos (\delta + \theta)$$

Also, $BF = I_d X_d = FD + DB = FD + BC \sin \psi$

or $I_d X_d = CK + X_q I_a \sin \psi = CK + X_q \cdot I_d$

$\therefore$ $CK = FD = I_d X_d - X_q I_d = I_d (X_d - X_q)$

$\therefore$ $\bar{E}_f = OC + CK = E_f' + I_d (X_d - X_q)$

$$= \bar{V}_t + \bar{I}_a r_a + j\, \bar{I}_a X_q + j\, I_d (X_d - X_q) \quad ...(5.27)$$

5.13.2. Determination of Load Angle

Here phasor diagram 5.24 is used to determine load angle δ. It is seen from this phasor diagram that

$$E_f = V_t \cos \delta + r_a \cdot I_a \cos (\delta + \theta) + I_d X_d$$

or $E_f = V_t \cos \delta + r_a \cdot I_q + X_d I_d$ ...(5.28)

Phasor diagram also shows that

$$\tan \psi = \tan (\delta + \theta) = \frac{AC}{OA} = \frac{V_t \sin\theta + I_a X_q}{V_t \cos\theta + I_a r_a} \quad ...(5.29)$$

Power factor angle θ is usually known. Therefore, load angle δ can be obtained from Eq. (5.29). If armature resistance is neglected, it is seen from Fig. 5.24 that

$$V_t \sin \delta = I_q X_q = X_q \cdot I_a \cos (\theta + \delta)$$

$$= X_q I_a [\cos \theta \cos \delta - \sin \theta \sin \delta]$$

or $V_t = X_q I_a \cdot \cos \theta \cot \delta - X_q \cdot I_a \sin \theta$

or $X_q I_a \cdot \cos \theta \cot \delta = V_t + I_a X_q \sin \theta$

$\therefore$ $$\tan \delta = \frac{I_a X_q \cos\theta}{V_t + I_a X_q \sin\theta} \quad ...(5.30)$$

If armature resistance is not neglected, then Fig. 5.24 gives

$$V_t \sin \delta = I_q X_q - r_a I_d$$

$$= X_q \cdot I_a \cos (\delta + \theta) - r_a \cdot I_a \sin (\delta + \theta)$$

$$= X_q I_a [\cos \delta \cos \theta - \sin \delta \sin \theta] - r_a I_a [\sin \delta \cos \theta + \cos \delta \sin \theta]$$

or $V_t \sin \delta = X_q I_a \cos \delta \cos \theta - X_q \cdot I_a \sin \delta \sin \theta - r_a I_a \sin \delta \cos \theta - r_a I_a \cos \delta \sin \theta$

or $V_t = X_q I_a \cos \theta \cdot \cot \delta - X_q I_a \sin \theta - r_a I_a \cos \theta - r_a I_a \sin \theta \cdot \cot \delta$

or $\cot \delta [X_a I_a \cos \theta - r_a I_a \sin \theta] = V_t + X_q I_a \sin \theta + r_a I_a \cos \theta$

$\therefore$ $$\tan \delta = \frac{I_a X_q \cos\theta - I_a r_a \sin\theta}{V_t + I_a [X_q \sin\theta + r_a \cos\theta]} \quad ...(5.31)$$

If armature resistance is neglected, then Eq. (5.31) becomes

$$\tan \delta = \frac{I_a X_q \cos\theta}{V_t + I_a X_q \sin\theta} \quad ...(5.30)$$

Example 5.4. *A 1000 kVA, 3300 V, star-connected salient-pole alternator has per phase reactances of X_d = 3 Ω and X_q = 2.5 Ω. Armature resistance is neglected. Calculate per-phase excitation voltage and voltage* *regulation under rated kVA load at pf 0.8 lagging.*

Solution. Per-phase terminal voltage, $V_t = \dfrac{3300}{\sqrt{3}} = 1905.3$ V

Per-phase rated armature current, $I_a = \dfrac{1000 \times 1000}{\sqrt{3} \times 3300} = 174.96$ A

Take V_t as reference phasor, $\therefore\ V_t = 1905.3 \angle 0°$

$$\cos\theta = 0.8,\ \sin\theta = 0.6,\ \text{angle } \theta = 36.87°$$

$$\therefore \quad \bar{I}_a = \bar{I}_a \angle{-\theta} = 174.96 \angle{-36.87} = 139.97 - j\,104.98$$

From Fig. 5.24 and Eq. (5.26), we get

$$OC = E_f' = V_t \angle 0° + j\,\bar{I}_a \cdot X_q$$

or
$$\begin{aligned} E_f' &= 1905.3 \angle 0° + j\,(2.5) \times 174.96 \angle{-36.87} \\ &= 1905.3 + j\,0 + j\,(2.5) \times [139.97 - j\,104.98] \\ &= 1905.3 + 262.45 + j\,349.93 \\ &= 2167.75 + j\,349.93 = 2195.8 \angle 9.17° \end{aligned}$$

This shows E_f' leads V_t by load angle $\delta = 9.17°$

$$\text{Now } \psi = \delta + \theta = 9.17 + 36.87 = 46.04°$$

$$\therefore \quad I_d = I_a \sin\psi = 174.96 \sin 46.04° = 125.94 \text{ A}$$

and
$$I_q = I_a \cos\psi = 174.96 \cos 46.04 = 121.45 \text{ A}$$

From Eq. (5.27), excitation voltage is

$$\begin{aligned} E_f &= E_f' + I_d\,(X_d - X_q) = 2195.8 + 125.94\,[3 - 2.5] \\ &= 2258.77 \text{ V} \end{aligned}$$

$$\therefore \quad \text{Per-phase excitation voltage} = 2258.77 \text{ V}$$

$$\text{Voltage regulation} = \frac{E_f - V_t}{V_t} \times 100 = \frac{2258.77 - 1905.3}{1905.3} \times 100 = 18.536\%$$

Alternatively : From Eq. (5.29),

$$\tan(\delta + \theta) = \frac{V_t \sin\theta + I_a X_q}{V_t \cos\theta + I_a r_a} = \frac{1905.3 \times 0.6 + 174.96 \times 2.5}{1905.3 \times 0.8 + 0}$$

$$= 1.0369°$$

$$\therefore \quad \delta + \theta = 46.04° \text{ and } \delta = 46.04 - 36.87 = 9.17°$$

$$\therefore \quad I_d = I_a \sin(\delta + \theta) = 174.96 \sin 46.04 = 125.94 \text{ A}$$

From Fig. 5.23, with $r_a = 0$, we get

$$E_f = V_t \cos\delta + I_d X_d = 1905.3 \times \cos 9.17° + 125.94 \times 3$$

$$= \mathbf{2258.77\ V}$$

Example 5.5. *A 10 kVA, 400 V, 3-phase star-connected salient-pole alternator has $X_d = 6\ \Omega$ and $X_q = 4\ \Omega$. Alternator resistance per phase is 0.5 Ω. The generator delivers rated load at 0.8 pf lagging at rated terminal voltage. Determine (a) direct-axis and quadrature-axis components of armature current (b) excitation voltage of alternator and (c) its voltage regulation.*

Solution. Here $r_a = 0.5\ \Omega$, $X_d = 6\ \Omega$, $X_q = 4\ \Omega$

Power factor = $\cos\theta = 0.8$, $\sin\theta = 0.6$ and $\theta = \cos^{-1}(0.8) = 36.87°$

Therminal voltage per phase, $$V_t = \frac{400}{\sqrt{3}} = 230.95 \text{ V}$$

Armature current per phase, $$I_a = \frac{kVA \times 1000}{\sqrt{3} \times V_L} = \frac{10 \times 1000}{\sqrt{3} \times 400} = 14.434 \text{ A}$$

From Eq. (5.29), $$\tan\psi = \tan(\theta + \delta) = \frac{V_t \sin\theta + I_a X_q}{V_t \cos\theta + I_a r_a}$$

$$= \frac{230.95 \times 0.6 + 14.434 \times 4}{230.95 \times 0.8 + 14.434 \times 0.5} = 1.02255$$

$\therefore$ $$\psi = \theta + \delta = 45.64° \text{ and } \delta = 45.64 - 36.87 = 8.77°$$

(*a*) Direct-axis component of $I_a = I_d = I_a \sin\psi = 14.434 \times \sin 45.64 =$ **10.3197** A

Quadrature-axis component of $I_a = I_q = I_a \cos\psi = 14.434 \times \cos 45.64 =$ **10.0917** A

(*b*) Excitation voltage, $$E_f = V_t \cos\delta + I_q \cdot r_a + I_d X_d$$

$$= 230.95 \times \cos 8.77 + 10.0917 \times 0.5 + 10.3197 \times 6$$

$$= 295.214 \text{ V}$$

$\therefore$ $$E_f \text{ (line to line)} = \sqrt{3} \times 295.214 = 511.31 \text{ V}$$

(*c*) Voltage regulation $$= \frac{295.214 - 230.95}{230.95} \times 100 = \mathbf{27.826\%}$$

5.14. PARALLEL OPERATION OF ALTERNATORS

In modern power systems, alternators are always operated in parallel so as to obtain economical and reliable operation of the system. The reasons for parallel operation of alternators are as follows.

(*i*) The total load requirement can be met by several alternators in parallel but not by a single alternator.

(*ii*) If an alternator breaks down, the remaining alternators can still supply the load though at a reduced level. Thus, parallel operation of alternators makes the power system more reliable.

(*iii*) With alternators operating in parallel, one or two alternators can be shut down for scheduled maintenance and inspection.

(*iv*) During light load periods, less efficient machines can be shut down. Now the remaining alternators in parallel would operate near their rated capacity leading to more efficient operation of the power system.

(*v*) In case load demand on power system rises, more alternators can be installed in parallel.

It can be stated from above that parallel operation of alternators leads to economical and reliable operation of a power system.

Infinite bus : Many alternators running in parallel constitute an infinite bus. Its voltage and frequency do not change even if one or two alternators are shut down or more load is put on the infinite bus. Even if one or two alternators are added to infinite bus, its voltage and frequency would not alter.

5.14.1. Synchronization

The process of connecting an alternator to an infinite bus or another alternator under voltage is called **synchronization**. The synchronous machine which is to be synchronized is called incoming machine. The following **conditions** must be fulfilled before an incoming machine can be synchronized.

(*i*) The terminal voltage of the incoming machine must be equal to the voltage of bus bars or already running alternator.

(*ii*) The frequency of the incoming alternator should be nearly the same as that of the bus bars or already running alternator.

(*iii*) The two voltages must be in the same phase with respect to the external circuit. This condition also means that the phase sequence of the incoming machine voltage and bus-bar voltage must be the same.

5.14.2. Synchronizing Methods

The methods of synchronizing an incoming machine to the existing alternator or bus bar are as follows:

(*i*) Synchronizing by dark-lamp method.

(*ii*) Synchronizing by synchroscope.

These are now described below:

5.14.2.1. Synchronizing by dark-lamp method

Connection scheme for synchronizing an incoming machine with an infinite bus by dark-lamp method is shown in Fig. 5.25. Lamps L_1, L_2, L_3 are connected respectively across *Aa*, *Bb*, *Cc* terminals as shown.

The incoming machine is started by a prime-mover and brought up to synchronous speed. Now the field winding of incoming machine is energized. Then, the field current is adjusted till the incoming machine voltage is equal to the bus voltage.

These voltages should be compared by the same voltmeter. Now the three lamps flicker at a rate equal to the difference in frequencies of incoming machine and the bus. For correct phase sequence, the three lamps would become either bright or dark at the same time. If the lamps do not flicker in agreement, then the phase sequence of the two voltages is incorrect. This can be corrected by interchaning two leads of either incoming machine or the bus bar. The speed of the prime-mover is adjusted until the lamps flicker in agreement at a **very slow rate**. At this time, adjust again incoming machine equal to the bus-bar voltage.

Observe the very slow flickering of lamps. Now close the synchronizing switch *S* when the lamps are in the **middle of their dark** period.

Advantages of dark-lamp method:

(*i*) The required equipment is cheap.

(*ii*) Proper phase sequence is easily determined by lamps and no phase-sequence indicator is required.

Disadvantages of dark-lamp method:

(*i*) The lamps become dark at about one-third of their rated voltage. As a consequence, it may happen that the synchronizing switch is closed when there is considerable voltage across the lamps. This voltage would give rise to the flow of high synchronizing current which may be harmful to the system.

(*ii*) It is stated in the literature that this method does not indicate whether the incoming machine is fast or slow. For proper synchronization, incoming machine must be a little fast, *i.e.*, the frequency of the incoming machine must be a little more than the bus-bar frequency. This drawback can, however, be overcome as follows.

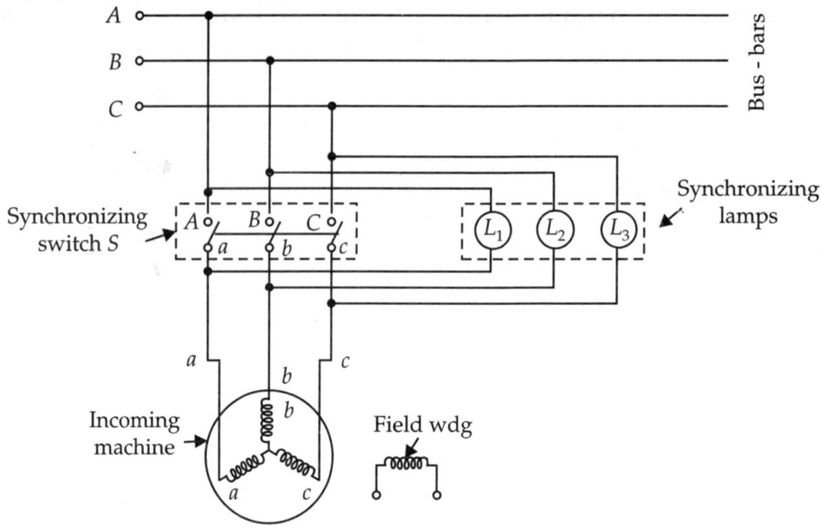

Fig 5.25: Synchronizing by dark-lamp method.

Increase the speed of incoming machine. If lamps flickering increases, it means the incoming machine is already running fast and this is what is required. Decrease the speed of the incoming machine till the lamps flicker very slowly and now close the synchronizing switch as described before.

For high-voltage alternators, lamps cannot be used directly. In such cases, lamps are connected through potential transformers.

5.14.2.2. Synchronizing by synchroscope

A synchroscope is an instrument which indicates the phase difference between voltage one phase of the incoming machine and the corresponding phase of the bus-bar voltage.

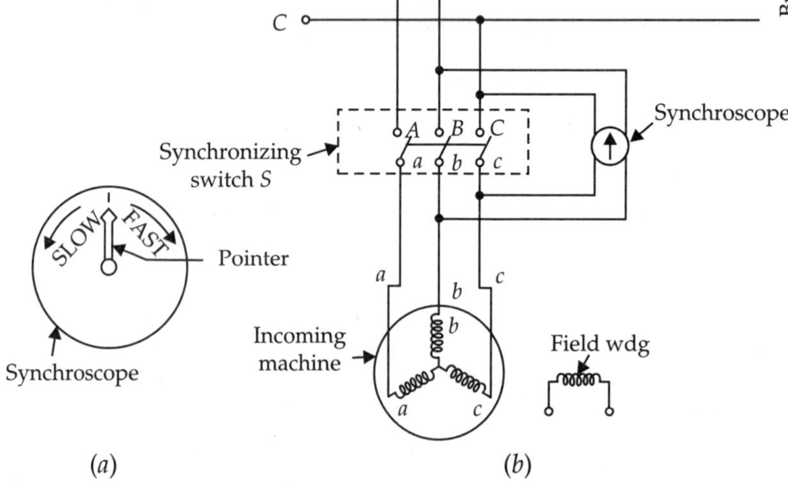

Fig 5.26: (*a*) Synchroscope and (*b*) synchronizing by means of synchroscope.

A simple connection scheme of synchronizing by means of a synchroscope is shown in Fig. 5.26 (*b*). It is connected to *B*, *C* terminals of infinite bus and *b*, *c* terminals of the incoming machine. Phase sequence of the bus-bar voltages and incoming machine voltages is checked with the help of a phase-sequence indicator. Since synchroscope is a single-phase instrument, it cannot check the phase sequence. Prime-mover speed is now adjusted so that pointer of synchroscope movers very slowly in the direction of arrow marked fast. This indicates that frequency of the incoming machine is a little more than bus-bar frequency which is required. Now the incoming machine voltage is made equal to bus-bar voltage. When the rotating pointer of synchroscope reaches the vertical up position (indicating zero degree difference between two voltages) as shown in Fig. 5.26 (*a*), the synchronizing switch *S* is at once closed. With this, the incoming alternator gets connected to the bus bar.

When the two frequencies are equal, the pointer of synchroscope would be stationary. In case the frequency difference is large, the pointer would not rotate but would vibrate at some random position. When the two frequencies are nearly the same, only then the pointer would rotate slowly indicating whether the incoming machine is running fast or slow.

The best synchronization is done if both lamps and synchroscope are used. In large alternators, synchronization is done automatically.

5.15. LOAD DIVISION

Let us consider two synchronous generators running in parallel. When these alternators are loaded, they share the entire load depending upon their excitation emfs and synchronous impedances. In this article, we will examine the load division between two alternators under loaded conditions.

Consider two alternators running in parallel as shown in Fig. 5.27. Here E_{f1} and E_{f2} are the excitation emfs of two alternators 1 and 2. Synchronous impedances of alternators 1 and 2 are Z_{s1} and Z_{s2} respectively. Here Z_L is the load impedance.

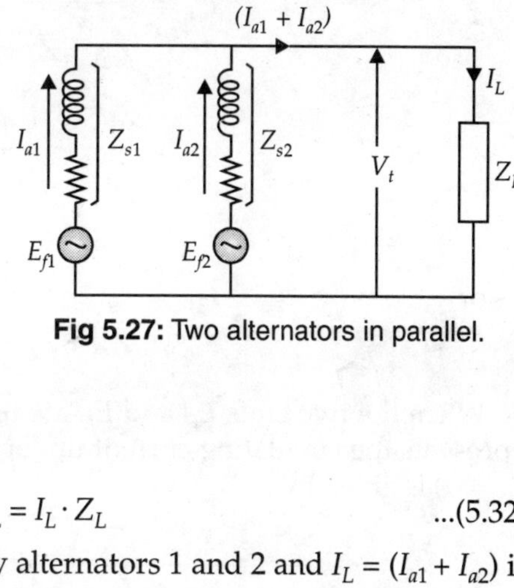

Fig 5.27: Two alternators in parallel.

It is seen from Fig. 5.27 that

$$V_t = (I_{a1} + I_{a2})\, Z_L = I_L \cdot Z_L \qquad ...(5.32)$$

where I_{a1} and I_{a2} are the current shared respectively by alternators 1 and 2 and $I_L = (I_{a1} + I_{a2})$ is the load current. This figure also gives

$$\overline{E}_{f1} - \overline{I}_{a1}\,\overline{Z}_{s1} = \overline{E}_{f2} - \overline{I}_{a2}\,\overline{Z}_{s2} = \overline{V}_t$$

$$\therefore \qquad \overline{I}_{a1} = \frac{\overline{E}_{f1} - \overline{V}_t}{\overline{Z}_{s1}} \text{ and } \overline{I}_{a2} = \frac{\overline{E}_{f2} - \overline{V}_t}{\overline{Z}_{s2}}$$

Substitution of I_{a1} and I_{a2} in Fig. (5.32) gives

$$\overline{V}_t = \left[\frac{\overline{E}_{f1} - \overline{V}_t}{\overline{Z}_{s1}} + \frac{\overline{E}_{f2} - \overline{V}_t}{\overline{Z}_{s2}}\right] \cdot Z_L$$

or

$$\overline{V}_t \left[\frac{1}{\overline{Z}_L} + \frac{1}{\overline{Z}_{s1}} + \frac{1}{\overline{Z}_{s2}}\right] = \frac{\overline{E}_{f1}}{\overline{Z}_{s1}} + \frac{\overline{E}_{f2}}{\overline{Z}_{s2}} \qquad ...(5.33)$$

When more than two alternators are running in parallel, Eq. (4.33) can be written as

$$\overline{V}_t \left[\frac{1}{\overline{Z}_L}+\frac{1}{\overline{Z}_{s1}}+\frac{1}{\overline{Z}_{s2}}+\frac{1}{\overline{Z}_{s3}}+...\right] = \frac{\overline{E}_{f1}}{\overline{Z}_{s1}}+\frac{\overline{E}_{f2}}{\overline{Z}_{s2}}+\frac{\overline{E}_{f3}}{\overline{Z}_{s3}}+...$$

It is seen from Fig. 5.27 that

$$\overline{E}_{f1} - \overline{I}_{a1}\,\overline{Z}_{s1} - (\overline{I}_{a1}+\overline{I}_{a2})\,\overline{Z}_L = 0 \qquad ...(5.34)$$

and

$$E_{f2} - \overline{I}_{a2}\,\overline{Z}_{s2} - (\overline{I}_{a1}+\overline{I}_{a2})\,\overline{Z}_L = 0 \qquad ...(5.35)$$

Eq. (4.34) minus Eq. (4.35) gives

$$\overline{E}_{f1} - \overline{E}_{f2} = \overline{I}_{a1}\,\overline{Z}_{s1} - \overline{I}_{a2}\,\overline{Z}_{s2}$$

or

$$\overline{I}_{a2} = \frac{(\overline{E}_{f2}-\overline{E}_{f1})+\overline{I}_{a1}\cdot\overline{Z}_{s1}}{\overline{Z}_{s2}}$$

Substitution of this value of I_{a2} in Eq. (4.34) gives

$$\overline{E}_{f1} - \overline{I}_{a1}\,\overline{Z}_{s1} - \overline{I}_{a1}\,\overline{Z}_L - \left[\frac{(\overline{E}_{f2}-\overline{E}_{f1})+\overline{I}_{a1}\cdot\overline{Z}_{s1}}{\overline{Z}_{s2}}\right]\overline{Z}_L = 0$$

or

$$\overline{I}_{a1}\left[\overline{Z}_{s1}+\overline{Z}_L+\frac{\overline{Z}_{s1}\cdot\overline{Z}_L}{\overline{Z}_{s2}}\right] = \overline{E}_{f1} + \frac{\overline{E}_{f1}-\overline{E}_{f2}}{\overline{Z}_{s2}}\cdot\overline{Z}_L$$

$\therefore$

$$\overline{I}_{a1} = \frac{\overline{E}_{f1}}{\overline{Z}_{s1}+\overline{Z}_L+\frac{\overline{Z}_{s1}\overline{Z}_L}{\overline{Z}_{s2}}} + \frac{(\overline{E}_{f1}-\overline{E}_{f2})\overline{Z}_L}{\overline{Z}_{s2}} \times \frac{1}{\overline{Z}_{s1}+\overline{Z}_L+\frac{\overline{Z}_{s1}\cdot\overline{Z}_L}{\overline{Z}_{s2}}}$$

$$= \frac{\overline{E}_{f1}}{\overline{Z}_{s1}+\overline{Z}_L+\frac{\overline{Z}_{s1}\overline{Z}_L}{\overline{Z}_{s2}}} + \frac{(\overline{E}_{f1}-\overline{E}_{f2})\overline{Z}_L}{\overline{Z}_{s2}} \times \frac{\overline{Z}_{s2}}{\overline{Z}_{s1}\cdot\overline{Z}_{s2}+\overline{Z}_L\cdot\overline{Z}_{s2}+\overline{Z}_{s1}\cdot\overline{Z}_L}$$

or

$$\overline{I}_{a1} = \frac{\overline{E}_{f1}}{\overline{Z}_{s1}+\overline{Z}_L+\frac{\overline{Z}_{s1}\overline{Z}_L}{\overline{Z}_{s2}}} + \frac{(\overline{E}_{f1}-\overline{E}_{f2})}{\overline{Z}_{s1}+\overline{Z}_{s2}+\frac{\overline{Z}_{s1}\cdot\overline{Z}_{s2}}{\overline{Z}_L}} \qquad ...(5.36)$$

When the two emfs E_{f1} and E_{f2} are unequal or are out of phase, then second term of Eq. (5.36) represents the circulating current under loaded conditions. The circulating current under no load ($Z_L = \alpha$) is given by

$$\overline{I}_c = \frac{\overline{E}_{f1}-\overline{E}_{f2}}{\overline{Z}_{s1}+\overline{Z}_{s2}} \qquad ...(5.37)$$

Example 5.6. *Two 3-phase star-connected alternators, running in parallel, supply a load of 3000 kW at 6.6 kV at power factor of 0.8 lagging. The load is shared equally by the two alternators. Synchronous impedances are 0.3 + j 9 Ω for alternator 1 and 0.4 + j 12 Ω for alternator 2. The excitation emf of second alternator is adjusted so that it delivers 140 A at a lagging pf. Calculate the current, pf, excitation emf and power angle of each alternator.*

Solution. Load shared by each alternator $= P_1 = P_2 = \frac{3000}{2} = 1500$ kW.

Here current shared by alternator 2 is $I_{a2} = 140$ A

$\therefore$ For alternator 2,

$$P_2 = \sqrt{3}\,V_t I_{a2}\cos\theta_2 = 1500 \text{ kW}$$

$$\sqrt{3}\times 6.6\times 140\times\cos\theta_2 = 1500 \text{ kW}$$

$$\therefore \qquad \cos\theta_2 = \frac{1500}{\sqrt{3}\times 6.6\times 140} = 0.937,$$

$$\therefore \qquad \theta_2 = 20.4° \text{ and } \sin\theta_2 = 0.3486.$$

$$\therefore \qquad \overline{I}_{a2} = I_{a2}(\cos\theta_2 - j\sin\theta_2) = 140\,[0.937 - j\,0.3486]$$

$$= [131.18 - j\,48.8]\text{ A}$$

Total load current $= I_{a1} + I_{a2} = \dfrac{3000}{\sqrt{3}\times 6.6\times 0.8}$

$$= 328.05 \text{ A at pf} = 0.8 \text{ lagging}$$

$$= 328.05\,[\cos\theta - j\sin\theta] = 328.05\,[0.8 - j\,0.6]$$

$$= 262.44 - j\,196.83 \text{ A}$$

Current shared by alternator 1 is $\overline{I}_{a1}$ = total current $- \overline{I}_{a2}$

$$= [262.44 - j\,196.83] - [131.18 - j\,48.8]$$

$$= 131.26 - j\,148.03 = 197.84\,\angle{-48.44°}\text{ A}$$

∴ Power factor of alternator 1 $= \cos 48.44 = 0.6634$ lagging.

Excitation emf of alternator 1 is $\overline{E}_{f1} = \overline{V}_t + \overline{I}_{a1}\,\overline{Z}_{s1}$

Here $Z_{s1} = 0.3 + j\,9\,\Omega$. With V_t as reference, $\overline{V}_t = \dfrac{6.6}{\sqrt{3}}\angle 0°$ kV

$$\therefore \qquad \overline{E}_{f1} = \frac{6.6}{\sqrt{3}}\angle 0° + \frac{(131.26 - j\,148.03)(0.3 + j\,9)}{1000}$$

$$= 3.81 + j\,0 + \frac{39.378 + 1332.27 - j\,44.41 + j\,1181.34}{1000}$$

$$= (5.182 + j\,1.137) = 5.305\,\angle 12.375°$$

∴ E_{f1} per phase is 5.305 kV. E_{f1} is ahead of V_t by 12.375°

∴ Power angle of alternator 1 $= \delta_1 = 12.375°$

Excitation voltage of alternator 2 is $E_{f2} = \overline{V}_t + \overline{I}_{a2}\cdot\overline{Z}_{s2}$

Here $\overline{Z}_{s2} = 0.4 + j\,12$. Again with V_t as reference,

$$\overline{V}_t = \frac{6.6}{\sqrt{3}}\angle 0° \text{ kV}$$

$$\therefore \qquad E_{f2} = \frac{6.6\angle 0°}{\sqrt{3}} + \frac{(131.18 - j\,48.8)(0.4 + j12)}{1000}$$

$$= 3.81 + 0.638 + j\,1.555 = 4.448 + j\,1.555$$

$$= 4.712\,\angle 19.27° \text{ kV}$$

Therefore, excitation voltage of alternator 2 is 4.712 kV per phase and power angle $\delta_2 = 19.27°$.

5.16. POWER ANGLE CHARACTERISTICS OF SYNCHRONOUS MACHINES

For obtaining power angle characteristics of synchronous machines, first power expressions are derived for both type of synchronous machines from their respective phasor diagrams. Then their power-angle characteristics are drawn. For the sake of convenience, armature circuit resistance is neglected.

5.16.1. Cylindrical Rotor Alternator

The phasor diagram for a cylindrical rotor alternator operating at a lagging power factor is drawn in Fig. 5.28 (*a*). For this alternator,

$$\bar{E}_f = \bar{V}_t + \bar{I}_a \bar{Z}_s$$

and with $r_a = 0$, $\bar{E}_f = \bar{V}_t + j\,\bar{I}_a X_s$ or $\bar{I}_a = \dfrac{\bar{E}_f - \bar{V}_t}{jX_s}$

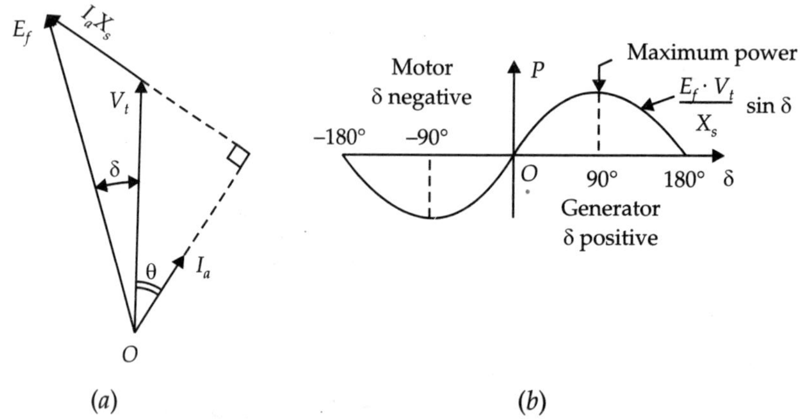

Fig 5.28: Cylindrical rotor alternator (*a*) phasor diagram with $r_a = 0$ and (*b*) power-angle characteristics.

Take V_t as the reference phasor. Then $\bar{V}_t = V_t \angle 0°$ and $\bar{E}_f = E_f \angle \delta$

$$\therefore \quad \bar{I}_a = \frac{E_f \angle \delta}{X_s \angle 90} - \frac{V_t \angle 0°}{X_s \angle 90°} = \frac{E_f}{X_s} \angle \delta - 90° - \frac{V_t}{X_s} \angle -90°$$

$$\bar{I}_a^* = \text{conjugated of } \bar{I}_a = \frac{E_f}{X_s} \angle 90 - \delta - \frac{V_t}{X_s} \angle 90°$$

Power output of alternator,

$$P = Re\,[\bar{V}_t\ \bar{I}_a^*] = Re\left[\frac{E_f V_t}{X_s} \angle 90 - \delta - \frac{V_t^2}{X_s} \angle 90°\right]$$

or

$$P = Re\left[\frac{E_f V_t}{X_s} \cdot \{\cos(90 - \delta) + j\sin(90° - \delta)\} - \frac{V_t^2}{X_s}(\cos 90 + j\sin 90°)\right]$$

$$= \frac{E_f \cdot V_t}{X_s} \cos(90 - \delta) - \frac{V_t^2}{X_s} \cos 90$$

$$= \frac{E_f \cdot V_t}{X_s} [\cos 90 \cdot \cos\delta + \sin 90 \sin\delta] - 0$$

$$\therefore \quad P = \frac{E_f \cdot V_t}{X_s} \cdot \sin\delta \qquad \text{...(5.38)}$$

With the help of Eq. (5.38), variation of power P with power angle δ is plotted in Fig. 5.28 (*b*). This power versus load-angle curve has a sinusoidal shape. This curve is usually called power-angle characteristics of a cylindrical-rotor synchronous machine. For generator mode, power is taken positive and therefore, for a motor mode, power is negative. It is seen from Fig. 5.28 (*b*) that maximum synchronous power occurs when power or load angle δ = 90°.

5.16.2. Salient-pole Alternator

Phasor diagram for a salient-pole alternator operating at a lagging power factor and with $r_a = 0$, obtained from Fig. 5.23, is shown in Fig. 5.29 (*a*). From this figure,

$$V_t \sin\delta = I_q X_q \text{ or } I_q = \frac{V_t \sin\delta}{X_q}$$

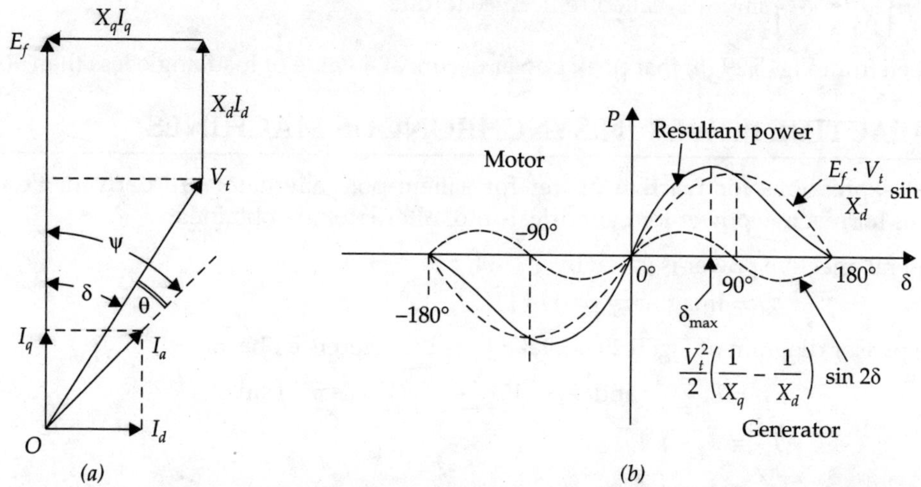

(*a*) (*b*)

Fig 5.29: Cylindrical rotor alternator (*a*) phasor diagram with $r_a = 0$ and (*b*) power-angle characterstics.

Also, $$V_t \cos\delta = E_f - I_d X_d \text{ or } I_d = \frac{E_f - V_t \cos\delta}{X_d}$$

In Fig. 5.29 (*a*), take E_f as reference phasor, then $\overline{E}_f = E_f \angle 0°$

and $\overline{V}_t = V_t \angle -\delta = V_t (\cos\delta - j\sin\delta)$. Also $\overline{I}_a = \overline{I}_q - j\,\overline{I}_d$

$$\therefore \quad \overline{I}_a^{\,*} = \overline{I}_q - j\,\overline{I}_d = \frac{V_t \sin\delta}{X_q} + j\,\frac{E_f - V_t\cos\delta}{X_d} \qquad ...(5.39)$$

Power output of alternator $P = Re\,[\overline{V}_t\, \overline{I}_a^{\,*}]$

or $$P = Re\,[V_t \angle -\delta \times (\overline{I}_q + j\,\overline{I}_d)]$$

$$= Re\left\{\left[(V_t\cos\delta - j\,V_t\sin\delta) \times \left[\frac{V_t\sin\delta}{X_q} + j\frac{E_f - V_t\cos\delta}{X_d}\right]\right]\right\}$$

$$= \frac{V_t^2}{X_q}\sin\delta\cos\delta + \frac{V_t \cdot E_f}{X_d}\sin\delta - \frac{V_t^2}{X_d}\sin\delta\cos\delta$$

$$\therefore \quad P = \frac{E_f \cdot V_t}{X_d}\sin\delta + \frac{V_t^2}{2}\left[\frac{1}{X_q} - \frac{1}{X_d}\right]\sin 2\delta \qquad ...(5.40)$$

With the help of Eq. (5.40), power versus load-angle characteristics of a salient-pole machine are plotted in Fig. 5.29 (*b*). The total power *P* consists of fundamental component $\frac{E_f \cdot V_t}{X_d}\sin\delta$ and a second harmonic component $\frac{1}{2} \cdot V_t^2\left[\frac{1}{X_q} - \frac{1}{X_d}\right]\sin 2\delta$.

The first term of P, *i.e.*, $\frac{E_f \cdot V_t}{X_d}$ is called electromagnetic power and $\frac{1}{\omega_s}\left[\frac{E_f \cdot V_t}{X_d}\sin\delta\right]$ is called reluctance torque.

The second of P, *i.e.*, $\frac{1}{2}\cdot V_t^2\left[\frac{1}{X_q}-\frac{1}{X_d}\right]$ sin 2δ is called reluctance power and $\frac{1}{\omega_s}\left[\frac{1}{2}\cdot V_t^2\left\{\frac{1}{X_q}-\frac{1}{X_d}\right\}\sin 2\delta\right]$ is called reluctance torque.

It is seen from Fig. 5.29 (*b*) that peak power occurs at a value of load angle less than 90°.

5.17. REACTIVE POWER IN SYNCHRONOUS MACHINES

Here, first expressions for reactive power for salient-pole alternator are derived. From these, expressions for reactive power for cylindrical-rotor alternator are obtained.

In general, reactive power is given by

$$Q = \text{Imaginary part of } [\bar{V}_t\ \bar{I}_a^*] \qquad ...(5.41)$$

In the phasor diagram of Fig. 5.29 (*a*), take E_f as the reference phasor.

$$\therefore \quad \bar{E}_f = E_f \angle 0^\circ \text{ and } \bar{V}_t = V_t \angle -\delta = (V_t\cos\delta - j\sin\delta)$$

$$\text{Also} \quad \bar{I}_a = \bar{I}_q - j\,\bar{I}_d$$

$$\therefore \quad \bar{I}_a^* = \bar{I}_q - j\,\bar{I}_d$$

From Eq. (5.39), $\bar{I}_a^* = \left[\frac{V_t\sin\delta}{X_q} + j\frac{E_f - V_t\cos\delta}{X_d}\right]$

Substituting these values in Eq. (5.41), we get

$$Q = Im\cdot\left[(V_t\cos\delta - j\,V_t\sin\delta)\times\left\{\frac{V_t\sin\delta}{X_q} + j\frac{E_f - V_t\cos\delta}{X_d}\right\}\right]$$

$$= \frac{V_t\cdot E_f}{X_d}\cos\delta - \frac{V_t^2}{X_d}\cos^2\delta - \frac{V_t^2}{X_q}\sin^2\delta$$

$$= \frac{E_f\cdot V_t}{X_d}\cdot\cos\delta - \frac{V_t^2}{X_d}(1-\sin^2\delta) - \frac{V_t^2}{X_q}\cdot\sin^2\delta$$

$$= \frac{E_f\cdot V_t}{X_d}\cos\delta - \frac{V_t^2}{X_d} - V_t^2\left[\frac{1}{X_q}-\frac{1}{X_d}\right]\sin^2\delta \qquad ...(5.42)$$

For a cylindrical-rotor alternator,

$$X_d = X_q = X_s$$

$$\therefore \quad Q = \frac{E_f\cdot V_t}{X_s}\cos\delta - \frac{V_t^2}{X_s} = \frac{V_t}{X_s}[E_f\cos\delta - V_t] \qquad ...(5.43)$$

Eq. (5.43) shows that if $E_f\cos\delta = V_t$, that is under normal excitation, $Q = 0$ and the alternator operates at unity pf, neither delivering nor absorbing reactive power.

If $E_f\cos\delta > V_t$, alternator is overexcited, Q is positive. Therefore, the alternator delivers reactive power to the bus bars.

When $E_f\cos\delta > V_t$, the alternator is underexcited, Q is negative. The alternator, therefore, absorbs reactive power from the bus bars.

In general (*a*) an overexcited alternator or synchronous motor delivers reactive power to bus bars, (*b*) an underexcited synchronous machine absorbs reactive power from the bus bars and (*c*) a normally excited synchronous machine neither delivers nor absorbs reactive power from the bus bars.

5.18. SYNCHRONOUS MOTOR OPERATING PRINCIPLE

A synchronous motor converts electrical energy into mechanical energy at a constant speed, called synchronous speed. Just like an alternator, a synchronous motor is a **doubly-excited** machine. Its field winding is fed from a dc source and armature winding from a 3-phase ac source. Some characteristic features of synchronous motors are as under :

1. It can run only at synchronous speed.
2. It has no inherent starting torque.
3. It can be made to operate at a lagging, unity and leading power factors just like an alternator.

5.18.1. Operating Principle

Consider a two-pole synchronous motor shown in Fig. 5.30. Field winding on stationary rotor produces two poles. When three-phase supply is given to 3-phase armature winding on stator, a rotating magnetic field having 2 poles is produced. Stator poles *N*, *S* rotating at synchronous speed n_s are shown in Fig. 5.30.

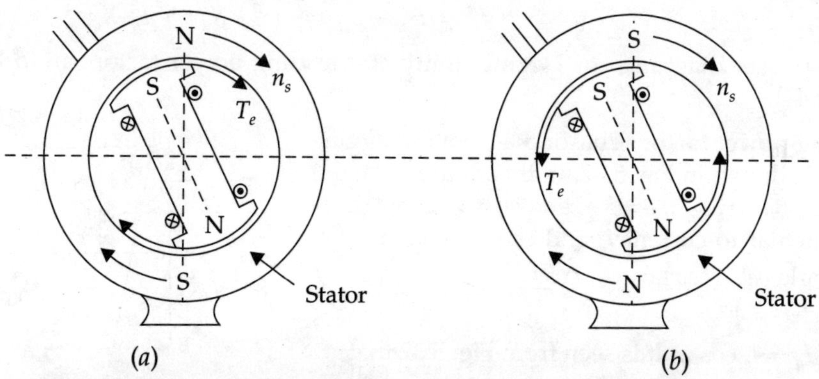

Fig 5.30: Development of starting torque in a 3-phase synchronous motor.

When the stator rotating poles occupy the position indicated in Fig. 5.30 (*a*), stator *N*, *S* poles, attract rotor *S*, *N* poles, thus producing a clockwise torque on the rotor. After half a cycle, *i.e.*, after 0.01 sec or 10 ms $\left(=\frac{1}{2f}\right)$ for a 50 Hz supply, the stator poles would occupy the position shown in Fig. 5.30 (*b*). Now stator *N*, *S* poles repel stationary rotor *N*, *S* poles, thus producing anticlockwise torque. In Fig. 5.30 (*a*), the rotor is urged to rotate clockwise, but soon after, *i.e.*, after 10 ms, the rotor is urged to rotate anticlockwise in Fig. 5.30 (*b*). The rotor, due to its inertia, cannot respond to such quick reversals of electromagnetic torque. As a result, the rotor remains at standstill position. This shows that in a synchronous motor, **net starting torque is zero.** In other words, a 3-phase synchronous motor has **no inherent starting torque**.

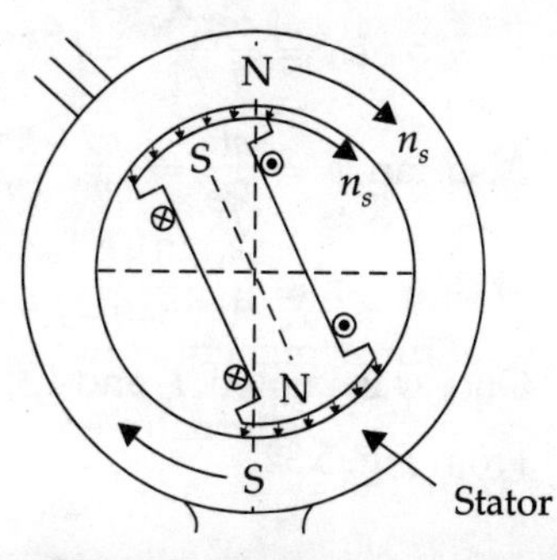

Fig 5.31: Development of continuous torque in a synchronous motor.

Now consider the situation depicted in Fig. 5.31. Stator poles N, S run clockwise at synchronous speed. Suppose rotor is also made to run clockwise at synchronous speed. Under these conditions, relative speed between stator field and rotor field would be zero. In other words, the stator and rotor fields are stationary with respect to each other. The stator poles now can attract rotor poles of opposite polarity, Fig. 5.31, and continue to pull the rotor along at synchronous speed. This **magnetic locking** between stator poles and rotor poles is essential for the development of steady torque. This shows that it is basically necessary to bring the rotor to synchronous speed by auxiliary means and then only steady torque would be developed in a synchronous motor.

5.19. PHASOR DIAGRAM FOR SALIENT POLE SYNCHRONOUS MOTOR

Phasor diagrams for cylindrical rotor synchronous motor are already drawn in Fig. 5.20 from its basic voltage equation $\bar{V}_t = \bar{E}_f + \bar{I}_a \bar{Z}_s$. Now, we shall describe how to draw the phasor diagrams for salient pole synchronous motors at different operating power factors.

For a salient-pole alternator, the voltage equation, from Eq. (5.24), is

$$\bar{E}_f = \bar{V}_t + \bar{I}_a r_a + j \bar{I}_d X_d + j \bar{I}_q X_q \qquad ...(5.24)$$

For a synchronous motor, the armature current flows opposite to that in an alternator. Therefore, voltage equation for a salient-pole synchronous motor is

$$\bar{E}_f = \bar{V}_t - \bar{I}_a r_a - j \bar{I}_d X_d - j \bar{I}_q X_q$$

or

$$\bar{V}_t = \bar{E}_f + \bar{I}_a r_a + j \bar{I}_d X_d + j \bar{I}_q X_q \qquad ...(5.44)$$

Now the phasor diagrams for lagging, unity and leading power factors are drawn with the help of Eq. (5.44).

(*i*) **Lagging power factor :** Phasor diagram for lagging power factor is drawn in Fig. 5.32. In this figure; take $OA = E_f$, $AB = I_q X_q$, $Bd = I_d X_d$, $dn = I_a r_a$ and $on = V_t$. Now draw db a perpendicular to current I_a and cb perpendicular to OAp. In triangle oab, $\angle aob = \psi$, $\angle oba = \angle dbp = 90 - \psi$. Therefore, $\angle cbd = \psi°$.

Now $\quad I_q = I_a \cos \psi$. It is seen from Fig. 5.32 that

$$bc = bd \cos \psi = AB = X_q I_q$$

$$\therefore \quad b_d = \frac{I_q \cdot X_q}{\cos \psi}. \text{ But } \cos \psi = \frac{I_q}{I_a},$$

$$\therefore \quad bd = \frac{I_q \cdot X_q}{I_q / I_a} = I_a X_q$$

$$\text{Also, } \tan \psi = \frac{ab}{oa} = \frac{ad - bd}{om - am} = \frac{mn - bd}{om - am}$$

$$= \frac{V_t \sin \theta - I_a X_q}{V_t \cos \theta - I_a r_a} \qquad ...(5.45)$$

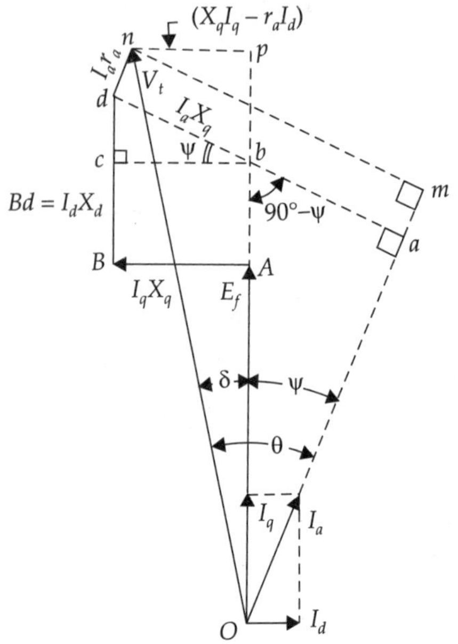

Fig 5.32: Salient-pole synchronous motor phasor diagram for lagging pf.

Once ψ is known, I_d and I_q can be calculated.

From Fig. 5.32, $\quad V_t \sin \delta = X_q I_q - r_a I_d$

$$= X_q I_a \cos (\theta - \delta) - r_a \cdot I_a \sin (\theta - \delta)$$

$$V_t \sin \delta = X_q I_a \cos \theta \cos \delta + X_q I_a \sin \theta \sin \delta - r_a I_a \sin \theta \cos \delta + r_a I_a \cos \theta \sin \delta$$

$\therefore \quad \sin\delta\,[V_t - I_a X_q \sin\theta - r_a I_a \cos\theta] = \cos\delta\,[I_a X_q \cos\theta - I_a r_a \sin\theta]$

$$\therefore \quad \tan\delta = \frac{I_a\left(X_q\cos\theta - r_a\sin\theta\right)}{V_t - I_a\left(X_q\sin\theta + r_a\cos\theta\right)} \qquad ...(5.46)$$

Also, $$E_f = V_t\cos\delta - I_q r_a - I_d X_d \qquad ...(5.47)$$

(*ii*) **Unity power factor :** Phasor diagram for unity power factor operation is drawn in Fig. 5.33, where $OA = E_f$, $AB = I_q X_q$, $Bb = I_d X_d$, $ba = I_a r_a$ and $Oa = V_t$. Now draw $b\,d$ perpendicular to V_t or I_a and bc perpendicular to E_f or OA. As before, $\angle cbd = \psi$. It is seen from Fig. 5.33 that

$$bc = I_q X_q = bd\cos\psi$$

or $$bd = \frac{bc}{\cos\psi}$$

But $$I_a\cos\psi = I_q \text{ or } \cos\psi = \frac{I_q}{I_a},$$

$$\therefore \quad bd = \frac{I_q X_q}{I_q/I_a} = I_a X_q$$

$$\tan\psi = \tan\delta = \frac{bd}{Ob} = \frac{bd}{Oa - ab} = \frac{I_a X_q}{V_t - I_a r_a} \qquad ...(5.48)$$

From angle ψ, I_d and I_q can be obtained.

Also, $$E_f = V_t\cos\delta - I_q\cdot r_a + I_d X_d \qquad ...(5.49)$$

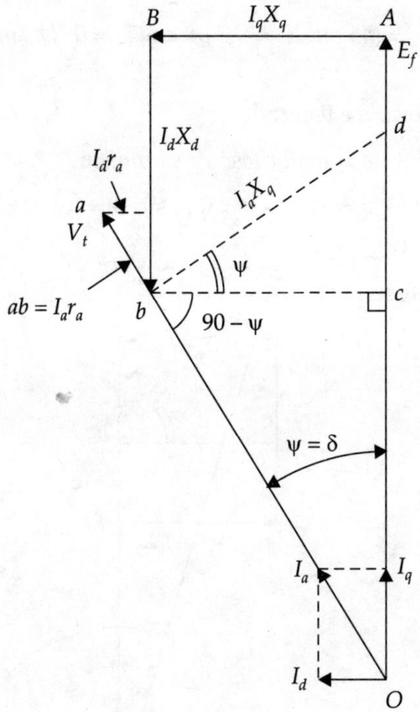

Fig 5.33: Salient-pole synchronous motor phasor diagarm at unity pf.

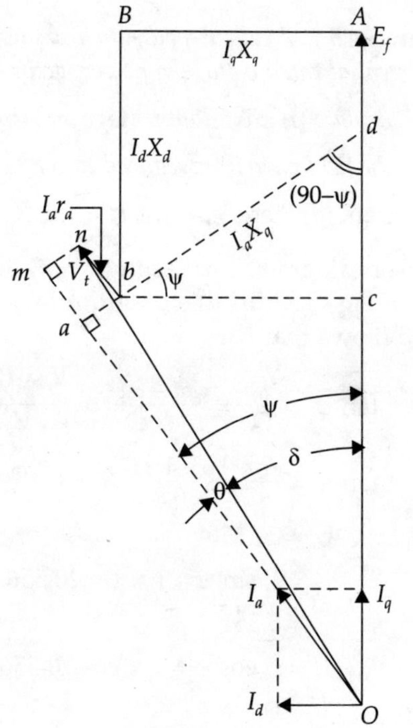

Fig 5.34: Salient-pole synchronous motor phasor diagram at leading pf.

(*iii*) **Leading power factor :** For leading power-factor operation, phasor diagram is drawn in Fig. 5.34, where $OA = E_f$, $AB = I_q X_q$, $Bb = I_d X_d$, $b\,n = I_a r_a$, $O\,n = V_t$ and I_a leads V_t by power-factor angle θ. In this figure, draw $a\,b\,d$ perpendicular to I_a and bc perpendicular to $OA = E_f$.

Here also $\angle cbd = \psi$ and $bc = AB = I_q X_q$

But $b\,c = bd \cos\psi$ and $I_q = I_a \cos\psi$

$$\therefore \quad bd = \frac{bc}{\cos\psi} = \frac{I_q X_q}{I_q / I_a} = I_q X_q$$

$$\tan\psi = \tan(\delta + \theta) = \frac{ad}{Oa} = \frac{ab + bd}{Om - ma}$$

$$= \frac{mn + bd}{Om - am} = \frac{V_t \sin\theta + I_a X_q}{V_t \cos\theta - I_a r_a} \quad ...(5.50)$$

From ψ, I_d and I_q can be calculated.

From Fig. 5.34, $\quad V_t \sin\delta = bc + I_d r_a = X_q I_q + I_d r_a$

$$= X_q I_a \cos(\delta + \theta) + r_a I_a \sin(\delta + \theta)$$

or $\quad V_t \sin\delta = X_q I_a \cos\delta \cos\theta - X_q I_a \sin\delta \sin\theta + r_a I_a \sin\delta \cos\theta + r_a I_a \cos\delta \sin\theta$

$$\sin\delta\,[V_t + I_a X_q \sin\theta - r_a I_a \cos\theta] = \cos\delta\,[I_a X_q \cos\theta + r_a I_a \sin\theta]$$

$$\therefore \quad \tan\delta = \frac{I_a[X_q \cos\theta + r_a \sin\theta]}{V_t + I_a[X_q \sin\theta - r_a \cos\theta]} \quad ...(5.51)$$

Also, $\quad E_f = V_t \cos\delta - r_a I_q + I_d X_d \quad ...(5.52)$

Example 5.7. *A salient-pole synchronous motor has $X_d = 0.5$ pu, $X_q = 0.3$ pu and $r_a = 0$. The motor takes rated current at rated voltage at power factor 0.8 lagging.*

(a) Calculate (i) excitation voltage and (ii) active and reactive powers.

(b) If the field current is reduced to zero, will the synchronous motor lose synchronism?

Solution. (*a*) Here $V_t = 1.0$, $I_a = 1.0$, $X_d = 0.5$, $X_q = 0.3$, $r_a = 0$, $\cos\theta = 0.8$, $\sin\theta = 0.6$, $\theta = 36.87°$.

Phasor diagram for lagging power factor load is shown in Fig. 5.35. In this diagram $bd = I_a X_q$ as before. Fig. 5.35 shows that

$$\tan\psi = \frac{ab}{Oa} = \frac{ad - bd}{Oa} = \frac{V_t \sin\theta - I_a X_q}{V_t \cos\theta}$$

$$\tan\psi = \frac{1 \times 0.6 - 1 \times 0.3}{1 \times 0.8} = 0.375$$

$$\therefore \quad \psi = 20.556°$$

$$I_d = I_a \sin\psi = 1 \times \sin 20.556 = 0.351$$

$$I_q = I_a \cos\psi = 1 \times \cos 20.556 = 0.9363$$

Also, $\quad \theta = \psi + \delta$,

$$\therefore \quad \delta = \theta - \psi = 36.87 - 20.556 = 16.314°$$

It is seen from Fig. 5.35 that

$$E_f = V_t \cos\delta - I_d X_d$$

$$= 1 \times \cos 16.314 - 0.351 \times 0.5$$

$$= 0.7842 \text{ pu}$$

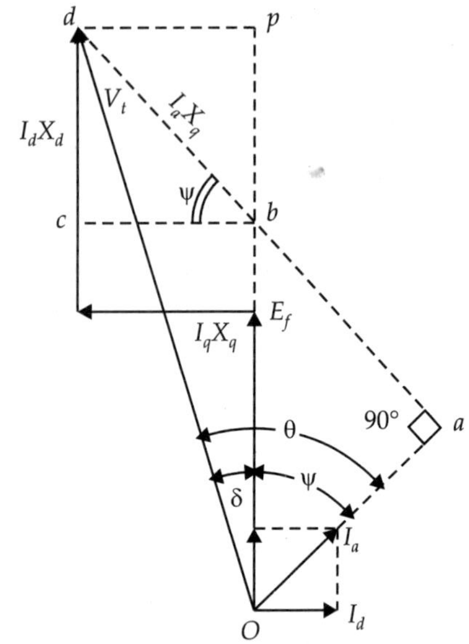

Fig 5.35: Phasor diagram for Example 5.7.

$$\text{Power} = \frac{E_f \cdot V_t}{X_d} \sin \delta + \frac{V_t^2}{2}\left[\frac{1}{X_q} - \frac{1}{X_d}\right] \sin 2\delta$$

$$= \frac{0.7842 \times 1}{0.5} \sin 16.314 + \frac{1}{2}\left[\frac{1}{0.3} - \frac{1}{0.5}\right] \sin (2 \times 16.314)$$

$$= 0.4406 + 0.3594 = 0.8 \text{ pu}$$

Reactive power output for a salient-pole alternator is given by Eq. (5.42). In a synchronous motor, current flow is opposite to that in an alternator. Therefore, reactive power expression for a motor can be obtained from Eq. (5.42) by putting negative signs before the terms on right-hand side.

$$\therefore \quad Q = -\frac{E_f \cdot V_t}{X_d} \cos \delta + \frac{V_t^2}{X_d} + V_t^2 \left[\frac{1}{X_q} - \frac{1}{X_d}\right] \sin^2 \delta$$

$$= \frac{V_t^2}{X_d} + V_t^2 \left[\frac{1}{X_q} - \frac{1}{X_d}\right] \sin^2 \delta - \frac{E_f \cdot V_t}{X_d} \cos \delta$$

$$= \frac{1}{0.5} + 1\left[\frac{1}{0.3} - \frac{1}{0.5}\right] (\sin 16.314)^2 - \frac{0.7842 \times 1}{0.5} \cos 16.314$$

$$= 2 + 0.1052 - 1.5052 = 0.6 \text{ pu}$$

(*b*) With zero field current, $E_f = 0$, now reluctance power is given by $\frac{V_t^2}{2}\left[\frac{1}{X_q} - \frac{1}{X_d}\right] \sin 2\delta$. Its maximum value occurs when load angle $\delta = 45°$.

$$\therefore \quad \text{Maximum reluctance power} = \frac{1}{2}\left[\frac{1}{0.3} - \frac{1}{0.5}\right] \sin 90° = 0.667 \text{ pu}$$

Since maximum reluctance power 0.667 pu is less than the rated power of 0.8 pu, the synchronous motor would lose synchronism.

Example 5.8. *A 10 MVA, 3-phase star-connected, 11 kV, 12 pole, 50 Hz, salient pole synchronous motor has $X_d = 6\ \Omega$, $X_q = 4\ \Omega$ and $r_a = 0.5\ \Omega$. If this motor is operating at 0.8 pf leading and at rated voltage, then calculate (a) the excitation voltage, (b) synchronous power and (c) maximum value of power angle and the corresponding power.*

Solution. (*a*) Here $V_t = \frac{11000}{\sqrt{3}} = 6351$ V, $X_d = 6\ \Omega$, $X_q = 4\ \Omega$,

$r_a = 0.5\ \Omega$, pf, $\cos\theta = 0.8$, $\sin\theta = 0.6$, $\theta = 36.87°$.

Armature current per phase, $I_a = \frac{10 \times 10^6}{\sqrt{3} \times 11000} = 524.88$ A.

Phasor diagram for salient-pole synchronous motor at 0.8 pf leading is shown in Fig. 5.36. Here $OA = E_f$, $AB = I_q X_q$, $Bb = I_d X_d$, $bn = I_a r_a$, $On = V_t$ and I_a leads V_t by pf angle θ. Draw *abd* perpendicular to I_a and *bc* perpendicular to $OA = E_f$.

It is seen from Fig. 5.36 that and Eq. (5.50) that

$$\tan \psi = \frac{V_t \sin\theta + I_a X_q}{V_t \cos\theta - I_a r_a}$$

$$= \frac{6351 \times 0.6 + 524.88 \times 4}{6351 \times 0.8 - 524.88 \times 0.5} = 1.2266$$

$$\therefore \quad \psi = 50.81°$$

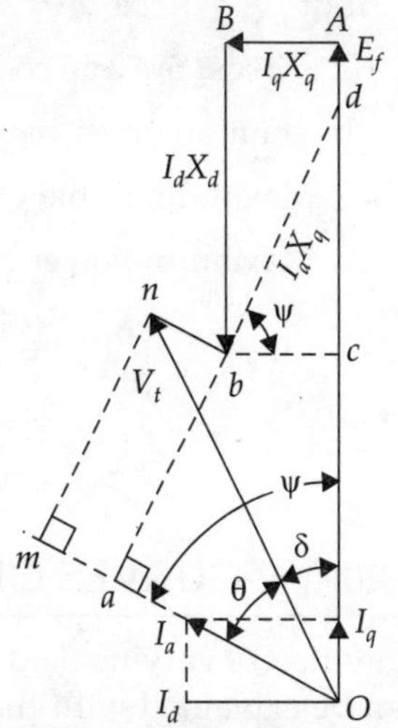

Fig 5.36: Phasor diagram for Example 5.8.

Now $I_d = I_a \sin\psi = 524.88 \times \sin 50.81 = 406.81$ A

$I_q = I_a \cos\psi = 524.88 \times \cos 50.81 = 301.67$ A

Also $\psi = \theta + \delta,$

$\therefore$ $\delta = \psi - \theta = 50.81 - 36.87 = 13.94°$

From Eq. (5.52),

$$E_f = V_t \cos\delta - r_a I_q + I_d \cdot X_d$$
$$= 6351 \times \cos 13.94 - 0.5 \times 331.67 + 406.81 \times 6$$
$$= 8438.9787 \cong 8439 \text{ V}$$

(*b*)
$$P = \frac{E_f \cdot V_t}{X_d} \sin\delta + \frac{V_t^2}{X_d^2}\left[\frac{1}{X_q} - \frac{1}{X_d}\right] \sin 2\delta$$
$$= \frac{8439 \times 6351}{6} \sin 13.94 + \frac{6351^2}{2}\left[\frac{1}{4} - \frac{1}{6}\right] \sin(2 \times 13.94)$$
$$= 2937833.6 \text{ W per phase}$$
$$= 8813500.777 \cong 8813.5 \text{ kW for 3-phases}$$

(*c*)
$$P = \frac{E_f \cdot V_t}{X_d} \sin\delta + \frac{V_t^2}{2}\left[\frac{1}{X_q} - \frac{1}{X_d}\right] \sin 2\delta$$

For maximum power,

$$\frac{dP}{d\delta} = 0, \therefore \frac{E_f \cdot V_t}{X_d} \cos\delta + V_t^2\left[\frac{1}{X_q} - \frac{1}{X_d}\right] \cos 2\delta = 0$$

or
$$\frac{E_f}{X_d} \cos\delta + V_t\left[\frac{1}{X_q} - \frac{1}{X_d}\right] \cos 2\delta = 0$$
$$\frac{8439}{6} \cos\delta + 6351\left[\frac{1}{4} - \frac{1}{6}\right] \cos 2\delta = 0$$

or $\cos 2\delta + \frac{1406.5}{529.25} \cos\delta = 0$

But $\cos 2\delta = 2\cos^2\delta - 1$

$\therefore$ $2\cos^2\delta + 2.66\cos\delta - 1 = 0$

Its solution gives $\cos\delta = 0.30568$

$\therefore$ Maximum stable power angle $\delta = \cos^{-1}[0.30568] = 72.20°$

$\therefore$ Maximum power is given by

$$P_{max} = \frac{8439 \times 6351}{6} \sin 72.20° + \frac{6351^2}{2}\left[\frac{1}{4} - \frac{1}{6}\right] \sin(2 \times 72.20°)$$
$$= 9483404 \text{ W per phase}$$
$$= 28450.212 \text{ kW for 3-phases.}$$

5.20. V-CURVES OF SYNCHRONOUS MOTORS

The effect of varying field current on the power factor and armature current of a synchronous motor can be explained with the help of its phasor diagram. For simplicity, armature circuit resistance is neglected. Synchronous reactance X_s and terminal voltage V_t are assumed constant. Per-phase power in a synchronous motor is given by

$$P = \frac{E_f \cdot V_t}{X_s} \sin \delta = V_t I_a \cos \theta$$

Since V_t and X_s are constant, for ϕ constant power output, $E_f \sin \delta \left[= \frac{P \cdot X_s}{V_t}\right]$ and $I_a \cos \theta \left[= \frac{P}{V_t}\right]$ must remain constant. In other words, under the assumptions stated above, $E_f \sin \delta$ = constant and also $I_a \cos \theta$ = constant.

When the field current is varied, excitation emf E_f varies but $E_f \sin \delta$, normal to V_t, must remain constant. Further, as E_f varies, $I_a X_s$ and therefore armature current I_a also varies under the condition that $I_a \cos \theta$ remains constant.

The effect of variation of field on the synchronous motor power factor and armature current can be explained with the phasor diagram of Fig. 5.37.

When the excitation emf is E_{f1}, the motor is underexcited and armature current I_{a1} lags V_t by pf angle θ_1 so that $E_{f1} + j\, I_{a1} \cdot X_s = V_t$ is satisfied. Load angle here is δ_1. When excitation voltage is increased to E_{f2} by increasing the field current, the angle δ_1 must decrease to angle δ_2 so that $E_{f1} \cdot \sin \delta_1 = E_{f2} \cdot \sin \delta_2$. In order to statisfy the relation $E_{f2} + j\, I_{a2}\, X_s = V_t$, the phase of armature current changes to I_{a2} as shown. Now the motor operates at unity power factor such that $I_{a2} \times$ pf 1 $= I_{a1} \cos \theta_1$. When the excitation is increased to E_{f3}, the load angle must decrease from δ_2 to δ_3 so that $E_{f1} \cdot \sin \delta_1 = E_{f2} \cdot \sin \delta_2 = E_{f3} \cdot \sin \delta_3$. For satisfying the relation $E_{f3} + j\, I_{a3}\, X_s = V_t$, the phase of armature current I_{a3} is pushed ahead of V_t as shown in Fig. 5.37, the motor now operates at a leading power factor cos θ_3. Note that active power components of armature current are equal, *i.e.* $I_{a1} \cdot \cos \theta_1 = I_{a2} \cdot \cos \theta_2 = I_{a3} \cdot \cos \theta_3$. It is seen from Fig. 5.37 that armature current is minimum at unity pf and more at leading and lagging power factors. This variation of armature current with change in field current is plotted in Fig. 5.38 (*a*).

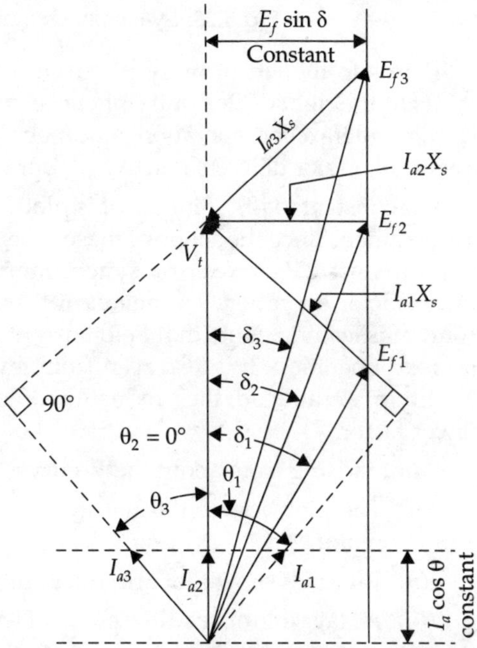

Fig 5.37: Phasor diagram showing the effect of field current on synchronous motor pf and armature current.

The lowest curve is a plot between armature current along vertical axis and field current along horizontal axis at no load. For higher mechanical loads on the motor, higher armature currents would be required. As a result, constant half-full load and constant full load curves are obtained one above the other as shown in Fig. 5.38 (*a*). Since the shape of these curves resemble the letter '*V*', these are called **V-curves of a synchronous motor**. Thus, *V*-curves are the plots of armature current and field current for different constant shaft loads. The point at which unity pf occurs is indicated by minimum armature current. A curve joining all the minimum armature current points is called **unity pf compounding curve**.

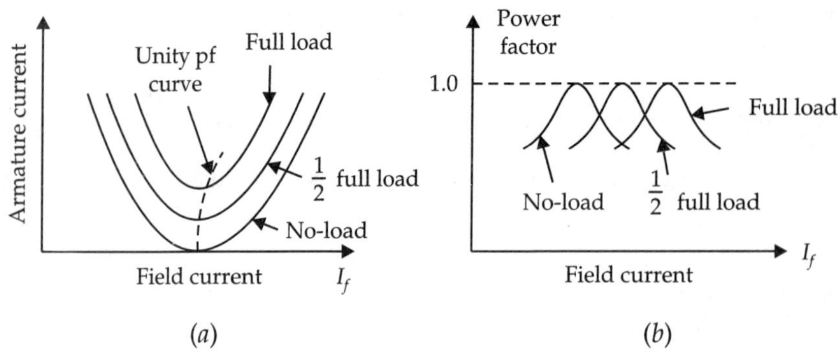

Fig 5.38: Synchronous motor (*a*) V-curves and (*b*) inverted V-curves.

Points to the left of unity pf curve correspond to underexcitation and lagging pf operation. Points to the right of this unity pf curve indicate overexcitation and leading pf operation. Further, during underexcited operation, motor absorbs reactive power from the bus and during overexcited operation, motor delivers reactive power to the bus.

For constant loads, if motor pf is plotted as a function of field current, the curves of Fig. 5.38 (*b*) are obtained. Since the shape of these plots resemble inverted letter '*V*', these curves are sometimes called **inverted V-curves of a synchronous motor**. The peak point of these curves indicate unity power factor operation. To the left of these peak points for any load, the pf is lagging and to the right, pf is leading. Note that field current for unity pf operation at no load is less than its value at full load operation. It is also seen from inverted *V*-curves that if synchronous motor is operating at unity pf at full load, then reduction of load to half would cause the motor to operate at leading power factor.

Summarising from about the *V*-curves, the following statements can be made :

(*i*) The plot between armature current and field current gives *V*-curves of a synchronous motor.

(*ii*) *V*-curves show that armature current is minimum at unity pf.

(*iii*) At lagging or leading power factors, armature current is more than its value at unity power factor.

(*iv*) Increasing the field current, above the level for minimum armature current, causes the motor to operate at leading pf. The motor is now overexcited and delivers reactive power to the system.

(*v*) Decreasing the field current, below that required for minimum armature current, causes the motor to operate at lagging pf. The motor is now underexcited and absorbs reactive power from the bus.

Example 5.9. *A 3-phase, 1000 kW, 3.3 kV, 10 pole, 50 Hz, star-connected synchronous motor has negligible armature resistance and synchronous reactance is 6 Ω per phase. Its field current is so adjusted that motor begins to operate at rated load at unity power factor. Calculate* (a) *the load angle and* (b) *the maximum torque the motor can develope.*

Solution. (*a*) Here, per-phase voltage,

$$V_t = \frac{3300}{\sqrt{3}} = 1905.3 \text{ V, power factor} = 1.$$

Per-phase armature current,

$$I_a = \frac{1000}{\sqrt{3} \times 3.3 \times 1} = 174.96 \text{ A}$$

Synchronous motor phasor diagram at unity power factor is drawn in Fig. 5.39. From this figure

$$\tan\delta = \frac{I_a X_s}{V_t}$$

$\therefore$ Load angle, $\delta = \tan^{-1}\left[\frac{I_a X_s}{V_t}\right] = \tan^{-1}\left[\frac{174.96\times 6}{1905.3}\right]$

$= \mathbf{28.853°}$

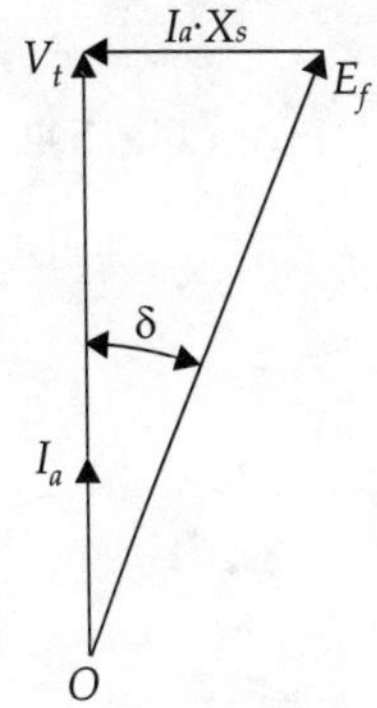

Fig 5.39: Phasor diagram pertaining to Example 5.9.

(*b*) It is seen from Fig.5.39 that

$$E_f = \sqrt{V_t^2 + (I_a X_s)^2}$$

$$= \sqrt{1905.3^2 + (174.96\times 6)^2} = 2175.35 \text{ V}$$

Synchronous speed, $N_s = \frac{120\times 50}{6} = 600$ rpm

$$\omega_s = 2\,\pi \times \frac{600}{60} = 20\,\pi \text{ rad/sec.}$$

$\therefore$ Maximum torque $= \left[\frac{3\cdot E_f\cdot V_t}{X_s}\cdot\sin 90°\right]\times\frac{1}{\omega_s}$

$= \left[\frac{3\times 2175.35\times 1905.3}{6}\right]\times\frac{1}{20\pi}$ Nm

$\therefore$ Maximum torque = 32982.43 Nm.

Example 5.10. (*a*) *A 3-phase, 15 kW, 400 V, 6-pole, 50 Hz, star-connected synchronous motor has* $Z_s = 0 + j\,6\,\Omega$ *per phase. If its field current is adjusted to make it operate at full load unity power factor, then find the load angle and excitation emf.*

(*b*) *Calculate the load angle, armature current and power factor of excitation emf found in part* (*a*) *is* (*i*) *increased by 20% and* (*ii*) *decreased by 20°. Motor load remains at rated value.*

Solution. (*a*) Here $V_t = \frac{400}{\sqrt{3}} = 231$ V, power factor = 1, $X_s = 6\,\Omega$, $r_a = 0$

$\therefore$ Per-phase armature current, $I_a = \frac{15\times 1000}{\sqrt{3}\times 400\times 1} = 21.65$ A

Synchronous motor phasor diagram at unity pf is drawn in Fig. 5.40. From this figure,

$$\tan\delta = \frac{I_a X_s}{V_t}$$

$\therefore$ Load angle $\delta = \tan^{-1}\left[\frac{I_a X_s}{V_t}\right] = \tan^{-1}\left[\frac{21.65\times 6}{231}\right] = 29.35°.$

It is seen from Fig. 5.40 that $E_f = \sqrt{V_t^2 + (I_a X_s)^2} = [231^2 + (21.65\times 6)^2]^{1/2} = 265.0$ V

(*b*) (*i*) When excitation emf is increased by 20%, its new value becomes $E_{f1} = 265 \times 1.2 = 318$ V. Emf E_{f1}, current I_{a1} and δ_1 are indicated in Fig. 5.40. Load remains constant, armature resistance is zero and V_t is also constant.

$\therefore$ $E_f \sin\delta = E_{f1}\sin\delta_1$

$\therefore$ $\delta_1 = \sin^{-1}\left[\frac{E_f\cdot\sin\delta}{E_{f1}}\right]$

$$= \sin^{-1}\left[\frac{265 \times \sin 29.35}{1.2 \times 265}\right]$$

$$\therefore \quad \delta_1 = 24.11°$$

From Fig. 5.40,

$$(I_{a1} \cdot X_s)^2 = E_{f1}^2 + V_t^2 - 2\,E_{f1} \cdot V_t \cdot \cos \delta_1$$

$$\therefore \quad I_{a1} = \frac{1}{6}\,[318^2 + 231^2 - 2 \times 318 \times 231 \times \cos 24.11°]^{1/2}$$

$$= 23.796 \text{ A}$$

$$\text{Load} = V_t\,I_a \cos\theta = V_t \cdot I_{a1} \cdot \cos\theta_1$$

$$\therefore \text{ Power factor } \cos\theta_1 = \frac{I_a \cos\theta}{I_{a1}} = \frac{21.65 \times 1}{23.796}$$

$$= 0.9098 \text{ leading}$$

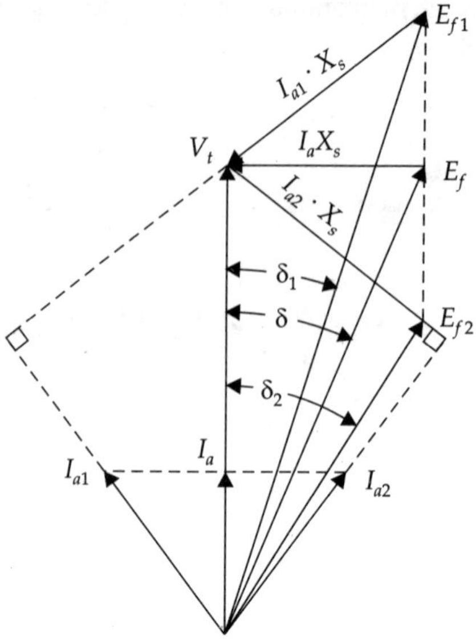

Fig 5.40: Phasor diagram pertaining to Example 5.10.

(*ii*) Here $E_{f1} = 0.8\,E_f = 0.8 \times 265 = 212$ V.

E_{f2}, I_{a2} and δ_2 are also shown in Fig. 5.40.

As in part (*i*),

$$\delta_2 = \sin^{-1}\left[\frac{E_f \sin\delta}{E_{f1}}\right] = \sin^{-1}\left[\frac{265 \times \sin 29.35}{212}\right] = 37.78°$$

Also $$(I_{a2}\,X_s)^2 = [\,E_{f2}^2 + V_t^2 - 2\,E_{f2}\,V_t \cos\delta_2]$$

$$\therefore \quad I_{a2} = \frac{1}{6}\,[212^2 + 231^2 - 2 \times 212 \times 231 \times \cos 37.78°]$$

$$= 24.091 \text{ A}$$

$$\text{Power factor, } \cos\theta_2 = \frac{I_a \cdot \cos\theta}{I_{a2}} = \frac{21.65 \times 1}{24.091} = 0.8987 \text{ lagging}$$

Example 5.11. *A 2200 V, delta connected synchronous motor has $X_s = 16\,\Omega$ per phase. Its excitation emf is adjusted to 3500 V so that its armature current is 100 A per phase. Find the power factor at which motor is operating.*

Solution. Here, $V_t = 2200$ V, $E_f = 3500$ V, $I_a = 100$ A, $X_s = 16\,\Omega$ and $r_a = 0$.

Phasor diagram of synchronous motor with these values is drawn in Fig. 5.41. In this figure, $OA = V_t = 2200$ V, $OB = E_f = 3500$ V, $BA = I_a X_s = 100 \times 16 = 1600$ V. Angle $OCA = 90°$. Therefore, in triangle OAC, $\angle OAC = 90 - \theta$. Further $\angle OAB = 180 - \angle OAC = 180 - (90 - \theta) = 90 + \theta$. It is seen from Fig. 5.41 that

$$E_f^2 = V_t^2 + (I_a\,X_s)^2 - 2\,V_t \cdot I_a X_s \cdot \cos \angle OAB$$

$$3500^2 = [2200]^2 + [100 \times 16]^2 - 2 \times 2200 \times 1600 \times \cos \angle OAB$$

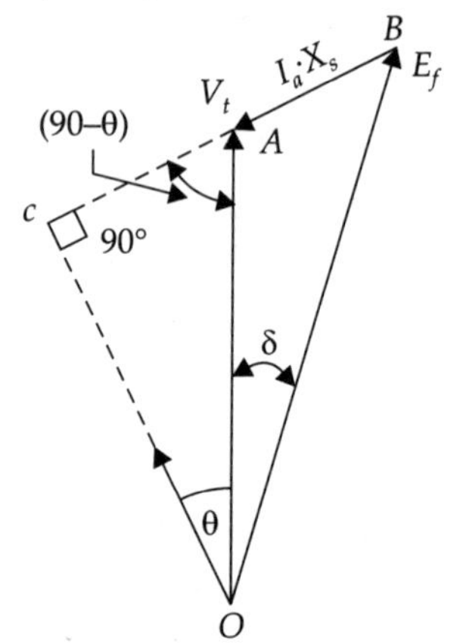

Fig 5.41: Phasor diagram pertaining to Example 5.11.

or $2 \times 2200 \times 1600 \cos \angle OAB = 2200^2 + 1600^2 - 3500^2 = -4850{,}000$

$\therefore \quad \cos \angle OAB = -0.688920453$

$\therefore \quad \angle OAB = \cos^{-1}[-0.688920453]$

$= 133.545°$

But $\quad \angle OAB = 90 + \theta = 133.545°$

$\therefore$ Power factor angle, $\theta = 133.545 - 90° = 43.545°$

$\therefore \quad$ Power factor $= \cos\theta = \cos 43.545°$

$= 0.7248$ leading

Example 5.12. *A 3-phase star-connected 400 V synchronous motor takes a power input of 8000 watts at rated voltage. It has $Z_s = 0 + j\,10\ \Omega$. If its excitation voltage is adjusted equal to the rated voltage of 400 V, then calculate the power angle, power factor and the armature current.*

Solution. Here $\quad V_t = E_f = \dfrac{400}{\sqrt{3}} = 230.95$ V, $r_a = 0$, $X_s = 10\ \Omega$.

With $V_t = E_f$, phasor diagram for the synchronous motor is drawn in Fig. 5.42.

With $r_a = 0$, we have

$$3\,\frac{E_f \cdot V_t}{X_s}\sin\delta = P$$

or $$3 \times \frac{400}{\sqrt{3}} \times \frac{400}{\sqrt{3}} \times \frac{1}{10} \cdot \sin\delta = 8000 \text{ W}$$

$\therefore$ $$\sin\delta = \frac{8000 \times 10}{400 \times 400} = 0.5$$

$\therefore$ Power angle, $\quad \delta = \sin^{-1}(0.5) = 30°$

Thus the motor operates with a power angle of 30°.

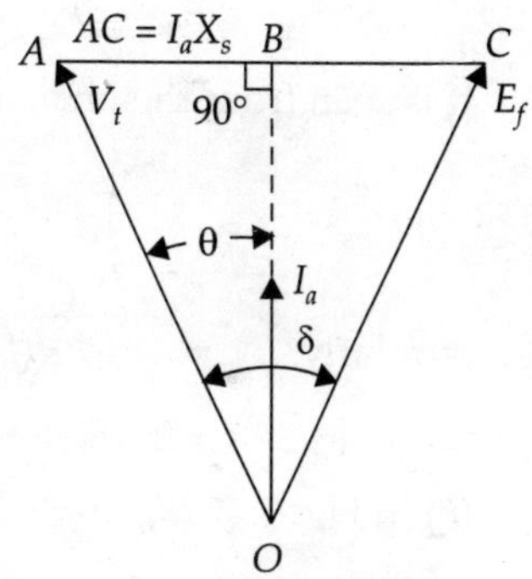

Fig 5.42: Phasor diagram pertaining to Example 5.12.

It is observed from Fig. 5.42 that I_a lags V_t, $V_t = E_f$ and $\theta = \frac{1}{2}\delta = \frac{1}{2} \times 30 = 15°$

$\therefore \quad$ Motor power factor $= \cos\theta = \cos 15° = 0.966$ lag

$\therefore$ It is also seen from Fig. 5.42 that $AB = V_t \sin\theta$.

Also, $\quad I_a X_s = AC = AB + BC = 2\,AB = 2\,V_t \cdot \sin\theta$.

$\therefore$ Armature current, $$I_a = \frac{2 \times 230.95 \times \sin 15°}{10} = 11.955 \text{ A}$$

Example 5.13. *A 1500 kW, 3-phase star-connected, 3300 V, 50 Hz synchronous motor has synchronous reactance $X_{sm} = 2\ \Omega$. Motor is fed from a 3300 V, 2000 kVA, star-connected alternator with $X_{sg} = 2.5\ \Omega$. Motor is operating at rated voltage and rated load at unity power factor at its terminals. Calculate (a) excitation emfs of both alternator and motor and (b) power transfer between alternator and motor.*

Solution. The equivalent cicuit for this example is shown in Fig. 5.43 (*a*) and its phasor diagram is drawn in Fig. 5.43 (*b*). Here E_{fg} and E_{fm} are the excitation emfs of alternator and motor respectively. V_t is the motor terminal voltage.

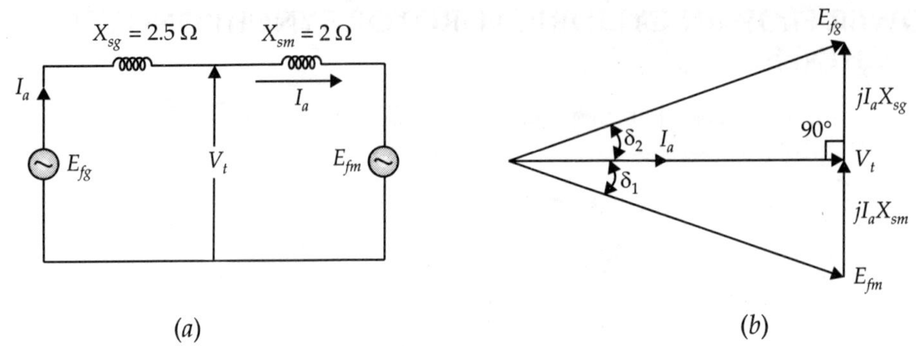

Fig 5.43: (*a*) Equivalent circuit and (*b*) phasor diagram for Example 5.13.

Here $\sqrt{3} \times V_t \times I_a \times \cos\theta = 1500$ kW

∴ Motor armature current, $I_a = \dfrac{1500 \times 1000}{\sqrt{3} \times 3300 \times 1} = 262.44$ A

(*a*) $V_t = \dfrac{3300}{\sqrt{3}} = 1905.3$ V,

$I_a = 262.44\ \Omega$, $X_{sm} = 2\ \Omega$, $X_{sg} = 2.5\ \Omega$.

It is seen from the phasor diagram of Fig. 5.43 (*b*) that

$$E_{fm} = \sqrt{V_t^2 + (I_a X_{sm})^2} = [(1905.3)^2 + (262.44 \times 2.)^2]^{1/2}$$
$$= 1976.28 \text{ V per phase}$$

Similarly, $E_{gg} = \sqrt{V_t^2 + (I_a X_{sg})^2} = [(1905.3)^2 + (262.44 \times 2.5)^2]^{1/2}$

$= 2015.10$ V perphase

(*b*) In Fig. 5.43 (*b*), angle bwteen E_{fm} and V_t is δ_1. Also, $E_{fm} \cos\delta_1 = V_t$

∴ Angle between E_{fm} and V_t is

$$\delta_1 = \cos^{-1}\left[\frac{V_t}{E_{fm}}\right] = \cos^{-1}\left[\frac{1905.3}{1976.28}\right] = 15.402°.$$

Similarly, angle between E_{fg} and V_t is

$$\delta_2 = \cos^{-1}\left[\frac{V_t}{E_{fg}}\right] = \cos^{-1}\left[\frac{1905.3}{2015.10}\right] = 19.0°$$

∴ Power angle between E_{fm} and E_{fg} is

$$\delta_{gm} = \delta_1 + \delta_2 = 15.402 + 19.0 = 34.402°$$

∴ Power transfer between alternator and motor

$$= \frac{E_{fg} \cdot E_{fm}}{X_{sg} + X_{sm}} \cdot \sin\delta_{gm} = \frac{2015.10 \times 1976.28}{2.5 + 2.0} \sin 34.402°$$
$$= 500000 \text{ W} = 500 \text{ kW per phase}$$
$$= 1500 \text{ kW for 3-phases}$$

5.21. POWER FLOW IN CYLIDRICAL ROTOR SYNCHRONOUS MACHINES

Expressions for synchronous power P and reactive power Q have already been derived in Art. 5.16 but with armature circuit resistance neglected.

Here we shall derive these expressions again for cylindrical rotor alternator but with armature resistance included.

5.21.1. Power Flow in Alternator

Equivalent circuit for a cylindrical-rotor alternator is shown in Fig. 5.44. Here per-phase values are; E_f = excitation emf, V_t = terminal voltage, I_a = armature current, $Z_s = r_a + j\,X_s$ = synchronous impedance and θ_Z = impedance angle.

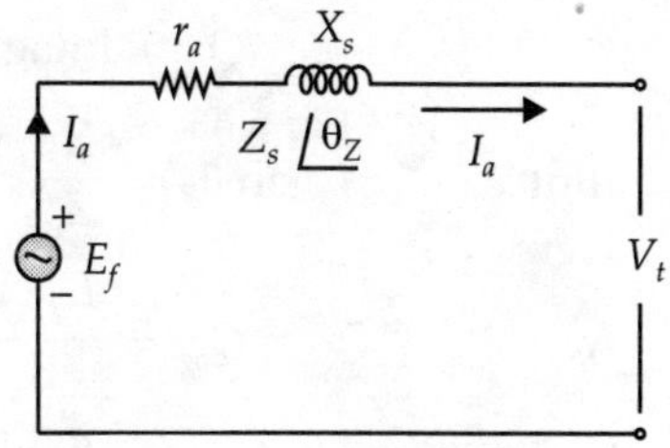

Fig 5.44: Equivalent circuit for a cylindrical-rotor alternator.

Alternator phasor diagram at lagging factor is drawn in Fig. 5.45 (*a*). Here E_f leads V_t by load angle δ. Take V_t as reference phasor. Then it can be written that $\overline{V}_t = V_t \angle 0°$ and $\overline{E}_f = E_f \angle\delta$. Synchronous impedance $Z_s = r_a + j\,X_s = Z_s \angle\theta_Z$ where impedance angle θ is given by $\theta_Z = \tan^{-1}\dfrac{X_s}{r_a}$.

From Fig. 5.45 (*b*), $\alpha_Z = 90 - \theta_z = \tan^{-1}\dfrac{r_a}{Xs}$

KVL for Fig. 5.44 gives $\overline{E}_f = \overline{V}_t + \overline{I}_a\,\overline{Z}_s$

or
$$\overline{I}_a = \frac{\overline{E}_f - \overline{V}_t}{\overline{Z}_s} = \frac{E_f \angle -\delta - V_t \angle 0°}{Z_s \angle\theta_Z} \qquad ...(5.53\ a)$$

$$\text{Conjugate of } \overline{I}_a = \overline{I}_a^{\,*} = = \frac{E_f \angle -\delta - V_t \angle 0°}{Z_s \angle -\theta_Z} \qquad ...(5.53\ b)$$

5.21.1.1. Complex power output of alternator

Complex power output S_{og} of an alternator is given by

$$\therefore \quad S_{og} = P_{og} + j\,Q_{og}$$

= [Output terminal voltage V_t] [Conjugate of armature current] = $\overline{V}_t\,\overline{I}_a^{\,*}$

$$= V_t \angle 0° \left[\frac{E_f \angle -\delta - V_t \angle 0}{Z_s \angle -\theta_Z}\right] = \frac{V_t \cdot E_f}{Z_s} \angle\theta_Z - \delta - \frac{V_t^2}{Z_s} \angle\theta_Z$$

$$S_{og} = P_{og} + j\,Q_{og} = \frac{V_t \cdot E_f}{Z_s} \cos(\theta_Z - \delta)$$

$$+ j\frac{V_t \cdot E_f}{Z_s} \sin(\theta_Z - \delta) - \frac{V_t^2}{Z_s}\cos\theta_Z - j\frac{V_t^2}{Z_s}\sin\theta_Z \qquad ...(5.34)$$

Real power output of alternator : From Eq. (5.34),

$$P_{og} = \text{Real component of } S_{og}$$

$$= \frac{E_f \cdot V_t}{Z_s}\cos(\theta_Z - \delta) - \frac{V_t^2}{Z_s}\cos\theta_Z$$

But $\cos\theta_Z = \dfrac{r_a}{Z_s}$ and $\theta_Z = 90 - \alpha_Z$

$$\therefore \quad P_{og} = \frac{E_f \cdot V_t}{Z_s} \cdot \cos(90 - \overline{\alpha_Z + \delta}) - \frac{V_t^2}{Z_s} \cdot \frac{r_a}{Z_s}$$

$$= \frac{E_f \cdot V_t}{Z_s} \cdot \sin(\delta + \alpha_Z) - \frac{V_t^2}{Z_s} \cdot r_a \qquad \text{...(5.35)}$$

Reactive power output of alternator : From Eq. (5.34),

$$Q_{og} = \text{Imaginary component of } S_{og} = \frac{E_f \cdot V_t}{Z_s} \sin(\theta_Z - \delta) - \frac{V_t^2}{Z_s} \cdot \sin\theta_Z$$

But $\sin\theta_Z = \dfrac{X_s}{Z_s}$ and $\theta_Z = 90 - \alpha_Z$

$$\therefore \quad Q_{og} = \frac{E_f \cdot V_t}{Z_s} \sin(90 - \overline{\delta + \alpha_Z}) - \frac{V_t^2}{Z_s} \cdot \frac{X_s}{Z_s}$$

$$= \frac{E_f \cdot V_t}{Z_s} \cdot \cos(\delta + \alpha_Z) - \frac{V_t^2}{Z_s^2} \cdot X_s \qquad \text{...(5.36)}$$

5.21.1.2. Complex power input to alternator

Complex power input to alternator is given by

$$S_{ig} = P_{ig} + j\,Q_{ig} = [\text{Excitation emf, } E_f] \times [\text{Conjugate of armature current } I_a]$$

$$= \bar{E}_g \cdot \bar{I}_a^{\,*}$$

With V_t as reference, $\bar{E}_f = E_f \angle\delta$, $\bar{V}_t = V_t \angle 0$ and $\bar{I}_a^{\,*}$, from Eq. (5.33 *b*) is

$$\bar{I}_a^{\,*} = \left[\frac{E_f \angle{-\delta} - V_t \angle{-0}}{Z_s \angle{-\theta_Z}}\right]$$

$$\therefore \quad S_{ig} = E_f \angle\delta \left[\frac{E_f}{Z_s} \angle\theta_Z - \delta - \frac{V_t}{Z_s} \angle\theta_Z\right] = \frac{E_f^2}{Z_s} \angle\theta_Z - \frac{E_f \cdot V_t}{Z_s} \angle\theta_Z + \delta$$

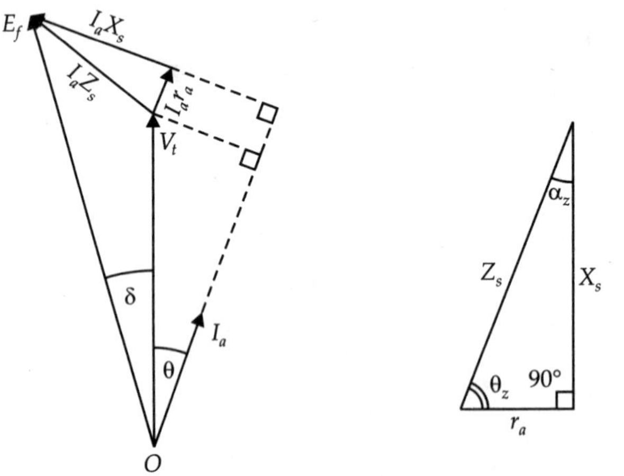

(*a*) (*b*)

Fig 5.45: (*a*) Alternator phasor diagram at lagging pf and (*b*) impedance triangle for Z_s.

$$\therefore\ S_{ig} = \frac{E_f^2}{Z_s}\cos\theta_Z + j\,\frac{E_f^2}{Z_s}\sin\theta_Z - \frac{E_f\cdot V_t}{Z_s}\cos(\theta_Z+\delta) - j\,\frac{E_f\cdot V_t}{Z_s}\sin(\theta_Z+\delta) \qquad ...(5.37)$$

$$= P_{ig} + j\,Q_{ig}$$

Real power input to alternator : From Eq. (5.37)

$$P_{ig} = \text{Real component of } S_{ig} = \frac{E_f^2}{Z_s}\cos\theta_Z - \frac{E_f\cdot V_t}{Z_s}\cdot\cos(\theta_Z+\delta)$$

But $\cos\theta_Z = \dfrac{r_a}{Z_s}$ and $\theta_Z = 90 - \alpha_Z$

$$\therefore\ P_{ig} = \frac{E_f^2}{Z_s}\cdot\frac{r_a}{Z_s} - \frac{E_f\cdot V_t}{Z_s}\cos(90 + \overline{\delta+\alpha_z})$$

$$= \frac{E_f^2}{Z^2}\cdot r_a + \frac{E_f\cdot V_t}{Z_s}\sin(\delta-\alpha_Z) \qquad ...(5.38)$$

Mechanical power input to alternator $= P_{ig}$ + rotational losses, where rotational losses
= F and W losses + core losses.

Reactive power input to alternator: From Eq. (5.37), we get

$$Q_{ig} = \text{Imaginary part of } [S_{ig}]$$

$$= \frac{E_f^2}{Z_s}\sin\theta_Z - \frac{E_f\cdot V_t}{Z_s}\cdot\sin(\theta_Z+\delta)$$

But $\sin\theta_Z = \dfrac{X_s}{Z_s}$ and $\theta_Z = 90 - \alpha_Z$

$$\therefore\ Q_{ig} = \frac{E_f^2}{Z_s}\cdot\frac{X_s}{Z_s} - \frac{E_f\cdot V_t}{Z_s}\cdot\sin[90 + (\delta-\alpha_Z)]$$

$$= \frac{E_f^2}{Z^2}\cdot X_s - \frac{E_f\cdot V_t}{Z_s}\cos(\delta-\alpha_Z) \qquad ...(5.39)$$

5.21.1.3. Maximum power output of alternator

For maximum power output from alternator $\dfrac{dP_{og}}{d\delta} = 0$. From Eq. (5.35), we get

$$\frac{dP_{og}}{d\delta} = \frac{E_f\cdot V_t}{Z_s}\cos(\delta+\alpha_Z) - 0 = 0$$

or $\cos(\delta+\alpha_Z) = 0 = \cos 90°$

$\therefore$ $\delta+\alpha_Z = 90°$ or $\delta = 90 - \alpha_Z = \theta_Z$

Therefore, maximum power output from alternator occurs when load angle δ = impedance angle θ_Z.

From Eq. (5.35), maximum power output from alternator is given by

$$P_{og\cdot(max)} = \frac{E_f\cdot V_t}{Z_s} - \frac{V_t^2}{Z_s^2}\,r_a \qquad ...(5.40)$$

5.21.1.4. Maximum power input to alternator

For maximum power input to alternator, $\frac{dP_{ig}}{d\delta} = 0$. From Eq. (5.38), we get

$$\frac{dP_{ig}}{d\delta} = 0 = 0 + \frac{E_f \cdot V_t}{Z_s} \cos(\delta - \alpha_Z).$$

$$\therefore \quad \cos(\delta - \alpha_Z) = 0 = \cos 90° \text{ or } (\delta - \alpha_Z) = 90°$$

$$\therefore \quad \text{Load angle } \delta = 90 + \alpha_Z = 90 + 90 - \theta_Z = 180° - \theta_Z$$

Therefore, for maximum power input to alternator,

$$\text{load angle } \delta = 180 - \text{impedance angle } \theta_Z.$$

From Eq. (5.38), maximum power input to alternator is

$$P_{ig\cdot(max)} = \frac{E_f^2}{Z_s^2} r_a + \frac{E_f \cdot V_t}{Z_s} \quad ...(5.41)$$

5.21.1.5. Power flow in alternator with armature resistance neglected

If armature circuit resistance r_a is neglected, then $Z_s = X_s$

From Eq. (5.35).
$$P_{og} = \frac{E_f \cdot V_t}{X_s} \sin\delta \quad ...(5.42)$$

From Eq. (5.36),
$$Q_{og} = \frac{E_f \cdot V_t}{X_s} \cos\delta - \frac{V_t^2}{X_s} \quad [\text{For } r_a = 0, \alpha_Z = 0]$$

$$= \frac{V_t}{X_s}[E_f \cos\delta - V_t] \quad ...(5.43)$$

From Eq. (5.38),
$$P_{ig} = \frac{E_f \cdot V_t}{X_s} \sin\delta = P_{og} \quad ...(5.44)$$

From Eq. (5.39),
$$Q_{ig} = \frac{E_f^2}{X_s} - \frac{E_f \cdot V_t}{X_s} \cos\delta$$

$$= \frac{E_f}{X_s}[E_f - V_t \cos\delta] \quad ...(5.45)$$

Example 5.14. *A 3-phase alternator has $Z_s = 0.06 + j\,0.6$ pu. The alternator delivers rated current at rated voltage when its excitation emf is 1.5 pu. Calculate the power angle and the power factor.*

Solution. Here rated voltage $V_t = 1.0$ pu, $I_a = 1.0$ pu, $r_a = 0.06$ pu, $X_s = 0.6$ pu, $E_f = 1.5$ pu.

With E_f more than V_t, take alternator operation at a lagging pf. Therefore, from phasor diagram Fig. 5.19 (*a*), we get

$$E_f^2 = (V_t \cos\theta + I_a r_a)^2 + (V_t \sin\theta + I_a X_s)^2$$

or
$$1.5^2 = [(1 \times \cos\theta + 1 \times 0.06)^2 + (1 \times \sin\theta + 1 \times 0.6)^2]$$

$$2.25 = \cos^2\theta + 0.0036 + 0.12\cos\theta + \sin^2\theta + 0.36 + 1.2\sin\theta$$

$$= 0.12\cos\theta + 1.2\sin\theta + 1.3636$$

or
$$0.12\cos\theta + 1.2\sin\theta = 0.8864$$

But
$$A\cos\theta + B\sin\theta = \sqrt{A^2 + B^2}\,\sin(\theta + \tan^{-1}\frac{A}{B})$$

$\therefore \quad 1.20598 \sin(\theta + 5.71) = 0.8864$

$$\therefore \quad \theta = \sin^{-1}\left[\frac{0.8864}{1.20598}\right] - 5.71° = 41.6°$$

$\therefore$ Power factor $= \cos\theta = \cos 41.6° = \mathbf{0.7478}$ **lagging.**

Fig. 5.19 (*a*) also gives

$$\tan(\theta + \delta) = \frac{V_t \sin\theta + I_a X_s}{V_t \cos\theta + I_a r_a} = \frac{1 \times \sin 41.6° + 1 \times 0.6}{1 \times 0.7478 + 1 \times 0.06}$$

$$\therefore \quad (\theta + \delta) = \tan^{-1}\left[\frac{1.263926212}{0.8078}\right] = \mathbf{57.42°}$$

$\therefore$ Power angle $\delta = 57.42 - 41.6 = \mathbf{15.82°}$

Phasor diagram of Fig. 5.19 (*a*) also gives

$$E_f \cos\delta = V_t + I_a r_a \cos\theta + I_a X_s \sin\theta$$

$$1.5 \cos\delta = 1 + 1 \times 0.06 \times 0.7478 + 1 \times 0.6 \times \sin 41.6$$

$$\delta = \cos^{-1}\left[\frac{1 + 1 \times 0.06 \times 0.7478 + 0.6 \times 0.664}{1.5}\right] = \mathbf{15.81°}$$

Example 5.15. *Draw the phasor diagram for a cylindrical-rotor alternator at a lagging power factor. From this diagram, derive the following relation :*

$E_f \cos\delta = V_t + I_a r_a \cos\theta + I_a X_s \sin\theta$

where $\cos\theta$ = *alternator power factor.*

Solution. Phasor diagram of alternator operating at a lagging pf is redrawn in Fig. 5.46 from Fig. 5.19 (*a*). Here $I_a r_a$, $I_a X_s$, $I_a Z_s$ are shown more than their actual values for the sake of clarity.

Extent the line $OA = V_t$ to C so that $OC = E_f \cdot \cos\delta$. Here $\angle OCD = 90°$. Now draw $I_a r_a = AB'$ parallel to I_a and $B'D = I_a X_s$ perpendicular to I_a. Draw $B'B$ and DC' perpendicular to V_t or OC.

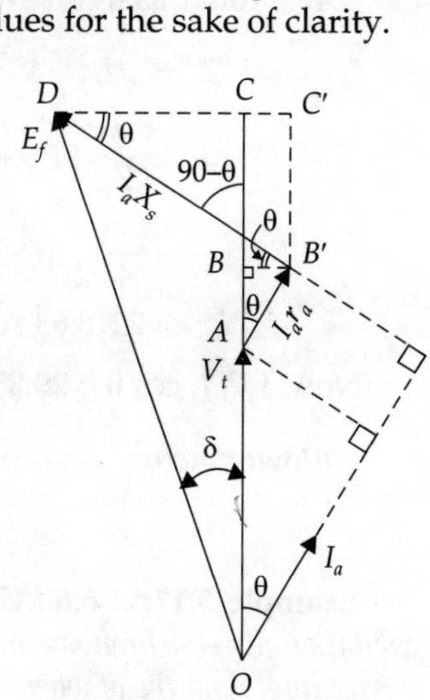

Fig 5.46: Phasor diagram pertaining to Example 5.15.

Since $I_a r_a$ is parallel to I_a $\angle BAB' = \theta$. Also $\angle AB'D = 90°$

$\therefore \quad \angle AB'B = 90 - \theta$

Here $\quad \angle AB'B + \angle BB'D = 90°$

or $\quad (90 - \theta) + \angle BB'D = 90°$

$\therefore \quad \angle BB'D = 90 - (90 - \theta) = \theta.$

As DCC' is parallel to BB', we have

$$\angle BB'D = \angle B'DC = \theta$$

But $\quad B'D = I_a X_s.$

$\therefore \quad B'C' = B'D \sin\theta$

$\qquad = I_a X_s \sin\theta = BC.$

It is seen from Fig. 5.46 that

$$OC = OA + AB + BC$$

$$= OA + AB + B'C'$$

$$\therefore \quad E_f \cos\delta = V_t + I_a r_a \cos\theta + I_a X_s \sin\theta.$$

Example 5.16. *A 10 kVA, 3-phase star-connected alternator, with $Z_s = 0.4 + j\,4\,\Omega$, is feeding 11 kV bus-bar. If its excitation emf is adjusted to 12 kV, then calculate*

(*a*) *maximum power output from the altenator and*

(*b*) *the armature current and power factor under maximum power output conditions.*

Solution. (*a*) Here $Z_s = 0.4 + j\,4 = 4.02\ \underline{/84.29°}$

Alternator phase voltage, $V_t = \dfrac{11000}{\sqrt{3}} = 6350$ V

Excitation emf per phase, $E_f = \dfrac{12000}{\sqrt{3}} = 6930$ V

Maximum power output from alternator is given by Eq. (5.40).

$$\therefore \quad P_{og(\max)} = \frac{E_f \cdot V_t}{Z_s} - \left[\frac{V_t}{Z_s}\right]^2 \cdot r_a = \frac{6930 \times 6350}{4.02} - \left[\frac{6350}{4.02}\right]^2 \times 0.4$$

$$= 9948584.8 \cong 9.95 \text{ MW per phase}$$

$$= 29.85 \text{ MW for 3-phases.}$$

(*b*) Under maximum power alternator output, $\delta = \theta_Z = 84.29°$

Here $\cos\theta_Z = \dfrac{r_a}{Z_s} = \dfrac{0.4}{4.02} \cong 0.1$

Phasor diagram of alternator under maximum power output can be drawn from Fig. 15.45 (*a*) with $\delta = \theta_Z$. This is illustrated in Fig. 5.47. From this figure, we get

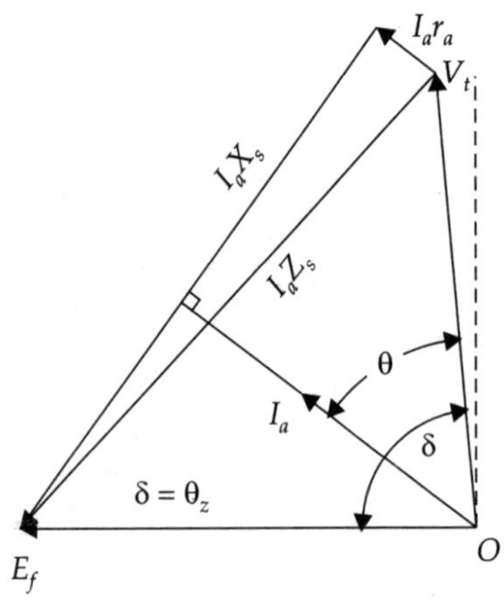

Fig 5.47: Alternator phasor diagram under maximum power output. Example 5.16.

$$I_a Z_s = \sqrt{E_f^2 + V_t^2 - 2E_f V_t \cos\theta_Z}$$

$$\therefore \quad I_a = \frac{1}{Z_s}\,[E_f^2 + V_t^2 - 2\,E_f\,V_t \cos\theta_Z]^{1/2}$$

$$= \frac{1}{4.02}\,[6930^2 + 6350^2 - 2 \times 6930 \times 6350 \times 0.1]^{1/2}$$

$$= 2218.63 \text{ A}$$

Now $3\,V_t I_a \cos\theta = 29.85$ MW

$$\therefore \text{ Power factor,} \quad \cos\theta = \frac{29.85 \times 10^6}{3 \times 6350 \times 2218.63}$$

$$= 0.70626 \text{ leading.}$$

Example 5.17. *A 6.6 kV star-connected synchronous motor works at constant voltage and constant excitation. Its synchronous impedance is $2 + j\,16\,\Omega$ per phase. When the input power is 1000 kW, the pf is 0.8 leading. Find the pf when input is increased to 1500 kW.*

Solution. Here $V_t = \dfrac{6600}{\sqrt{3}} = 3810.6$, pf = 0.8 leading,

$$Z_s = 2 + j\,16 = 16.125\ \underline{/82.87°}$$

$$\alpha_Z = 90 - \theta_Z = 90 - 82.87 = 7.13°,$$

$$I_a = \frac{1000 \times 10^3}{\sqrt{3} \times 6600 \times 0.8} = 109.35 \text{ A}$$

The phasor diagram for alternator working at a leading pf is shown in Fig. 5.20 (*c*). From this diagram and Eq. (5.20), we get

$$E_f = [(V_t \cos\theta - I_a r_a)^2 + (V_t \sin\theta + I_a X_s)^2]^{1/2}$$
$$= [(3810.6 \times 0.8 - 109.35 \times 2)^2 + (3810.6 \times 0.6 + 109.35 \times 16)^2]^{1/2}$$
$$= [(2829.78)^2 + (14035.96)^2]^{1/2} = 4931.62 \text{ V}$$

When the input is increased to 1500 kW, the load angle and current must increase. From Fig. 5.44, it is seen that equivalent circuit for a cylindrical rotor synchronous motor can be obtained by interchanging E_f and V_t. Therefore, power input to synchronous motor can be obtained from Eq. (5.38) by interchanging E_f and V_t. Thus, power input to synchronous motor is

$$P = \frac{E_f \cdot V_t}{Z_s} \sin(\delta - \alpha_Z) + \left[\frac{V_t}{Z_s}\right]^2 \cdot r_a$$

$$\frac{1500{,}000}{3} = \frac{4931.62 \times 3810.6}{16.125} \sin(\delta - 7.13°) + \left[\frac{3810.6}{16.125}\right]^2 \times 2$$

$$\sin(\delta - \alpha_Z) = 0.33319 \therefore \delta = 19.46 + 7.13 = 26.6°$$

It is seen from Fig. 5.20 (*c*) that $I_a Z_s = [E_f^2 + V_t^2 - 2 E_g V_t \cos\delta]^{1/2}$

$$\therefore \quad I_a = \frac{1}{16.125}[4931.62^2 + 3810.6^2 - 2 \times 4931.62 \times 3810.6 \times \cos 26.6°]^{1/2} = 141.9 \text{ A}$$

Input power per phase $= V_t I_a \cos\theta = 500$ kW

$$\therefore \quad \cos\theta = \frac{500{,}000}{3810.6 \times 141.9} = 0.9247 \text{ leading.}$$

Example 5.18. *A synchronous motor is connected to an infinite bus at 1.0 pu voltage and draws 0.6 pu current at unity power factor. Its synchronous reactance is 1.0 pu and resistance is negligible.*

(a) Calculate the excitation voltage and load angle.

(b) Keeping the excitation voltage same as found in part (a), the load on the motor is increased such that the motor current increases by 20%. Find the operating power factor of motor under these conditions.

[GATE, 2008]

Solution. (*a*) Here $V_t = 1.0$ pu, $r_a = 0$, $X_s = 1.0$ pu, $I_a = 0.6$ pu, pf = 1.0

Synchronous motor phasor diagram at unity pf is drawn in Fig. 5.48 (*a*). From this figure,

$$E_f = \sqrt{V_t^2 + (I_a X_s)^2} = [1^2 + (0.6 \times 1)^2]^{1/2} = 1.1662 \text{ pu}$$

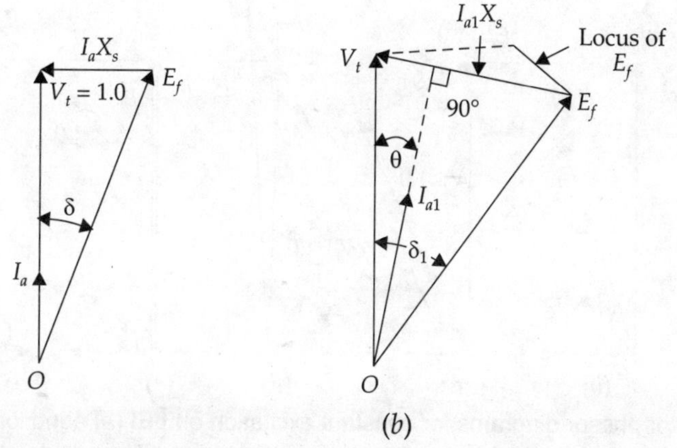

Fig 5.48: Synchronous motor phasor diagram at (*a*) unity pf (*b*) lagging pf with E_f constant. Example 5.18.

Also, $\tan \delta = \dfrac{I_a \cdot X_s}{V_t}$

$\therefore$ Load angle, $\delta = \tan^{-1}\left(\dfrac{I_a X_s}{V_t}\right) = \tan^{-1}\left[\dfrac{0.6 \times 1}{1}\right] = 30.964$ lag

(*b*) When load on motor is increased by keeping E_f constant, E_f falls back, load angle increases to δ_1 as shown in Fig. 5.48 (*b*). Motor now operates at a lagging pf with current $I_{a1} = 0.6 \times 1.2 = 0.72$ pu. It is seen from Fig. 5.48 (*b*) that

$$(I_{a1} \cdot X_s)^2 = E_f^2 + V_t^2 - 2\, E_f V_t \cos \delta_1$$

$$(0.72 \times 1)^2 = 1.1662^2 + 1^2 - 2 \times 1.1662 \times 1 \times \cos \delta_1$$

$$0.5184 = 2.36 - 2.3324 \cos \delta_1$$

$\therefore$ Load angle $\delta_1 = \cos^{-1}\left[\dfrac{2.36 - 0.5184}{2.3324}\right] = 37.854°$

Now power $P = V_t I_{a1} \cos \theta = \dfrac{E_f \cdot V_t}{X_s} \sin \delta_1$

$$1 \times 0.72 \times \cos \theta = \frac{1.1662 \times 1}{1} \cdot \sin 37.854°$$

$\therefore$ Motor operating power factor $= \cos \theta = \dfrac{1.1662 \cdot \sin 37.854}{0.72} = 0.9939 \cong 0.994$ lag.

5.22. OPERATING CHARACTERISTICS OF SYNCHRONOUS MACHINES

When a synchronous machine operates under steady state conditions on an infinite busbar, general features of its performance can be obtained from the operating characteristics. For synchronous motors, operating characteristics are already discussed in the form of *V*-curves and unity power factor compounding curve. Here, we shall describe the operating characteristics of alternators only.

5.22.1. Operating Characteristics of Alternators

Steady-state operating characteristics of an isolated cylindrical-rotor alternator can be obtained from its equivalent circuit shown in Fig. 5.12.

5.22.1.1. External load characteristics

The external load characteristics, or alternator **volt-ampere characteristics**, represent the variation of armature terminal voltage V_t with armature current I_a, for a **constant field current** or **constant excitation**.

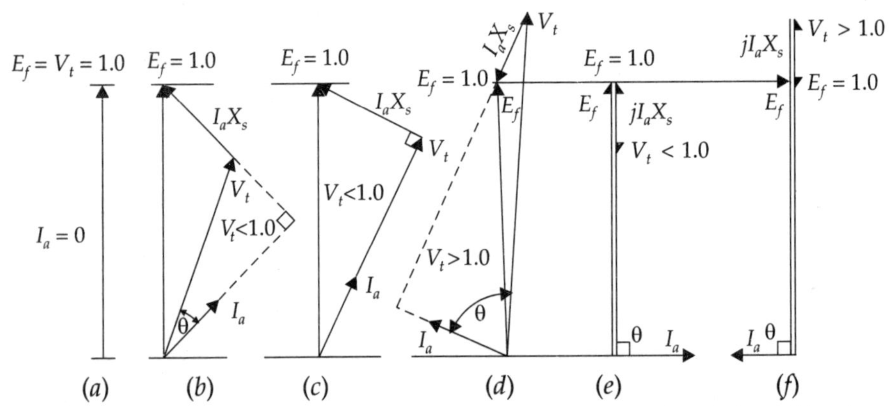

Fig 5.49: Alternator phasor diagrams for constant excitation emf Ef (*a*) at no load (*b*) at lagging pf (*c*) at unity pf (*d*) at leading pf (*e*) at zpf lag and (*f*) at zpf lead.

Consider an isolated alternator running at constant speed and with constant excitation, *i.e.* the alternator has constant E_f. At no load, $I_a = 0$, therefore, $E_f = V_t = 1.0$, Fig. 5.49 (*a*). The armature resistance drop, as usual, is neglected for convenience. For a lagging pf load, the phasor diagram is drawn in Fig. 5.49 (*b*) and here V_t is less than E_f. For unity pf load, V_t is again less than E_f but it is more than its value at a lagging power factor load. For a leading power-factor load, V_t is more than E_f. It is thus seen that the terminal voltage V_t falls on lagging power-factor loads and may rise on leading power-factor–loads this inference follows from Fig. 5.49. The variation of V_t with I_a for constant E_f, or constant I_f, is illustrated in Fig. 5.50 (*a*) for different power-factor loads. In this figure, when $I_a = 0$, $V_t = E_f = 1.0$. For unity pf load, $E_f^2 = V_t^2 + (I_a X_s)^2$ = constant. Therefore, plot of V_t and I_a for constant E is almost an ellipse for unity power factor.

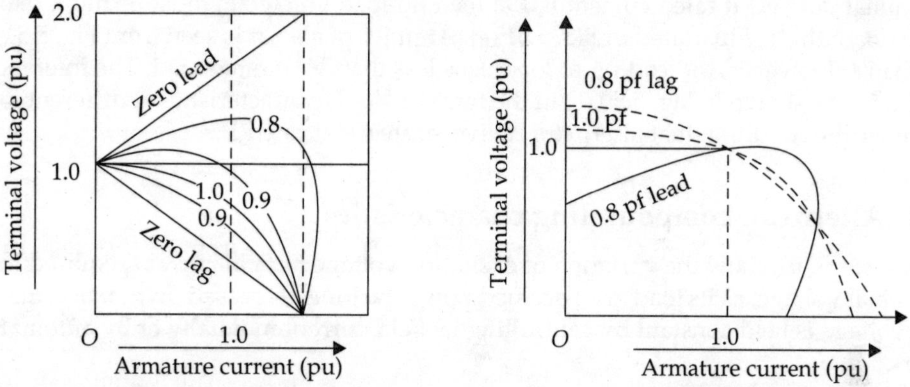

(*a*) Constant excitation (*b*) Constant excitation

Fig 5.50: Alternator external characteristics with I_f held constant (*a*) at its no-load value and (*b*) at its rated V_t and rated I_a.

The operation of alternator at zero power factor lagging and zpf leading is shown in Fig. 5.49 (*e*) and (*f*) respectively. For zero pf loads, it is observed that scalar relation $V_t = E_f \pm I_a X_s$ holds good. As $V_t = E_f \pm I_a X_s$ is the equation of a straight line, the variation of V_t with I_a are straight lines

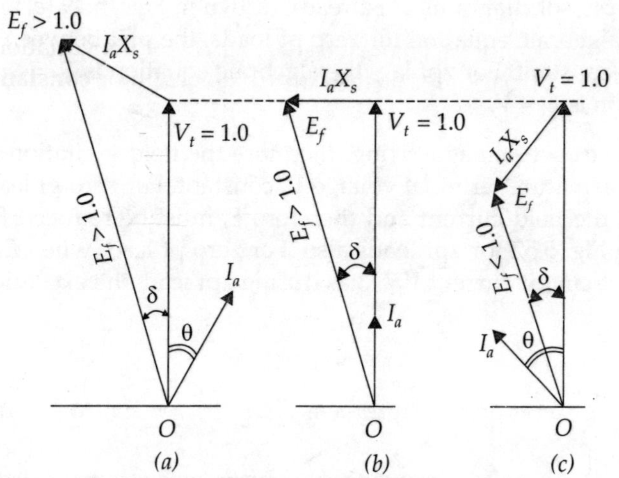

Fig 5.51: Alternator phasor diagrams for constant terminal voltage at (*a*) lagging pf (*b*) unity pf and (*c*) leading pf.

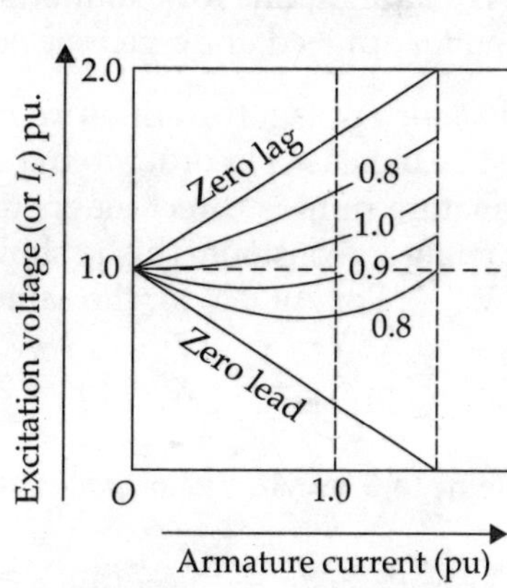

Fig 5.52: Alternator compounding curves for maintaining constant rated terminal voltage.

for both zpf lagging and zpf leading loads as shown in Fig. 5.50 (*a*). For zpf lagging, the algebraic equation is $V_t = E_f - I_a X_s$ and for zpf leading, the algebraic equation is $V_t = E_f + I_a X_s$. For zpf lag, when $V_t = 0$, $I_a = \dfrac{E_f}{X_s} = I_{sc}$. For zpf lead, for the same short-circuit current $E_f/X_s = I_{sc}$, as during the zpf lag, the terminal voltage for zpf leading load is $V_t = E_f + \dfrac{E_f}{X_s} \cdot X_s = 2\,E_f = 2.00$.

With alternator running at rated terminal voltage V_t and at rated armature current I_a (= 1.0), what happens if load current is now reduced to zero? No-load voltage, or excitation voltage E_f may rise or fall depending upon the nature of load power factor. This is discussed below.

If terminal voltage at rated current is 1.0, then no-load voltage E_f must be more than 1.0 for a lagging pf load; this is illustrated in Fig. 5.51 (*a*). At unity pf also, it is seen from Fig. 5.51 (*b*) that E_f is more than 1. However, for leading pf load, E_f is less than V_t at rated load. The inferences drawn from Fig. 5.51 are shown in Fig. 5.50 (*b*) in the form of $V_t - I_a$ characteristics at different load power factors under the condition that alternator delivers rated I_a at rated V_t.

5.22.1.2. Alternator compounding characteristics

These characteristics show the variation of excitation voltage or field current required to maintain rated terminal voltage, as its load at a specified power factor is increased. In practice, the alternator terminal voltage is held constant by controlling its field current manually or by automatic voltage regulators.

In order to illustrate the variation of E_f or I_f, for maintaining constant voltage V_t, refer to Fig. 5.51 again. At a lagging pf, E_f is more than one if $V_t = 1.00$. For unity pf, E_f is a little more than 1.00, but for leading pf in Fig. 5.51 (*c*), $E_f < 1.00$. In other words, for maintaining constant terminal voltage V_t; the excitation voltage E_f or the field current I_f should be increased for lagging pf loads and should be decreased for leading pf loads. For unity power factor loads, the increase in I_f with increases in I_a is small as compared with 0.8 pf lagging loads. Fig. 5.52 illustrates these compounding curves for alternators at 0.8 pf lag, unity pf, 0.9 pf lead and 0.8 pf lead.

For zero power-factor lag or lead, the phasor diagrams are already drawn in Figs. 5.49 (*e*) and (*f*) respectively. Since $E_f = V_t \pm I_a X_s$ is an algebraic equation for zero pf loads, the plot between E_f and I_a is a straight line for maintaining V_t constant. For zpf lag, the algebraic equation is $E_f = V_t + I_a X_s$ and for zpf lead, the algebraic equation is $E_f = V_t - I_a X_s$.

Also, for zpf lag, the armature mmf is direct demagnetizing; therefore the field excitation or E_f must be increased in order to maintain armature terminal voltage V_t constant. For zero pf lead, the armature mmf is direct magnetizing, the field current and therefore E_f must be reduced for maintaining V_t constant. This is shown in Fig. 5.52 for zpf loads also. For zero pf lead, when $E_f = 0$, $I_a = V_t/X_s$. For zpf lag, for the same short-circuit current V_t/X_s as during zpf lead, the excitation voltage is $E_f = V_t + \dfrac{V_t}{X_s} \cdot X_s = 2\,V_t = 2.00$ pu.

Example 5.19. *Alternator power input and power output expressions f_2 are* $\dfrac{E_f \cdot V_t}{Z_s}$ *sin* $(\delta - \alpha_Z) + \left[\dfrac{E_f}{Z_s}\right]^2 \cdot r_a = P_{ig}$ *and* $\dfrac{E_f V_t}{Z_s}$ *sin* $(\delta + \alpha_Z) - \left[\dfrac{V_t}{Z_s}\right]^2 \cdot r_a = P_{og}$. *From these expressions, obtain expressions for power input to motor and power output from motor. Hence, derive expressions for maximum power input and maximum power output for a cylindrical rotor synchronous motor.*

Solution. Equivalent circuit for a cylindrical rotor alternator and motor are shown in Fig. 5.53 (*a*) and (*b*) respectively.

An examination of Fig. 5.53 (*a*) reveals that power input to alternator P_{ig} is at the terminals where voltage is E_f. Power output of motor P_{om} is also at the same E_f terminals in Fig. 5.53 (*b*). The powers P_{ig} and P_{om} should therefore be equal. Since input power into alternator and output power in a motor flow in opposite directions, $P_{om} = -P_{ig}$.

Further, in an alternator, E_f is ahead of V_t whereas in a synchronous motor, E_f is behind V_t. This implies that power P_{om} can be obtained from power P_{ig} but with δ replaced by (– δ).

$$\therefore \quad P_{om} = -P_{ig} = -\frac{E_f \cdot V_t}{Z_s} \sin(-\delta - \alpha_Z) - \left[\frac{E_f}{Z_s}\right]^2 \cdot r_a$$

$$= \frac{E_f \cdot V_t}{Z_s} \sin(\delta + \alpha_Z) - \left[\frac{E_f}{Z_s}\right]^2 \cdot r_a \qquad ...(5.46)$$

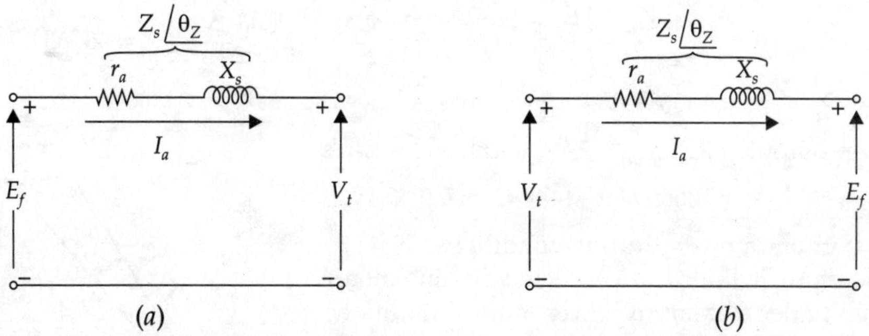

Fig 5.53: Equivalent circuit for cylindrical-rotor (*a*) alternator and (*b*) synchronous motor.

Similarly, power input to motor P_{im} at terminal voltage V_t can be obtained from power output of alternator P_{og} at the same V_t terminals.

$$\therefore \quad P_{im} = -P_{og} = -\frac{E_f \cdot V_t}{Z_s} \sin(-\delta + \alpha_Z) + \left[\frac{V_t}{Z_s}\right]^2 \cdot r_a$$

$$= \frac{E_f \cdot V_t}{Z_s} \sin(\delta - \alpha_Z) + \left[\frac{V_t}{Z_s}\right]^2 \cdot r_a \qquad ...(5.47)$$

With constant E_f, V_t and Z_s, the condition for maximum power output for a motor can be obtained by differentiating Eq. (5.46) with respect to δ.

$$\therefore \quad \frac{dP_{om}}{d\delta} = \frac{E_f \cdot V_t}{Z_s} \cos(\delta + \alpha_Z) - 0 = 0 = \cos 90°$$

$$\therefore \quad \delta + \alpha_Z = 90° \text{ or load angle } \delta = 90° - \alpha_Z = \theta_Z = \text{impedance angle}$$

Here $$\theta_Z = \tan^{-1}\left[\frac{X_s}{r_a}\right]$$

∴ Maximum power output from motor, from Eq. (5.46), is

$$P_{om\,(\max)} = \frac{E_f \cdot V_t}{Z_s} \sin 90 - \left[\frac{E_f}{Z_s}\right]^2 \cdot r_a = \frac{E_f \cdot V_t}{Z_s} - \left[\frac{E_f}{Z_s}\right]^2 \cdot r_a \qquad ...(5.48)$$

Similarly, for maximum power input to motor, from Eq. (5.47), we have

$$\frac{dP_{im}}{d\delta} = \frac{E_f \cdot V_t}{Z_s} \cos(\delta - \alpha_Z) + 0 = 0 = \cos 90° \text{ or } \delta - \alpha_Z = 90.$$

$\therefore$ Load angle $\delta = 90 + \alpha_Z = 90 + (90 - \theta_Z) = 180 - \theta_Z$

$\therefore$ Maximum power input to motor, from Eq. (5.47), is

$$P_{im\,(\max)} = \frac{E_f \cdot V_t}{Z_s} + \left[\frac{V_t}{Z_s}\right]^2 \cdot r_a \qquad ...(5.49)$$

Example 5.20. *A 400 V, 3-phase, mesh connected synchronous motor runs at rated voltage and with an excitation emf of 500 V. Its synchronous impedance per phase is 0.4 + j 4 Ω and friction, windage and iron losses are 900 W. Calculate the shaft power output, line current, power factor and efficiency for (a) maximum power output and (b) maximum power input.*

Solution. Here $V_t = 400$ V, $E_f = 500$ V, $Z_s = \sqrt{0.4^2 + 4^2} = 4.0\ \Omega$

$$\theta_Z = \tan^{-1}\left(\frac{X_s}{r_a}\right) = \tan^{-1}\left(\frac{4}{0.4}\right) = 84.29° \quad \therefore \alpha_Z = 90 - \theta_Z = 5.71°$$

(*a*) From Eq. (5.48), maximum power output is

$$P_{om\,(\max)} = \frac{E_f \cdot V_t}{Z_s} - \left[\frac{E_f}{Z_s}\right]^2 \cdot r_a = \frac{500 \times 400}{4.02} - \left[\frac{500}{4.02}\right]^2 \times 0.4 = 43563.3 \text{ W per phase}$$

$$= 130689.85 \text{ W for 3-phases.}$$

Shaft power output $= P_{om\,(\max)}$ – F.W. and Iron losses

$= 130689.85 - 900 = 129789.85$ W.

Under maximum power output conditions, $\delta = \theta_Z = 90 - \alpha_Z$. Therefore, cylindrical rotor synchronous motor phasor diagram under maximum power output conditions is as shown in Fig. 5.54. In this figure,

$$I_a Z_s = [E^2 + V_t^2 - 2 E_f V_t \cos \delta]^{1/2}$$

Here $\delta = \theta_Z$.

$$\therefore \quad I_a = \frac{1}{4.02}[500^2 + 400^2 - 2 \times 500 \times 400 \times \cos 84.29°]^{1/2}$$

$$= 151.354 \text{ A/phase}$$

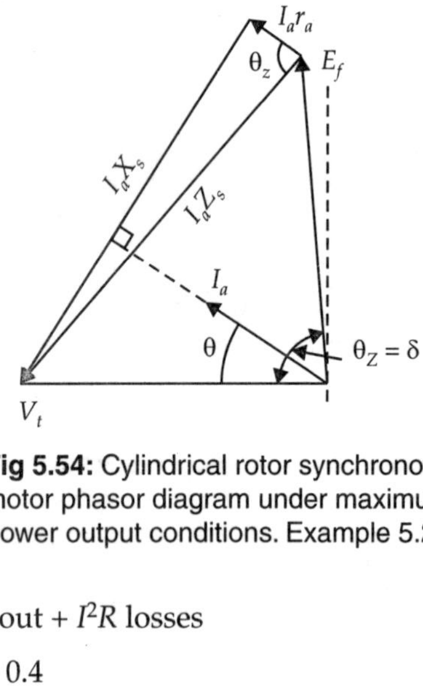

Fig 5.54: Cylindrical rotor synchronous motor phasor diagram under maximum power output conditions. Example 5.20

$\therefore$ Line current $= \sqrt{3} \times 151.354 = 262.145$ A

Power input to motor $= \sqrt{3}\, V_L I_L \cos\theta$ = maximum power out + I^2R losses

$$\therefore \quad \sqrt{3} \times 400 \times 262.145 \times \cos\theta = 130689.85 + 3\,(151.354)^2 \times 0.4$$

$$\therefore \quad \cos\theta = \frac{130689.85 + 3(151.354)^2 \times 0.4}{\sqrt{3} \times 400 \times 262.145}$$

$$= 0.871 \text{ lag}$$

$$\text{Efficiency} = \frac{\text{Power output}}{\text{Power input}} = \frac{129789.85}{158179.4} \times 100 = 80.052\%$$

(*b*) Maximum power input can be obtained from Eq. (5.49).

$\therefore$ Maximum power input to motor is

$$P_{im\,(\max)} = \frac{E_f \cdot V_t}{Z_s} + \left[\frac{V_t}{Z_s}\right]^2 \times r_a = \frac{500 \times 400}{4.02} + \left[\frac{400}{4.02}\right]^2 \times 0.4$$

$$= 53711.54 \text{ W per phase} = 161134.62 \text{ W for 3-phases}$$

Maximum power input to motor occurs when $\delta = 90 + \alpha_Z$

$$\therefore \quad [I_a Z_s]^2 = E_f^2 + V_t^2 - 2\,E_f \cdot V_t \cdot \cos(90 + \alpha_Z)$$

$$\therefore \quad I_a = \frac{1}{4.02}\,[500^2 + 400^2 - 2 \times 500 \times 400 \cos(90 + 5.71)]^{1/2} = 166.833 \text{ A}$$

$$\therefore \quad \text{Line current} = 166.833 \times \sqrt{3} = 288.96 \text{ A}$$

Maximum power input to motor is given by

$$V_a I_a \cos\theta = 53711.54 \text{ W per phase}$$

$$\therefore \quad \cos\theta = \frac{53711.54}{400 \times 166.833} = 0.8049 \text{ lag}$$

$$\text{Shaft power output} = 53711.54 \times 3 - 3 \times (166.833)^2 \times 0.4 - 900$$

$$= 126834.72 \text{ W}$$

$$\therefore \quad \text{Efficiency} = \frac{\text{Power output}}{\text{Power input}} = \frac{126834.72}{53711.54 \times 3} \times 100 = 78.714\%$$

5.23. SYNCHRONOUS MACHINE APPLICATIONS

Synchronous machines have wide variety of applications listed below.

Synchronous Generators : Synchronous generators or alternators are used universally for the generation of three-phase power in the whole world.

Large power stations use cylindrical rotor alternators (up to about 150 MVA or so) in thermal stations salient-pole alternators in hydro-stations. Synchronous generators are also used in ships and air-crafts. The range of ratings and speeds of synchronous generators is very wide.

All synchronous generators are invariably three-phase star-connected machines.

Synchronous Motors : These are usually made in sizes above about 50 kW, because in small sizes they are more expensive than induction motors.

Its principal advantages are as under.

(*i*) An overexcited synchronous motor can generate reactive power to improve the system power factor and at the same time, drive a constant-speed load.

(*ii*) It has high operating efficiency and constant speed.

(*iii*) For operating speeds less than about 500 rpm and for power requirements from 35 kW up to about 2500 kW; size, weight and cost of synchronous motors are much less than those of induction motors of the same speed and kW rating. It is because of these reasons that synchronous motor applications are on the rise for such speed and power requirements.

In view of the above, synchronous motors are preferred for driving the loads requiring high powers at low speeds ; for example, large low-head pumps, reciprocating pumps and compressors, rolling mills, ball mills, mixers, crushers, pulp grinders etc.

PROBLEMS

5.1. (*a*) Give the constructional features of stator of three-phase synchronous machines.

(*b*) Derive an expression for the frequency of emf generated in a synchronous generator. Hence define synchronous speed.

5.2. Give the constructional details of rotor of salient-pole and cylindrical-rotor synchronous machines.

5.3. Derive an expression for the emf generated in an alternator. What are their expressions for phase and line voltages for star-connected and delta-connected alternators.

5.4. A 3-phase, 16 pole, star-connected alternator has 192 stator slots with 8 conductors per slot and conductors of each phase are connected in series. Coil span is 150°. Determine the phase and line voltages if the machine runs at 375 rpm and the flux per pole is 64 mWb distributed sinusoidally over the pole. [**Ans.** 3366.13 V, 5830.14 V]

5.5. (*a*) Write an expression for the generated emf in an alternator. Discuss about the various terms involved in this expression.

(*b*) What are the various causes for the voltage drop in an alternator when it is loaded.

(*c*) Draw alternator phasor diagram showing air-gap voltage, terminal voltage etc. How is armature leakage flux accounted for? Write an equation in phasor form for E_r, V_t, I_a etc.

What are other names for air-gap voltage?

(*d*) Draw alternator phasor diagram at no load showing field flux, excitation emf etc. Explain it briefly.

5.6. What is armature reaction?

Describe the effect of armature reaction for unity pf load on an alternator. Obtain space-phasor diagram and time-phasor diagram separately and then combine these to obtain single space and time phasor diagram.

Discuss about the nature of armature reaction under these conditions.

5.7. Draw space and time phasor diagrams for zero pf lagging and zero pf leading loads on an alternator.

Discuss the effect of armature mmf for these two types of load on an alternator main field flux.

5.8. (*a*) Draw space and time phasor diagram for a lagging pf load on an alternator. Discuss the effect of armature mmf on the alternator main field.

(*b*) Repeat part (*a*) in case load on alternator is a leading power factor load.

5.9. (*a*) Explain about armature reaction in 3-phase synchronous motors.

(*b*) Discuss about the nature of armature mmf in an alternator and synchronous motor in case

(*i*) of lagging pf operation (*ii*) of leading pf operation

(*iii*) internal pf is zero pf lagging (*iv*) internal pf is zero pf leading.

5.10. Draw alternator phasor diagram for a lagging power factor load showing mmfs, excitation emf and air-gap emf. From this diagram, derive the concept of synchronous reactance, synchronous impedance and hence obtain equivalent circuit of a cylindrical-rotor alternator.

5.11. Describe the various tests for determining the synchronous impedance of a synchronous machine. Illustrate your anwser with appropriate diagrams.

5.12. Draw phasor diagrams for cylindrical rotor alternator for lagging, unity and leading power factors. From these diagrams, obtain expressions for calculating excitation emfs, internal pf angles and power angles.

5.13. Draw phasor diagrams for cylindrical rotor synchronous motor for lagging, unity and leading power factors. From these diagrams, obtain expressions for calculating excitation emfs, internal power factor angles and load angles.

5.14. Define voltage regulation of an alternator.

Describe how voltage regulation of an alternator can be determined for lagging, unity and leading power factor loads by synchronous-impedance method.

Discuss why synchronous-impedance method is also called emf method.

5.15. A 100 kVA, 1100 V, 3-phase, star-connected alternator gave the following test data :

DC resistance test : E between lines = 6 V dc

I in lines = 10 A dc

Open circuit test : Field current = 12.5 A dc

Line voltage = 420 V ac

Short circuit test : Field current = 12.5 A dc

Line current = rated current.

Calculate voltage regulation of this alternator at 0.8 pf lagging **[Ans.** 28.46%]

5.16. Explain two-reaction theory of salient-pole synchronous machines. Draw the phasor diagram at a lagging power factor according to this theory.

5.17. Draw the phasor diagram for a salient-pole alternator working at a lagging pf and explain how armature current can be resolved into *d*-axis and *q*-axis current components. From this phasor diagram, show that

$$\tan \delta = \frac{I_a[X_q \cos\theta - r_a \sin\theta]}{V_t + I_a[X_q \sin\theta + r_a \cos\theta]}$$

5.18. A salient-pole alternator has $X_d = 0.8$ pu, $X_q = 0.5$ pu, $r_a = 0.0$.

If this alternator delivers rated kVA at rated voltage at 0.8 pf lagging, then calculate load angle, excitation emf and voltage regulation. **[Ans.** 17.102°, 1.6027 pu, 60.27%]

5.19. (*a*) Enumerate the reasons for the parallel operation of alternators.

(*b*) What is an infinite bus?

5.20. What is synchronization? State the conditions to be fullfilled for synchronizing an alternator with an infinite bus.

Describe the method of synchronization of an alternator with an infinite bus by the use of a synchroscope.

5.21. Describe dark-lamp method of synchronizing an alternator with an infinite bus.

How can you ascertain with dark-lamp method that the incoming machine is a little too fast with respect to infinite bus.

5.22. Two synchronous generators, with excitation emfs E_{f1} and E_{f2} and synchronous impedances of Z_{s1} and Z_{s2}, are operating in parallel. If load impedance is Z_L and $E_{f1} = E_{f2}$, then show that currents shared by two alternators are

$$I_{a1} = \frac{\overline{E}_{f1}}{\overline{Z}_{s1} + \overline{Z}_L + \dfrac{\overline{Z}_{s1}\overline{Z}_L}{\overline{Z}_{s2}}} \text{ and } I_{a2} = \frac{\overline{E}_{f1}}{\overline{Z}_{s2} + \overline{Z}_L + \dfrac{\overline{Z}_{s2}\cdot\overline{Z}_L}{\overline{Z}_{s1}}}$$

5.23. Two alternators with excitation emfs E_{f1} and E_{f2} and synchronous impedances of Z_{s1} and Z_{s2} are operating in parallel. If load impedance is Z_L and E_{f1} is not equal to E_{f2}, then show that current shared by alternator 1 is

$$I_{a1} = \frac{\overline{E}_{f1}}{\overline{Z}_{s1} + \overline{Z}_L + \dfrac{\overline{Z}_{s1} \cdot \overline{Z}_L}{\overline{Z}_{s2}}} + \frac{E_{f1} - E_{f2}}{Z_{s1} + Z_{S2} + \dfrac{Z_{s1} \cdot Z_{s2}}{Z_L}}$$

5.24. Two 3-phase star-connected synchronous generators running in parallel supply a total load of 1000 kW at 6.6 kV at power factor 0.8 lagging. The load is shared equally by the two alternators. Synchronous impedance is $1 + j\,20\ \Omega$ for each machine. The field current of first alternator is so adjusted that it delivers 50 A at a lagging power factor. Calculate the current, excitation emf and power angle of each alternator.

[**Ans.** Altr. 1 : 50 A, 0.875 lag, 4.4205 kV per phase, 11.09°;
Altr. 2 : 60.23 A, 0.726 lag, 4.755 kV per phase, 10.09°]

5.25. Write voltage equation for cylindrical-rotor synchronous generator in terms of excitation voltage, terminal voltage, synchronous reactance etc. From this, derive an expression for power using $P = Re\left[\overline{V}_t \overline{I}_a^{\,*}\right]$ relation and hence obtain power-angle characteristics of synchronous machine.

5.26. From the phasor diagram of a salient-pole alternator with negligible armature resistance, derive an expression for power in terms of load angle etc. by using $P = Re\left[\overline{V}_t \overline{I}_a^{\,*}\right]$ relation. Hence obtain power angle characteristics of salient-pole synchronous machine.

5.27. Draw phasor diagram for a salient-pole alternator and derive an expression for reactive power using the relation $Q = I_{mg}\left[\overline{V}_t \overline{I}_a^{\,*}\right]$. Neglect armature resistance.

Hence obtain reactive power expression for cylindrical rotor alternator.

Discuss about the flow of reactive power in case of unity, lagging and leading power factors in alternator and synchronous motor.

5.28. Give some salient features of 3-phase synchronous motors. Describe the operating principle of 3-phase synchronous motors. What is magnetic locking in a synchronous motor? Show that a synchronous motor has no inherent starting torque.

5.29. Draw salient-pole synchronous motor phasor diagram for lagging power factor and obtain the following relations :

$$\tan\delta = \frac{I_a\left[X_q \cos\theta - r_a \sin\theta\right]}{V_t - I_a\left[X_q \sin\theta + r_a \cos\theta\right]} \quad \text{and} \quad E_f = V_t \cdot \cos\delta - I_q \cdot r_a - I_d \cdot X_d$$

5.30. Obtain the following relations from salient-pole synchronous motor phasor diagrams for

(*a*) Unity pf : $\tan\delta = \dfrac{I_a X_q}{V_t - I_a r_a}$

and $E_f = V_t \cos\delta - I_q \cdot r_a - I_d \cdot X_d$

(*b*) Leading pf : $\tan\delta = \dfrac{I_a\left[X_q \cos\theta + r_a \sin\theta\right]}{V_t + I_a\left[X_q \sin\theta - r_a \cos\theta\right]}$

5.31. A 3-phase salient-pole synchronous motor has $X_d = 0.6$ pu, $X_q = 0.4$ pu and $r_a = 0$. The motor takes rated current at rated voltage at power factor 0.8 lagging.

(*a*) Calculate (*i*) excitation voltage and (*ii*) active and reactive powers.

(*b*) If the field current is reduced to zero, will the synchronous motor lose synchronism?

[**Ans.** (*a*) (*i*) 0.7761 pu (*ii*) 0.8 pu, 0.6 pu (*b*) yes]

5.32. Describe the effect of varying field current upon the armature current and power factor of a cylindrical-rotor synchronous motor connected to an infinite bus and under the conditions of constant power output. Neglect armature resistance.

Hence, draw *V*-curves of this synchronous motor.

5.33. What are *V*-curves of a synchronous motor? What information can be obtained from these curves?

Draw unity power-factor compounding curve. It is not vertical but bends to the right. Explain.

5.34. What are inverted *V*-curves of a synchronous motor? How can these be obtained from the *V*-curves? What information can be obtained from inverted *V*-curves?

5.35. A cylindrical-rotor synchronous motor is connected to an infinite bus and drives a constant load.

(*a*) If its field current is increased, armature current decreases. Is the motor working at a lagging or leading power factor? Illustrate your answer with the help of phasor diagrams.

(*b*) If its field current is increased, the armature current increases. Is the motor working at unity pf or leading pf? Give reasons.

5.36. A 3-phase, 440 V, 6 pole, 50 Hz star-connected synchronous motor has synchronous impedance of $0.2 + j\,2\ \Omega$ per phase. The motor operates at rated voltage with a power angle of 20° and excitation emf of 240 V per phase. Calculate armature current, power factor and power output.

[**Ans.** 43.225 A, 0.9727 lag, 30.92 kW]

5.37. From the equivalent circuit of a cylindrical-rotor alternator with synchronous impedance Z_s, derive expression for complex power output. From this, obtain expressions for real power and reactive power outputs from alternator.

5.38. Draw equivalent circuit of a cylindrical-rotor alternator with synchronous impedance Z_s. From this, derive expression for complex power input to alternator. Then, obtain expressions for real power and reactive power inputs to alternator.

5.39. Derive expression for the power output from a cylindrical rotor alternator in terms of E_f, V_t, Z_s, load angle etc. Hence derive an expression for maximum power output and the corresponding load angle.

5.40. Derive expression for the power input to a cylindrical rotor alternator in terms of E_f, V_t, Z_s, load angle etc. Hence derive an expression for maximum power input and the corresponding load angle.

5.41. What are external load characteristics of alternators?

Draw cylindrical rotor alternator phasor diagrams at no load and also at different operating power factors with armature resistance neglected. From these diagrams, plot external load characteristics of an alternator in case

(*a*) excitation emf is kept constant at its load value and

(*b*) excitation emf is kept constant at its rated terminal voltage and rated armature current.

5.42. What are alternator compounding curves?

Draw cylindrical rotor alternator phasor diagrams at lagging, unity and leading power factors for constant terminal motor voltage and obtain therefrom the alternator compounding characteristics.

5.43. A 2200 V, delta-connected synchronous motor has $X_s = 16\ \Omega$ per phase. It operates at a power factor of 0.707 lagging when taking 250 kW from the supply mains. Calculate the excitation emf. **[Ans.** 3415.3 V**]**

5.44. (*a*) Give some applications of 3-phase synchronous generators.

(*b*) Enumerate the principal advantages of 3-phase synchronous motors.

Discuss the type of applications where 3-phase synchronous motors are preferred over 3-phase induction motors.

Also, list some of the applications of three-phase synchronous motors.

Objective Type Questions

1. In a synchronous machine, the generated emf at no load depends on
   (*a*) speed (*b*) speed and flux
   (*c*) dc field current (*d*) load on the machine.
2. In a 3-phase alternator, air-gap voltage is given by
   (*a*) $\overline{V}_t + \overline{I}_a \cdot r_a$ (*b*) $\overline{V}_t + j\overline{I}_a \cdot x_{al}$
   (*c*) $\overline{V}_t + \overline{I}_a \overline{Z}_s$ (*d*) $\overline{V}_t + \overline{I}_a\ r_a + j\ I_a \cdot x_{al}$
3. In a synchronous generator operating at zero pf lagging, the effect of armature reaction is
   (*a*) magnetizing (*b*) demagnetizing
   (*c*) cross-magnetizing (*d*) both magnetizing and cross-magnetizing
   [*I.A.S.*, 1995]
4. In a synchronous generator operating at zero pf leading, the effect of armature reaction is
   (*a*) magnetizing (*b*) demagnetizing
   (*c*) cross-magnetizing (*d*) both magnetizing and cross-magnetizing.
5. In an alternaor operating at lagging power factor, the effect of armature reaction is
   (*a*) magnetizing
   (*b*) both magnetizing and cross-magnetizing
   (*c*) cross-magnetizing
   (*d*) both demagnetizing and cross-magnetizing
6. In a synchronous motor operating at zero power factor lagging, the effect of armature reaction is
   (*a*) magnetizing (*b*) de-magnetizing
   (*c*) cross-magnetizing (*d*) both magnetizing and cross-magnetizing.
7. In a synchronous motor operating at a leading power factor, the effect of armature reaction is
   (*a*) magnetizing
   (*b*) both demagnetizing and cross-magnetizing

(*c*) cross-magnetizing
(*d*) both magnetizing and cross-magnetizing.

8. In a synchronous machine, the armature reaction reactance takes care of

(*a*) leakage flux (*b*) mutual flux
(*c*) armature-current flux (*d*) field flux

9. Read the following statements about a cylindrical-rotor alternator.

1. Emf generated by armature reaction mmf lags armature current by 90°
2. Air-gap voltage lags terminal voltage
3. Air-gap voltage lags field flux by 90°
4. Armature reaction mmf lags field flux by (90° + internal pf angle).

From above, the correct answer is

(*a*) 1, 4 (*b*) 2, 3, 4 (*c*) 1, 3, 4 (*d*) 1, 2, 4

10. Consider the following statements regarding an alternator.

1. Armature mmf leads the field flux
2. Air-gap flux lags the field flux
3. Air-gap flux leads the armature mmf
4. Field mmf leads the air-gap flux.

From above, the correct answer is

(*a*) 1, 3 (*b*) 1, 3, 4 (*c*) 2, 3, 4 (*d*) 2, 4

11. Read the following statements about a cylindrical-rotor alternator.

1. Terminal voltage lags the field flux by (90 + δ)
2. Angle between excitation emf and air-gap voltage is called load angle
3. Angle between excitation emf E_f and air-gap voltage is called torque angle
4. Angle between E_f and armature current is called internal power factor angle.

From above, the correct answer is

(*a*) 1, 2, 4 (*b*) 1, 3, 4 (*c*) 3, 4 (*d*) 2, 4

12. A 3-phase alternator delivers power to a balanced 3-phase load of power factor 0.707 lagging. It is observed that the open-circuit emf phasor leads the corresponding terminal voltage phasor by 15°. Neglecting the effect of harmonics, the angle between the axis of main field mmf and the axis of armature mmf will be

(*a*) 30° electrical (*b*) 60° electrical (*c*) 90° electrical (*d*) 150° electrical

[I.A.S., 1997]

13. A 3-phase alternator has negligible star resistance. A short-circuit test is conducted on this alternator. At a particular speed, a field current of I_{f1} is required to drive the rated armature current. If the speed of the alternator is reduced to half, the field current required to maintain rated armature current

(*a*) would be equal to I_{f1} (*b*) would be equal to 2 I_{f1}
(*c*) would be equal to $\frac{1}{2} \cdot I_{f1}$
(*d*) cannot be predicted due to insufficient data *[GATE; 1993]*

14. A 3-phase, 400 V, delta connected alternator has a synchronous impedance of $(0 + j\,20)$ ohms per phase. If it delivers a balanced load of 12 kVA at zero pf lagging, then the percentage voltage regulation of the alternator is equal to

(*a*) –50 (*b*) +50 (*c*) –150 (*d*) 150

15. In a salient-pole alternator, the voltage in phase with *q*-axis is given by

(*a*) $V_t + I_a r_a + I_a x_{al}$ (*b*) $V_t + I_a r_a + I_a X_d$

(*c*) $V_t + I_a r_a + I_a X_q$ (*d*) $V_t + I_a r_a + I_a (X_d + X_q)$

16. A synchronous motor is operating on no load at unity power factor. If the field current is increased, then pf will become

(*a*) leading and the current will decrease (*b*) lagging and the current will increase

(*c*) lagging and the current will decrease (*d*) leading and the current will increase

17. A synchronous motor, fed from an infinite bus, is working at half-full load. If an increase in its field current causes a reduction in the armature current, then the motor is

(*a*) delivering reactive power to the bus at leading pf

(*b*) delivering reactive power to the bus at lagging pf

(*c*) absorbing reactive power from the bus at lagging pf

(*d*) absorbing reactive power from the bus at leading pf

18. A 3-phase synchronous motor is operating at a load angle of 20° and with excitation voltage equal to applied voltage. The synchronous reactance drop in terms of the excitation voltage will be

(*a*) 69.46% (*b*) 34.73% (*c*) 32.9% (*d*) 38.2%

19. In a synchronous machine,

(*a*) both I_d and I_q are in phase with E_f

(*b*) I_q is in phase with E_f and I_d is at 90° to E_f

(*c*) I_d is in phase with E_f and I_q is at 90° to E_f

(*d*) both I_d and I_q are at 90° to E_f

20. For a salient-pole synchronous machine with negligible armature resistance,

1. $E_f = V_t \cos\delta + I_d X_d$; generator at a lagging pf
2. $E_f = V_t \cos\delta - I_d X_d$; motor at a lagging pf
3. $E_f = V_t \cos\delta + I_d X_d$; motor at a leading pf
4. $E_f = V_t \cos\delta - I_d X_d$; generator at a leading pf

From above, the correct statements are

(*a*) 1, 3 (*b*) 2, 4

(*c*) 1, 2 (*d*) 1, 2, 3, 4

21. The phasor diagram shown in the figure pertains to

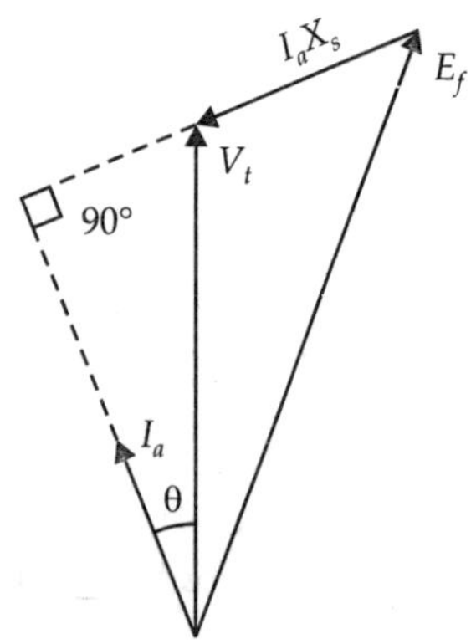

(*a*) overexcited alternator

(*b*) underexcited synchronous motor

(*c*) overexcited synchronous motor

(*d*) underexcited alternator

22. A synchronous motor is working at unity power factor. If the load on the motor is increased, keeping excitation and terminal voltages constant, then the power factor

(*a*) will remain the same (*b*) will become leading

(*c*) will become lagging

(*d*) may become leading or lagging depending on the applied load

23. The direct axis and quadrature axis reactances of a salient-pole alternator 1.2 pu and 1.0 pu respectively. The armature resistance is negligible. If this alternator is delivering rated kVA at UPF and at rated voltage, then its power angle is

(*a*) 30° (*b*) 45° (*c*) 60° (*d*) 90° *[GATE, 2011]*

24. A synchronous motor is connected to an infinite bus at 1 pu voltage and draws 0.6 pu current at unity pf. Its synchronous reactance is 1.0 pu and resistance is negligible.

The excitation voltage (E_f) and load angle will respectively be

(*a*) 0.8 pu and 36.86° lag (*b*) 0.8 pu and 36.86° lead

(*c*) 1.17 pu and 30.96 lead (*d*) 1.17 pu and 30.96° lag

25. A cylindrical-rotor alternator has a terminal voltage of 1 pu at a pf of 0.8 lagging. Its synchronous reactance is 1 pu on machine rating as the base. Its excitation voltage, with terminal voltage as the reference, is

(*a*) $1 + j\,0.8$ (*b*) $1.8 + j\,0.6$ (*c*) $1.6 + j\,0.8$ (*d*) $1.6 - j\,0.8$

26. Synchronous motor *V*-curves show the relation between

(*a*) armature current and load (*b*) armature current and terminal voltage

(*c*) armature current and field-current (*d*) armature current and power factor.

27. A synchronous motor is working at unity power factor at rated load. If its excitation is increased, then

(*a*) load on motor would increase (*b*) power factor would become lagging

(*c*) power factor would become leading (*d*) power factor would remain the same.

28. A salient-pole synchronous motor is running at no load. If its excitation is switched off, then

(*a*) motor would stop

(*b*) motor would continue running at a speed less than synchronous speed

(*c*) motor would continue running at synchronous speed

(*d*) motor may or may not continue to run

29. An alternator is connected to an infinite bus. If its prime-mover gets de-coupled accidently, then alternator will

(*a*) come to standstill

(*b*) continue to work as an alternator with direction of rotation reversed

(*c*) begin to work as an induction motor

(*d*) begin to work as synchronous motor in the same direction

30. In a 3-phase alternator, working on constant values of excitation and terminal voltages, for maximum power output and maximum power input, the relation between load angle δ and synchronous impedance and θ_Z is as under

(*a*) $\delta = \theta_Z$ and $\delta = 90 - \theta_Z$ (*b*) $\delta = 90 + \theta_Z$ and $\delta = \theta_Z$

(*c*) $\delta = \theta_Z$ and $\delta = 180 - \theta_Z$ (*d*) $\delta = 180 - \theta_Z$ and $\delta = 90 - \theta_Z$

31. In a 3-phase synchronous motor, working on constant values of excitation and terminal voltages, for maximum power out and maximum power input, the power angle δ is related to synchronous impedance angle θ_Z as under.

(*a*) $\delta = \theta_Z$ and $\delta = 90 - \theta_Z$
(*b*) $\delta = \theta_Z$ and $\delta = 180 - \theta_Z$
(*c*) $\delta = 180 - \theta_Z$ and $\delta = \theta_Z$
(*d*) $\delta = 90 + \theta_Z$ and $\delta = 180 - \theta_Z$

Answers

1. (*b*)	**2.** (*d*)	**3.** (*b*)	**4.** (*a*)	**5.** (*d*)
6. (*a*)	**7.** (*b*)	**8.** (*c*)	**9.** (*a*)	**10.** (*c*)
11. (*b*)	**12.** (*d*)	**13.** (*a*)	**14.** (*b*)	**15.** (*c*)
16. (*d*)	**17.** (*c*)	**18.** (*b*)	**19.** (*b*)	**20.** (*d*)
21. (*c*)	**22.** (*c*)	**23.** (*b*)	**24.** (*d*)	**25.** (*c*)
26. (*c*)	**27.** (*c*)	**28.** (*c*)	**29.** (*d*)	**30.** (*c*)
31. (*b*)				